6063090

ARTIFICIAL LOVE

ARTIFICIAL LOVE

A Story of Machines
and Architecture

Paul Shepheard

WITHDRAWN

The MIT Press
Cambridge, Massachusetts
London, England

This book was set in Univers and Melior by Graphic Composition and was printed and bound in the United States of America.

Library of Congress Cataloging-in-Publication Data
Shepheard, Paul
  Artificial love: a story of machines and architecture / Paul Shepheard.
    p.   cm.
  Includes bibliographical references and index.
  ISBN 0-262-19485-6 (hc. : alk. paper), 0-262-69285-6 (pb. : alk. paper)
    1. Architecture and technology. 2. Architecture—Aesthetics. 3. Mechanical engineering. I. Title.
  NA2543.T43 S52   2003
  720′.1′05—dc21

                                                              2002032134

CONTENTS

This book is three books sandwiched between one set of covers. When I say sandwich I don't mean one of those tight kid's party triangles—I'm thinking of the relaxed basketfuls of elements that arrive when you order a club sandwich in Houston, Texas, U.S.A. Buns, fries, rings, patties, salads, garnishes, dressings—they come splayed across the platter like tourists sunbathing round a pool. They are meals in kit form, ready for you to assemble yourself. Your glue is the wide selection of condiments twinkling in their jars and bottles, like the towers of a city center, right there in the middle of the table.

When I started out, the meal I wanted to offer here was machines. Machines as architecture. The contemporary world, I thought, is to its machines as the ancient world was to its temples and tombs. That Boeing jetliner up there may not be a building, but it is architecture. It's part of the refabrication of the material world. Part of the *human artifice*. The first part of my three-part sandwich is the four seminars: the story of me following up that idea. It expanded as I went until I found I was considering the entire range of human artifacts from the first pot shard from Jericho to the last titanium bracket of the Hubble telescope; and as I worked, technology, that fabulous, denigrated subject, changed from being the grubby end product of applied science to become the entire field of human desire to change and improve the world. I discovered that the contemporary world has the tombs and the temples in it as well as the machines. What I think now is that technology is a force of nature. It is the force of the human presence in the world.

Buildings and machines have been playing tag for a hundred years now, and the period of wishing buildings were machines—and the idea of a machine aesthetic—is over. But buildings have not been let off the hook of contemporaneity. Far from it. Architects are using machines to design them and theories of machinic processes to explain them. Buildings no longer have to look like machines because now they can look like anything, even themselves. And there's that word *now* again.

There is a fierce resemblance between Le Corbusier's "eyes that cannot see" and Greg Lynn's claim that "architecture remains as the last refuge of the flat earth society." But why do those beasts of the past—pyramids, Parthenon, Pantheon— still exert such power? Is it that they are great because they are confidently of their own time, and that's what we need to find for our time now? Or is it that they are great because they are great, and we should be striving to emulate their instructive forms? My proposition—hardly unexpected in the current climate of philosophies of emergence—is that there is no past. We and the tombs and temples all exist in the emerging present together with the jetliners and the computers and everything in between, just as the species *Homo sapiens* exists alongside archaic forms like the snail and the jellyfish. The strategies of other human beings, no matter how long ago they were made, are still with us. Their continuing presence in the world is the wonderful, ever-increasing accumulation of techniques that we live with. And the flat earth was the landscape from which the wheel and axle emerged, without which the machine I'm writing with would have to forego its fans and disc drives.

So the four seminars, tracking conversations I've had about machines and architecture with students, is the first part of the sandwich. The second is a soap opera. It is another way of exploring the same material. It came to me when my third child was born, with me already at the back end of middle age, and my own father right at the other end of his life to the baby, deep into his stroke-struck oldness. I used to present the two of them to each other, stroller to wheelchair, and marvel at how we spanned the last century, we three. We were personal witnesses to the coming of the automation that has changed everything, and that is now about to change politics itself; now that we have finally come to the point of automating human relationships. The opera spread until it had a full cast of men, seven of us, all humming to the five-hundred-year-old words of Shakespeare's *As You Like It,* about the seven ages of man. I think it is fascinating the way we occupy our ever-changing world with bodies that evolved a hundred thousand years ago to run and hunt and have joy in the chase; the way we embody that evolved history by carrying our own little salt-sea oceans with us, our seventy-percent water contents, wherever we go; the way we play out in the womb the entire heritage of animal beginnings with our embryonic gills and tails. All the shifts and changes of technology are made in the emotional flow of these evolved realities. And every generation has to learn from scratch the whole truth about the world for itself. That's the opera.

The third book here is the index; a thing that grew and grew until it took on itself all the mechanics of annotation. It is scatty and free-range, but I hope it is useful. It will be if, like me, you are a skip reader. It stands in for references, footnotes, asides, and qualifications in the other two parts. It is a glossary and a dictionary of quotations as well as an index. It dots the i's and crosses the t's and says who's who and what's what. It supplements the inquiry and the soap opera with postures of its own.

Seminars, soap opera, annotated index, and lastly the condiments: speculations. They are sprinkled throughout these pages like the salt and the ketchup on that club sandwich. At the end of last year I sat on a review in the architecture school of a studio that had given itself to speculating on the qualities special to suburbs. They wanted to accentuate the positive, not least that the garden-city alternative suburbs offer to the world had been smelted in the slums of industrial Europe. One of the other critics immediately waded in with a deep criticism of suburbia—unsustainable sprawl, he called it—that threatened to stall the whole conversation. I reflected then that there should be some other way of doing things that would allow some difficult assumptions to remain intact for the sake of investigation. The opposite of 'deep' is unfortunately 'shallow' so I needed another word to call it and came up with 'fast'. "What about 'fast criticism'?" I said. "Think of this study as a high-speed reconnaissance flight across disputed terrain."

For example, in the preface of my book about landscape, *The Cultivated Wilderness,* I said that architects did not need theories of being so much as they needed theories of action. And then a little while ago someone showed Hannah Arendt's

Vita Activa to me. "It's both being and action," she said, adding: "And what a surprise that people are reading Hannah Arendt again!" It's not hard to see why. The pious reassurance of Arendt's writing is like reentering the sea after that first cold dip. That picture of technology as the 'human artifice' is hers. The *Vita Activa* is a piece on the human condition, and it's an active one—the human condition is what humans do. It's a trilogy, as gentle as wisdom itself. Labor, work, and action are her three activities. *Labor* is the mundane profundity of being a living animal, the washing and the eating and the sex, those actions that repeat endlessly throughout your life and guarantee its meaning. *Work* is the refabrication of the material world that houses us and protects us against the stream of natural forces, and in its objectivity, explains the world to us: there's the architecture. *Action* for Arendt is politics: the activity of ensuring that "Me! Me! Me!" always adds up to "Us."

It is so measured and considerate, it's beautiful. It's an attempt to reconcile the blown-apart character of modern life with our ancient desires for eternity by harnessing the movement of action. I want to believe it, even though it's a matrix, not a recipe. Even though toil, pollution, and war fit as easily into it as the dignity, security, and peace that are intended. But I can't believe it because I think that there is more than one Us. We humans savor our differences. We live in complexes of tribal affinities just as we always have. The hegemonies that have periodically tried to resolve that difficulty have all let their fences deteriorate in the end. And then the rest of the world rushes in and disperses the unity all over again. This is my point—globalization is not a unity, it's not a 'global village', it's a multiplicity. And it has always been so.

Globalization is the original, recurring condition, the *wilderness* to hegemony's *cultivation*.

So here we have seminars, soap opera, glossary plus speculations, mostly concerning the special in the general, all on the subject of machines and architecture. Machines and landscapes, machines and buildings, machines and machines and, because everything in here is coming out not in threes but in fours, machines and sculpture. That is the meal offered in this book. It is set in Texas, where I have been teaching at the School of Architecture at the University of Texas at Austin while writing it; the book is dedicated with thanks to all the students who've taught me what I know. And to anyone who's loved a machine. And also to William Shakespeare—long dead, still with us—who gave the words that follow to his melancholic character Jaques, in *As You Like it*, act 3, scene 2:

All the world's a stage, and all the men and women merely players: they have their exits and their entrances; and one man in his time plays many parts, his acts being seven ages. At first the infant, mewling and puking in the nurse's arms. And then the whining schoolboy, with his satchel, and shining morning face, creeping like a snail unwillingly to school. And then the lover, sighing like furnace, with woeful ballad made to his mistress' eyebrow. Then a soldier, full of strange oaths, and bearded like the pard, jealous in honour, sudden and quick in quarrel, seeking the bubble reputation even in the canon's mouth. And then the justice, in fair round belly with good capon lin'd, with eyes severe, and beard of formal cut, full of wise saws and modern instances: and so he plays his part. The sixth age shifts into the lean and slipper'd pantaloon, with spectacles on nose and pouch on side, his youthful hose well saved, a world too wide for his shrunk shank: and his big manly voice, turning again toward childish treble, pipes and whistles in the sound. Last scene of all, that ends this strange eventful history, is second childishness and mere oblivion, sans teeth, sans eyes, sans taste, sans everything.

JAQUES

In the middle of the black Texas night, Jaques—the lover of machines—sits fast asleep, his face illuminated by the flicker of a television.

A few hundred yards away Interstate 10 is humming with the sound of a thousand cars and trucks and pickups and buses, a multitude as dense as a stampede, traffic that speeds in and out and round about the city all day and all night long, like the blood running in its veins. Houston. This modern, mobile place is not like those futuristic high-rise dream cities of the 1920s, with their hovering airplanes nudging up to cloud-high balconies and their men and women sunbathing nude together on suspended decks. Houston is not like that at all. When you're driving in along the interstate you can sense the city from forty miles out, the first glimpse of its distant towers turning out to be merely some of the towers that stand on a piece of the periphery. Every day the city grows a little more, adds another roll of fat to its hundred-mile girth, fanning out across the blank Texas ground like an oil slick.

And out here on the edge of it in his factory-made house sits Jaques, curled up in his motorized reclining chair, fast asleep. The scatter of hard study is all around him. His pads and pencils and hi-liters, his folders and files and the transcripts he has torn from the web, and all the gay panoply of his books as

well, with their cover designs so interesting and full of signif-
icance—all this stuff lies scattered around the place, piled
everywhere and every which way. They are the litter of a
moraine of stuff pushed there by the glacier Jaques in his
slow, waking moments, who is now temporarily retreated into
slumber. There is no 'all glass office' here. No clean, keyboard-
tapping Microsoftian all glass office, no six-inch shelf of
CDs containing all the knowledge of the known world, no
trashcan full of cellophane wrappers. This is an artist's garret.
Look at Jaques: he is no information age puppy; he is a dis-
tracted lover of verse, a Shakespearean, who wanders through
forests of dispute looking for an answer to the question, *what
are machines?* So this doublewide paradise he lives in—one-
hundred-ninety-nine dollars a month, all ready to go—is his
artist's garret. Of course, it has no stairs like garrets used to
have in the days of Paris. This is the New World, and life out
here is unified by the flat ground and the machinery. *Hey,
buddy!* Goes the refrain, *If you want to go up—use the
elevator!*

The temperature of Jaques's doublewide is set at seventy degrees. In the middle of the roof, just to one side of the seam that
joins the two halves of the thing together, is a small air-cooler.
When it runs it sounds like the barking of distant dogs. At two
A.M. everything is quiet, save the hum of the traffic on the freeway, and the cooler's fan stands idle in the humid Texas night,
while Jaques sleeps and the television plays ghosts on his
eyelids—but at one second past the hour, the thermostat clicks
open and the motor starts up with a woof and a clatter and the

faint chill of conditioned air starts to fill the room. Jaques wakes up. He squints at the television screen across his sloping chest and inches his fingers forward and presses *volume up* on the remote. He hears the soft sounds of the veldt, all the way from Africa. There is the thump of vulture's wings, and the tick-tick of insects, and the shuffling of ten thousand hooves as a herd of wildebeest grazes in the white-hot sunshine. He touches a lever and the chair, big, leather bound, automatic, slowly powers out of recline and he sits forward to give closer attention to the screen.

Everything is brown and ochre under a sheer blue sky. Even the grass is the color of sand. The big brown cattle have shoulders like buffalo and legs like antelopes, bulky and dainty at the same time. They stand and nudge each other in the hot wind and bat at the flies with their ears. In the foreground, you can see the glisten of the drool on their snouts, and in the distant background their shining flanks pick up the reflection of the sky and broadcast a blue haze around their brown bodies, just like the shimmering mirages on the ground itself. The herd is so big that it has become the landscape. It stretches out to the horizon as though it could fill the entire dusty sphere of Africa. Jaques rubs his eyes and eases himself out of the chair onto his hands and knees in front of the television. He turns the sound off again and boosts the color and the contrast and the scene becomes a dense metallic pastoral, like a summer traffic jam on a hot road. He is two feet from the screen. The cattle graze on under Jaques's close attention, baleful and primitive, as unmoved as they should have been had he been there in their real lives.

As he watches a hyena comes trotting back and forth beneath the bellies of the wildebeest. Then another, doing the same thing, then another; and soon a whole little pack, right in among the legs of the herd. They move in a continuous trot, changing direction constantly, their long pink tongues hanging down and their shaggy coats swinging with the rhythm of the pace. Suddenly they single out one of the wildebeest and attack it. Everything accelerates into chaos. The big animal breaks into a shambolic run, kicking out in all directions, but the hyenas are fast and aggressive and they work in concert. Four of them harry the wildebeest's legs, biting and snapping to slow it down while the other two go in at its belly, tearing away bits of it with their teeth, disembowelling it on the move. Jaques watches riveted, appalled, shocked to stillness by the sight. The wildebeest's mouth opens wide in a roar as its belly splits open. The shining grey-pink of its guts spill out into the ochre dust cloud put up by the fight, and it sinks to the ground like a ship going under. The hyenas career over the big animal, making for its throat to finish it off, and starting, in their frenzy, to eat: before the carcass has even finished with its life.

Jaques snapped the switch off and plunged himself into darkness. The horror of it froze his sweat. As soon as the hyenas had chosen their prey and cut it off, the rest of the herd had moved straight back into their steady grazing rhythms, not even lifting their heads to watch the spectacle.

Television! The wonder of it! So emotional—so affective—so global! Switch a television on and you are shown your place in the world. Little children know that—they cluster round televisions instinctively, like wasps at a honey pot. At two years old they stand with their noses pressed to the screen watching the white noise at the end of the channel band, as if it were Christmas Eve and they were watching for Santa Claus in the snow. Meanwhile, at the other end of life, in retirement homes, the televisions are left running all the time, like getaway cars. The visitors try to converse in spite of it; but all the time they are talking, their old folks keep one eye on the screen in the corner, which spills out its mixture of celebrity and massacre as disinterestedly as an oracle telling the future. They look like they are watching out for news of their own final catastrophe.

———————

Jaques is twenty-one. He has just started the middle part of his life. He is in the third age of his manhood—he is *the lover*. He is not yet encumbered with the company of children or old folks. He lives detached and alone, with his own little family of machines to help him. He has the automatic chair, the television, and the air-cooler. Over there in the corner is the refrigerator, humming its monotonous tune, cavernously nurturing his beer and his bread and butter. On the desk is his computer, the abstract machine, as infuriating and brainy as his best friend. On the floor in the corner is his stereo, with its stack of compact discs oozing romance, and outside on the grass in front of the trailer is his car. There are times when everything is quiet, all motors silent, all pilot lights off, when Jaques feels as though he is the only one awake in a sleeping house. He is the lover: and he loves these machines as if they were his people. He polishes them, he nurtures them. He spends whole days poking at their insides with screwdrivers. If you ask him, he can tell you the exact moment he fell in love with them all. Like the car: he woke up in the wilderness one day on a camping trip in the northwest and looked out of the tent to see it standing there, in among the pine trees, all still and quiet and ready to go. It seemed incandescent with potential. It was covered all over its metallic gray skin with a million identical drops of dew, each one with its own internal rainbow, which gave the car the luster of the dawn itself. Do you remember that peculiar empathy with mechanical toys you feel as a child, when perceiving for the first time their pathetically limited capacity for action? So dopey and faithful that they could be dogs? Falling in love with the car was like that feeling.

How can machines be lovable? We cleave the world into organic and inorganic, alive and dead, the spirited and the blank. It's easy to assume that machines are nothing but assemblages of blank matter, put together with the same clumsy hands with which we do everything else. So how can they be lovable? Would they not have to be alive to be lovable?

Jaques's friend Maria says that machines are indeed alive. "Machines aren't *in*organic, they're *non*organic." She tells him. "They are *artificial life.*"

"Artificial life?" repeats Jaques, "Does that mean there's artificial love? Is that what I've been feeling for these creatures? Artificial love?"

Maria is tall enough to look him in the eye, a dark-browed woman with a double demeanor. Stiff as a walnut but forever caving in to softness. And she talks all the time. "It's like having the radio on," says Jaques—"you almost feel like taking notes." The first time he met her she was leaning against a doorframe rattling the ice cubes in her glass and metaphorizing particle physics. She insisted that she could feel the spaces between the atoms of her flesh. She said she could feel the music going right through her and coming out the other side. He thought it was just party talk, something to go with the clash of glass and the roar of voices and the cigarette smoke. "If you knew how to look, you could see right through me," she said. "If you were small enough, you could get right into my bones!" Standing there in her white silk Spanish shirt and her prism-cut hair.

Now here she is sitting at his little plastic kitchen table drinking his whisky and telling him that machines are alive. She says she loves the whole spooky contradiction of the idea—as though machines could have an afterlife! And as though they have a sex life, too—"Which they *do,*" she says, but by using us to reproduce for them. We are midwives to the machines, she says. "Not Frankensteins, but midwives." To think that machines are alive you only have to think of the opposite, as utilitarian medical men do, that living things are machines. That food is fuel, that cells are building blocks, that sleep is maintenance downtime. And dreams are hard drive reconfigurations.

So machines are alive, says Maria. They are not *in*organic, they are *non*organic. She pulls Jaques's book of warships to the surface of the pile and thumbs through it until she comes to a picture of the aircraft carrier *U.S.S. Nimitz* cruising through the Strait of Hormuz in all its massive complexity. It looks like some thirteenth-century fantasy, a floating city on the move, is Jaques's opinion—you can almost see the big red crusader's cross fluttering on virtual masts a thousand feet high.

No, it looks like a huge living beast, says Maria. The rumble of digestion deep inside the hull as the beast consumes its food lulls its town-size crew asleep. The jets up on the deck gulp down kerosene and fart out heat—and back in California in Boeing's factories, other machines are busy reproducing more of them. She pauses for another pull at the bottle and Jaques makes his notes—*Machines don't have sex with each other like we do but they do reproduce / they use us to do it for them.*

"So what?" says Maria. "Now that the machines are sharing our world as though they were our cousins? When we make machines we aren't playing God. We are like the bees, pollinating flowers."

Frankenstein haunted by idea that he was playing God / at start of nineteenth century, this was big issue. "Or like warblers," says Jaques. "Hatching out huge cuckoos' eggs of new technologies in our little old-fashioned nests."

She smiles at that, because they're talking about the birds and the bees. "Artificial life," she says again. "People get so scared of it, like all the bombs are going to set themselves off on artificial purpose. I guess it's because they think machines are slaves, and that means that one day they're going to have to rebel." So let's give them their freedom now, she says. Lets call them our equals now.

So—chair, television, air-cooler, refrigerator, computer, stereo, and car. Jaques's family. Nonorganic but lovable. You want the names of Jaques's machines? Laz-y-boy, Toshiba, Lennox, Westinghouse, Dell, Denon, and Chevrolet. You want more specific names? The Chevrolet is a Lumina.

What? Said Maria in a horrified tone, when she first found out, suddenly full of Boston snobbery. *You mean, you no-balls, you drive a Lumina?*

"That's right. You should see it covered in the sparkle of dawnlight."

The next day Jaques was in the closet hunting for his no. 3 cross-head screwdriver. In shifting boxes he suddenly exposed a small brown spider, which dashed for cover under his shoe and made him jump back in terror. He watched, palpitating, as it scuttled off under the cover moulds. On his first arrival in Texas Jaques had been told about the brown recluse spider, an ordinary looking arachnid the size of a penny whose bite is as deadly as a rattlesnake. *If you find one,* they said, *kill it! Douse the place in bleach and burn all the rugs! You gotta kill the eggs!* The bite from this beast leaves an instant gangrene around the wound that rapidly grows until your whole body is consumed by stinking rot. You turn into a ghoul. *If you can't kill it first blow,* they told him, *run like hell!* That's what they said to him—and now maybe he had one lurking somewhere in the house!

The brown recluse, *Loxosceles reclusa,* is not quite the fiend it has been described as. The bite doesn't have to be fatal, if you move fast enough, but the wound can turn gangrenous and leave a dent in your flesh the size of an ice hockey puck. There are other Loxosceles spiders, mostly in Mexico and the southwestern United States, and all of them are poisonous. They belong to the arachnid family *Loxoscelidae.* 'Arachnids' are the class of spiders, plus scorpions, mites and ticks, within the phylum 'arthropods'—which also includes insects, centipedes and millipedes, and all of the crustaceans, from crabs to sowbugs.

Phylum *Arthropoda*, class *Arachnida*, order *Araneae*, family *Loxoscelidae*, genus *Loxosceles*, species *Reclusa*. This is how the living creatures on earth have been classified. That wildebeest that fell foul of the hyenas was *Connochaetes taurinus* of the family *Bovidae*, order *Artiodactyla*, class *Mammal*, phylum *Chordata*. A phylum is the second-penultimate division in the biological classification that groups together everything similarly constructed. Phylum *Arthropoda* are invertebrates with segmented bodies and jointed appendages; Phylum *Chordata*, ineffably more complex, include the ones with a spinal column, like us.

Maria appears in the street outside and beckons to Jaques from the open window of her Volkswagen. Her angular joints protrude from it like a stack of lumbar. She wants Jaques to go to the bookstore to help her resolve what she calls a "man-in-the-loop experience."

"Why do you need me for this?" says Jaques.

"You give me an alibi," says Maria, as he buckles up his safety belt.

On the drive to the mall, he tells her about the spider. He says it's interesting that this creature was living in his cupboard—living like a human in an artificial environment. Does that make his natural life an artificial thing? *Her* life, probably, says Maria—and anyway, the poor creature is just adapting— she says that all life could be described as artificial in the way it socializes and adapts. This is why, when talking about 'nature', one could try distinguishing between the inert nature of the inorganic universe, with its rocky planets spinning and colliding in the echo of the Big Bang, and the nature of the biomass, the evolving stew of life, full of desire and experiment: a nature that includes ourselves. If you had the math and the physics, she says, you might be able to compute the future of the first. But the second kind—that's plain unpredictable.

And machines? Nonorganic life? "They're with us. They're riding along in the biomass with us." To say it again—it's not that animals are like machines, it's that machines are like animals.

While Maria went off to debate her beef, Jaques went browsing in the natural history department, looking for spiders. He found hyenas first, in *A Field Guide to the Mammals of East Africa*. It had page after page of immaculately detailed paintings of all the safari familiars, the elephants, the lions, the zebras and giraffes; omitting, of course, the millions of mammal primates, family *Homonidae*, genus *Homo*, species *sapiens*, which swarm across Africa as they do over all the other continents. The guide to spiders that sat a little further down the shelf had color plates of every spider and its close similars all laid out in immaculate hand-painted detail, so true to life they looked ready to spring. Jaques stared at them with disgusted delight. There were thumbnail maps that showed where each species lived, and hundreds of tiny ink drawings of their intestines and mandibles and leg joints, each one littered with little markers showing the differences.

They are things of great beauty, these guides, but they are archaic. Compared to the Web's information wilderness, they are like information concentration camps. They are as straight as arrows. They try to show things exactly as they appear to be. Every volume is a huge compression of years of patient observation by naturalists and hunters, who went out into the long grass with their notebooks and cameras and telescopes and elephant guns to capture the great diversity of organic life. Every order of animal and plant has its own book, the whole of evolution's fund of forms, the currently surviving experiments and mutations of two and a half billion years of it, all laid out on the page in immaculate order, and painted by hand.

As Jaques looked and read, and saw how spider after spider was laid out in the edifice of biological taxonomy, he began to wonder *what if you could classify machines like this*? What if you could set out the whole complex dynamic of our machine dependency in one structure? What if you could make a field guide, not to the works of nature, but to the works of humankind? You could lay the whole artificial world out by observation and classification and eliminate the mysteries that surround it. You could dish the antiquated politics of power and control that we still use to frighten each other about what we have wrought—all those new inventions and processes that crowd in on us, scaring the people with the pace of change and creating unseen havoc in the atmosphere. "They disturb the peace," said Jaques aloud to the rows of books, "and yet they are lovable!" A field guide to machines could pin it all down, he thought. And this is how the lover of machines began the project that has littered his room with inquiry and felled his philosophical notions one by one, leaving him trembling and clueless, a rank atheist standing naked before his maker—*A Field Guide to the Machines*.

———————— THANKSGIVING ————————

The little girl stands with her feet on the air-conditioner grate and lets the cold air shiver up her naked body. Just one of a hundred shifts in position in the last fifteen minutes. She is busy showing the world to her doll, who is called Juliet, just like herself.

"Ah!" she says, "This is Juliet!" The doll has a purple satin dress so long that it comes down over her owner's wrist. It looks like a glove puppet, but inside the dress is a pair of Barbie-perfect pink plastic legs that you grip if you want to show the doll the world.

"Ah, Juliet!" she says, "Let's give John a kiss!" and John gets wearily to his twelve-year-old feet and backs off round the room, slowly waving his plastic assault rifle to cover his retreat. Juliet and Juliet skip after him. The little girl, my sister's daughter, is three feet high, four years old, naked, pink, and bony with blond curls all over her head. John, my son, in his ragged preteen clothes looks like a fugitive. Juliet goes racing round the place barking her shins and stubbing her toes and wailing and recovering and sitting her bare backside on the sharp shards of toy bits that litter the floor and wailing all over again, waving her long-skirted doll around like it was a fire extinguisher and the room was engulfed in flames.

John is detailed to look after Juliet because he's the only one with his hands free. I'm in the kitchen wrestling with the pink corpse of a turkey and my wife B is out in the yard chopping logs for the fire. Once a year we stack the fireplace and ignite it to celebrate the family hearth; it is the time when we compress our far-flung clan into one room and enact the ritual of Thanksgiving.

My piece of the family lives in a huge rented house in Houston, Texas, our temporary home for three years. This is how we know Jaques. It consists of myself and John, my first son; my second wife—the axe-wielding B—and our baby, who is just eleven months old. He still has a patchy shock of baby hair and it makes him look like a chimpanzee. Juliet and her mother and her mother's new husband, who is as deaf as a post and used to be in aerospace, are now in Switzerland, in a place they call "Zook." Our old folks live in London, England, *a city so dark,* as David Byrne's song says, *that people sleep in the daytime if they want to*—which is just what the old folks do. The last member of the family is Juliet's father, my sister's ex-husband, who wanders the world looking for someplace that isn't oppressed by hierarchy. Will he ever find it? At present, he lays his head to sleep in eastern Africa, Tanzania, where he grew up. He is in the city of Dar-es-Salaam, *Which shares its name,* says this postcard of concrete and glass office towers overlooking the Indian Ocean, *with Jerusalem: the "city of peace."*

Dear Paul, he writes. *I left London and went to Delhi because I could not bear the racism that pervades your country.*

He is what the English call an east-African Asian. We in the family all call him "Ex." *I left Delhi because I could not bear to live in a democracy so compromised by caste. And now, back in Tanzania, I find that all that counts is your father's name. Where is left?*

Ex, I wrote back. *It has to be Canada. You speak French, don't you?*

———————

London, Houston, Zurich, and Dar-es-Salaam. My literally extended family. Can you call this little diaspora a family? We maintain it using the machines that distort space and time, the airliners, the modems, the ATMs. They are the triumphs of the modern world that enable us to respond to our hundred-thousand-year-old impulse to belong to a tribe but still manage the globonomics of plenty. We meet once a year, kiss and give thanks, and then carry that memory of each other around with us the rest of the time like snapshots in a wallet; so when we meet again we are shocked by the realities—by how much our children have grown, by the zits and whiskers appearing on the teenagers, by the lines of age and failure and success on each other's faces, and by the alarming decline in the old folks. And then we carry on like we always did.

Sometimes when I sit out on the porch in the evening of a hot south-central Texas day, with the fragrant smell of baked chlorophyll still hanging in the air, I fall to thinking of the days when humans lived like the other primates do, roving and foraging in packs. Back then they lived in a plurality in which there were no individuals; everyone was distributed through everyone else. As we lounged in the planetwide forest the strands of family would have glimmered like threads of Lurex in the plaid. And then, in the days of Montague and Capulet I imagine great bricks of bone reared up in extended familial edifices, cemented by the new technology of banking, a literal inheritance. But now? In the *Summer Bay* wilderness of the present times? When families are loose connections of people scattered across the globe, truly extended, consisting of people as different from each other as granite is from groceries? Good news. We have the possibility of redistributing again. The egalitarian family. My sons and my brothers and my father are versions of myself, living different versions of each other's lives, at slightly shifted periods of time. We brook no hierarchy, we inherit no power. Together we span the last century. Ex at thirty-six, John at twelve, and chimp still zero; my new deaf brother in law, sixty-five years old, my aged father, *sans eyes, sans teeth* and pushing ninety, and myself at what B calls *Hawaii-five-O:* the six ages of man. If I include Jaques, the twenty-one-year-old lover of machines, because he's in our Thanksgiving clan as well this year, we are the bunch that Shakespeare wrote about. We are *The Seven Ages of Man.*

The first thunderstorms of the fall burst upon Texas out of hot blue skies, like bombs of rain. They deluge the nests of the tiny chestnut brown ants in our yard and provoke furious activity. John and I spent hours this year watching the ants clear out debris from one of the nests. The entrance was a hole as round as a bullet and about the same diameter as the barrel of a vermin gun. The ants emerged from this hole in a continuous procession, each one carrying a grain of sand the size of its own body in its pincers, holding it high in the air to clear the ground. They were piling these minute nuggets outside the nest in a fan-shaped cuesta about four inches wide and maybe two inches high at the tip of the scarp. Some of the ants would drop their loads on the dip slope of this little hill, while others would clamber all the way up it to teeter on the edge and hesitate for a moment, securing their footing, before casting theirs down the cliff. Then it was back down and into the gun barrel to fetch another grain of sand. The continuous stream of workers entering and leaving the hole meant that queues were perpetually forming, and all the ants as they passed touched antennae with the others who were waiting, affirming their intricate pheromonic pattern of bondage to each other. Ants— and bees, which belong to the same insect order—have an acute sense of smell, and each nest has its own particular odor. Possession of the odor is the password to the nest.

Is this complex social chemistry the evolutionary forerunner of our own human emotional bonds to each other? The social insects' sense of smell might be concentrated in their antennae or in the thousands of hair sensors that sprout all over their bodies; nobody knows. A similar perplexity surrounds the origin of the emotional triggers in humans. Strong candidates, as you might expect, are the smooth muscles of our hearts and guts. Another mystery about the ants and bees is the different physical forms that they can assume. The drones, queens, soldiers and winged males all hatch out of the same eggs. Entomologists think it is done by adjusting the type and quantity of food given to each larva as it nestles in its sculpted lodge within the nest, all delivered by handmaid insects, by instinct, as though some dietary program were running inside their tiny heads. Can it be so?

The intense social conformity of the ants' nest, which at first seems so mechanical, so *Hymenopteran Fascist,* turns out to have the full-blown emphasis of organic life as humans know it. The ants farm like us, they strive like us, they go to war like us, some even capture the nests of other ants and put them to work as slaves like us—and they care for their young ones so much it changes them completely. Just like us.

So my son and I watched over the spectacular industriousness of the brown ants for two whole days. We watched the steady accumulation of the little hill and the strident threat of the soldier ants as they patrolled the perimeter of the works. The soldiers are easily twice as big as the others and they have heads shaped like shovels, with huge pincers that glinted in the evening sun. Whenever one of us got too close, hanging our heads over their nest and blotting out their ant sky, the soldiers rushed over, clattering their weapons and forcing us back. At first it was funny to see them threaten with maximum ferocity and nil danger, like villains in a video game. But then John got a hair too close, and one of them ran up his leg, cleared the deep folds of his socks, and bit him on the bare skin of his calf. It spit a shot of acid in the wound that made him howl and swear like a Mississippi deckhand. Imagine this twelve-year-old, with his hair still as-trimmed-by-stepmom-on-bathnight, in his flapping skate pants and his size ten sports shoes, jumping up and down and mouthing obscenities at the top of his voice. I just stood there and guffawed like Goofy. John went little-boy mad, stamping crazily all over the nest and bringing forth a boiling swarm of vengeance that had us both fleeing for the pool. He stayed angry for hours. He spent the rest of the day in revenge. He fetched one of his old shoes and started systematically working his way across the yard, swatting every ant in sight. By nightfall he was hooting like a monkey, delighted with the results. He called me over to inspect the battlefield of wasted ant bodies, most of them half-crushed but still waving their legs around in their antish tenacity. *It's like trying to kill the Terminator!* he shouted, alluding to their strange machinic qualities of endurance, and started whacking them all over again. I should have stopped him doing it, I suppose, but I wanted him to learn the magnitude of his task. It was hopeless. No success was possible. No stirring songs could be written about the failure, even; no difference in the numbers of ants could be seen. They just kept on coming.

It is three days before Thanksgiving. John and Juliet and I are stashed in the front seat of B's pick-up on the way to the airport, looking at the jets gliding in across the city. Rumor has it that at any time of the day there are three hundred thousand people in the air over the continental United States. We wonder which one of them is carrying Juliet's mom and stepdad in from their stopover in California. My sister Liberty and her new husband Duke, who was a turbine engineer, and is now retired and—with his silver crewcut and his wrinkled jowl—much too old for her. Or is it much too good for her? The ferocious Texas sun is trying to bore through the dark green swipe across the top of the windshield and we are shivering in our T-shirts, because Juliet has decreed the internal temperature of the cab and is maintaining it with her foot planted firmly on the A/C dial. We have slipped through Houston's roadways as easily as a coin traveling through a slot machine, past towers and mansions and construction sites and slums, past art galleries and greensward lawns and past the tall gray hospital that looks like a U.S. Navy task force stuck stern first into the ground. I love the cheek-by-jowl cosmos of Houston. Its fresh-faced energy generates urban theory like a baby generates theories of parenthood. Joel Garreau's *Edge City* sees in it a bottom-line-driven metropolism of the suburbs that springs direct from desire and that is growing like algae on the so-new-it's-still-hot-surface of America. Lars Lerup's *After the City* calls Houston "now": he says we should sluice the old idea of cities clean out of our architecture and realize that the transformational technologies of the times—the cell-phones, I guess, the cars especially, the redistributed money—make our Paris-heavy ideas of city planning, the vistas and public spaces, the statues and the café life, just plain obsolete. I would not argue against these analyses of emergence—but right now, against the background of squabbling kids and the glory of the sun piercing my heart, I think that all cities, including this turbulent, machinic, Houston, are no more or less than human nests. They are fragments of the *Cultivated Wilderness,* localities in the *Human Artifice.*

We pass the Central Business District's blue and brown glass towers, which almost every city in North America has. They are so ubiquitous you could call it the *continental style.* I try to engage John and Juliet with John McPhee's description of mimicry in urban America—these high towers, he says, are an imitation of downtown New York, the paradigm of all Central Business Districts, just as golf courses all over the world are imitations of the glacial moraine landscape around St. Andrews, Scotland, where the game was invented. In Saudi, I have heard, there are golf courses where the greens as well as the bunkers are made of sand! The globe is scattered with these little pieces of Scotland, as it is with imitations of New York. The special bite of McPhee's observation is that New York's towers are founded on the rock of Manhattan Island. It's easy to build tall just there. In Houston, now, the ground beneath the beating wheels of our pickup is a fathomless depth of oil shale—sloppy ground, and no match for an eighty-storey building. Consequently, and all in pursuit of this chimera of economic power, Houston's towers go down into the fluid ground almost as far as they go up, like fishing floats on the Golden Pond.

Of course, Houstonites would not agree that economic power is in any way chimerical. They have turned these vast basements into a subterranean paradise, where the air is cool and the streets are safe and you can buy whatever you want. So the *Hymenopotera* don't go shopping—but does that not sound like an ant's nest? John and Juliet could not care less, being engrossed in the battle of the cooling dial—but the idea of the urban nest grows on me the more I think about it. So does Houston, incidentally. Fourth largest city in the United States after New York, Los Angeles, and Chicago—and catching up fast.

We are close enough to the airport to smell the kerosene. We slide open the moonroof so John and Juliet can stand on the seat with their heads stuck out into the slipstream and scream at the jets as they drop onto the runway across Airport Boulevard. We park in the short-term lot and cross the sun-baked desert of cement toward the cool mirage of the terminal buildings. We are way too early. We get chips and candy and make a temporary camp outside the baggage claim area, and while John and Juliet slide up and down the polished floor like hooligans, I allow myself to muse to myself on the nature of airports. Are airports machines? Can you call something so loosely connected a machine? It would include everything from the signs on the freeways through the auto-barriers on the car parks, and the departure terminals with all their integrated checking and sorting devices and their baggage handling and people processing machinery, and then through the airplanes themselves with their crystal-block inertial guidance gyros and hydraulic flaps and autopilots and vacuum-powered toilets and machines for heating up airline meals; and on through the flight traffic control systems that guide the airplanes themselves via automated waypoint markers and landing radars into other airports; and on again through the baggage reclaims and the immigration service torture chambers and into the parking lots and out on to the streets again. Are airports machines? Are they miniature cities in their own right? Or are they just pieces of that giant human nest that I can't get out of my head?

Eventually, our flight, in the shape of one of Continental's busy MD-80s, noses into the concertina. Its conservative gray livery bears every grease mark and squashed bug of the last fifteen turn-arounds. All of us waiting crowd up to get a good view of our loved ones as they emerge. There is plenty of antenna-touching going on here. I hoist Juliet up on my shoulders so she can witness the emotion of the scene. When she catches sight of her mother she shrieks and punches the air with both fists and digs her heels into my chest. All around us people are kissing and laughing and greeting and crying, and here is Liberty, smiling and hugging us all, her face creased in relief that soon, very soon now, she will be able to light up a cigarette. The grizzled figure of Duke looms up behind her, pulling their little wheeled cabin baggage carts behind him. He is wearing a cowboy hat! To fly to Texas! As the English say—it's like *bringing coals to Newcastle*.

"I know," he says, pulling his jaw tight like Cary Grant, "It's like carting lumber to the forest. It's for Juliet." He plucks it off his head and places it on hers, where it settles huge and loose, and she spins off across the lounge looking like a flying saucer. John gets a handshake, a slap on the arm and a twenty-dollar bill.

"Boy, that was a rough flight," he says. "Choppy over Phoenix. Big thunderheads over El Paso. Damn pansies in the seats behind us kept throwing up!" I tell him about the techno-hippie idea dreamed up in the sixties by Cedric Price, the same man who invented that machine for swinging Londoners, the Fun Palace. It was that air travel would be safer and quicker if the passengers were turned into machine components. Sedated and packed in Styrofoam containers and loaded by forklift trucks onto cargo planes. Hijacking would be a thing of the past.

"Styrofoam, you say?" said Duke. "Doesn't sound much fun to me. What do you have at the gate? A recovery ward? Flowers? Hell of a thing!"

Airports and hospitals: both are semipublic, highly serviced, full of human bodies undergoing transfers, both loaded with the requirements of professional scripts. There are similarities. Are machine buildings still interesting? You would have thought the whole thing had been hammered into the ground by the Hi-Tek crew: *this is modernism,* they say. *It is steel and glass: it is as simple as falling off logs.* But I remember visiting one of the shrines of the industrial revolution, Arkwright's cotton mill at Cromford, England, an eighteenth-century building in which the human workers had been reduced to machine parts and spent their days lashed to the unrelenting pace of the looms. The building was not steel and glass; it was fortified with solid stone. It was an armored machine, built as thick as a castle to fend off the Luddites, who wanted to smash mechanical tyranny to smithereens.

"What was that?" said Duke, turning up the volume on his hearing aid.

"Smithereens," I said. "It's an Irish word. It means bits of smithery."

"Huh?"

"Blacksmithery!" I yelled, and he roared with laughter as if I'd told a joke. We set off toward carousel five, where the first pieces of CO1825's baggage were forlornly tumbling onto the belt.

All the way back home I can't stop thinking about the urban nest. It is not a planning idea—it's not what they call 'urbanism'. The point about it is that you concern yourself only with the immediate locality. The greater whole of the city is like a contemporary version of the Oriental Caliphates—fabulous and infinite and beyond your control. Our cities are like the complex patterns of persian carpets. Like the global modern world itself, the urban nest is made of partial pictures, not whole ones. It is intricate and flexible. It is anonymous, like the freedom of the airport traveler to be just another ant. And it's local thanks to the machines, which are the product of our specific desires. The machines carry pieces of our lives for us. They are with us here in the nest like the drones. They are part of the family. They have levered open the casks of ancient secrets and scattered them wide. No one knows what else they are up to—but here's one question—what is more frightening? The unpredictable syntheses our machines put together without our knowledge, or the way we turn machines against our fellow human beings?

I try to speak of all this to my sister Liberty who is dreamily cruising her way through her third cigarette on the bench seat of the pickup. The doughty Duke is bundled up with the kids outside in the back, enjoying a Houston sky full of towering clouds and silver-rose splashes of color.

"Why worry?" she says. "It's Thanksgiving. So don't think about it. Just give thanks." What, me not worry? I am in the fifth age of man, I am the Justice, it is up to me to arbitrate the thanks this year. So what am I giving thanks for now? A terrible thought appears in my head: I want to make this a thanksgiving for the human invasion of the world. For our complex, accreted cultured world. Our partial, human, modern world. The ants and the bees, I think to myself, have nothing on us.

Here it is: a Thanksgiving: the humans have invaded the planet. And with our machines, we moderns have an inside track on cause and effect that renders the ancient world, however much more profound it seems than ours, as blind as a maze. We have planted robots on Mars that can teach themselves to walk on alien surfaces. We have isolated the things we want to kill and developed the tools we needed and carried through the extermination. We have invaded with intent to conquer: and now, like an army of occupation, we have only ourselves to manage. It is a big job, that management. An army of occupation is not carried forward by its mission, like the army that does the fighting. Complacency and corruption, and sloth and superstition, are the demons that plague it. And all the time, we must keep a watch out for the resistance.

Liberty looks at me curiously, picking pieces of tobacco off her tongue like smokers do. "Oh my, Pauly, you have it bad." *Pauly* is what she used to call me when we were little children. But this isn't bad, I start to say. This is just facing up to things. "I'll tell you what this is," she says, interrupting. "This is the new nihilism. As if the old one wasn't bad enough. You need to watch your mouth."

How can I explain? All this year I've been ending my lectures with some version of the *army of occupation,* and it's had a universally lousy reception. You would think I had been cheating my audiences to look at the discomfort and denial on their faces. But I think it's just facing up to things. History, for one—and taking responsibility for what we've done. Nihilism for me would be to say that the whole edifice of the cultivated world is a disaster and needs to be dismantled and that we should go back to living like the aborigines did, in harmony with nature. I don't think that at all. I think the reality is that with every breath we take we are in harmony with nature. And that the change that humans have wrought in the world is a wonderful thing.

. . . plains of open inquiry rolling out to the horizon like Texas itself . . . Route 349, fourteen miles south of Midland, Texas. Photograph by the author.

SEMINAR ONE

RIGHT-BAM-NOW!

Can Can! It's eighteen ninety eight—with tumbling billows of silk petticoats, black fishnets and red knickers! The military thrust of the music, with its suggestive blasts of brass, and the air sweet with pheromones and the smell of lust! The Naughty Nineties!

And one hundred years later, after a cold hard century of global wars and genetic experiments and the metaphysics of nothingness—it is *nineteen* ninety eight. I am at the University of Texas and these nineties are not naughty at all. The entire faculty has just been issued with a pamphlet defining sexual harassment and inappropriate behavior. Do not have sex with the students, it says. Do not talk about sex in class. No touching, no sympathetic hugs, no pats on the back. And be economical with your handshakes. That's okay. Sex with students is not what I'm here for. I'm here for knowledge. The limestone tower that dominates this paradise of a campus here in Austin, Texas has the words "Ye shall know the truth and the truth shall make you free" inscribed in letters thirty inches high on the facade. That's what I'm here for. I know they are the words of Jesus and that the truth they refer to is that Christ was the son of God, but the motto suggests to me plains of open inquiry rolling off to the horizon like Texas itself: that's why I'm here.

I am sitting in a seminar room at a cedar wood table surrounded by Eames chairs with three thousand series aluminum alloy frames and green leather upholstery; two thousand bucks apiece. The University of Texas is loaded. The floor is polished brown stone. It feels like the boardroom for some huge oil company. And here are seven graduate students, all as thirsty for knowledge as I am—anything to give them an edge in what's called *the real world*. We are reading the enigmatic brilliance of the philosophy of Gilles Deleuze and Felix Guattari because it's 1998 and high time we did so. We call them D&G in class, because of the amusing coincidence of their initials with those of the Italian fashion house Dolce e Gabbana.

I've started off, however, by raising a problem with the idea of 'process'—in architecture, that would be the idea that the building is not an object in space but part of a continuum of processes, one of which is the designer. As its protagonists say, the word 'building' is not a *noun*, it's a *verb*. The contemporary carriers of the modernist torch are mostly in that basket. I guess all the sustainability people would be in it too. The ever sharp Stewart Brand with his *How Buildings Learn* would be in it. So the problem is difficult, or delicate, to frame. The problem is what happens when process flips into consumption: we consume in practice when we use images as shortcuts. We consume in the academies when we use the works of philosophers as fuel instead of as a parallel investigation. It's like burning the roof of the house to keep warm. What I'm driving at is that in a few years Deleuze and Guattari's books may languish collecting dust in the architecture libraries, rather as Derrida's do now. And as the works of Melvin Webber, the network-age prophet of Los Angeles, have been doing since 1973.

What are we doing with all this philosophy in schools of art and architecture? I tell the students that it's because we have been let down by the artists, who have become stuck in an innovative groove. I tell them about Gertrude Stein's account of the first time her companion, Alice B. Toklas, saw Picasso's paintings. This was back in 1907 when painting was strange and new and was the medium by which culture was being levered out of the naughty nineties. Toklas doesn't know what to think of the paintings; she says they are *ugly.*

"Of course they are ugly!" Stein replies. "Picasso says that when you make a thing for the first time it is so complicated it is bound to be ugly—but those who follow, who do the same thing after you, do not have the worry of making it, so they can make it pretty and then everyone can like it!"

But this is not what happened. The artists of the succeeding generations have done nothing of the sort. They have gone on thrashing through dungeons of confusion chopping the heads off ever more complex inversions until the world of art has become sodden with irony. Picasso was wrong, it turns out—he was not the end as well as the beginning of the making. There is too much turbulence in the modern to solve it, I tell my students. So, losing patience with the artists, we turn to the philosophers.

The subject of the seminar is machines as architecture. As in: machines *are* architecture rather than machines *and* architecture. To do the latter, one could start with Le Corbusier's

Airplane! and examine the whole twentieth-century project of machine mimicry in buildings. All of it. From the stripped clean aesthetics of modern buildings whose style imitates the invisibility of machine functions—via the procedural, where design inputs are used like wind in a tunnel to shape the aesthetic equivalent of a low drag coefficient—to the silent majority of contemporary architecture, which is caught in the consumption trap, traded like slaves, using the built equivalent of a good set of teeth or a submissive attitude to confer a little value on the utilitarian frame. You can see that I am in no condition for that undertaking: no, this seminar is machines *are* architecture, and I hope to get a result by taking the philosophers and crashing them into my students' architectural assumptions. And mine.

So we start with D&G's *Nomadology*. It's just a fragment of their colossus, but we start with it because it describes the Mongol war machine shaping itself in the careering eastward momentum like molten metal shooting through the air. It embodies a huge analogy of the machine world slicing through human history on its own trajectory.

For D&G, analogies are not some literary nicety, they are bombs in a war. Their writing is all dynamic and emergence, quite unlike this class, which plods through the heavy translation like kittens in a blizzard. I am as bad as the rest of them. As philosophically naive as Bambi. I had to have it pointed out to me that *Nomadology* is a pun on Leibniz's *Monadology*—which becomes a byway to be explored, with its description of the bright cells of being and their strange relationships to each other. Our human brains as well, hurtling through an infinity whose space is made up of a multitude of personal galaxies.

One of the students, a gentle giant named John who sports one of those tufts of hair on his lower lip like a bebop jazz-hound, says it is a three-hundred-year-old explanation of the market economy. He puts it like this: he says that there is scarcely a thing in his apartment that doesn't have swarms of identical partners located elsewhere on planet earth. His Toshiba computer, his toy airliners by Shabak, his Fugees records, his Motorola telephone, his Pilot EasyTouch ballpoint pen. We get the picture. He says he may have constructed their particular monadic relationship, he may live in the space they configure, but there are parallel universes, other homes, in which the same things are permutated in different ways. How does that sound?

My position at this time is what it is in *What Is Architecture?* and *The Cultivated Wilderness.* Architecture is not just buildings; it is more than that. It is not everything, but it is more than just buildings. At one end of the scale of architecture are landscapes, which are long-term strategies that underlie all architectural action. In the center are the buildings, which stand for a few generations and give us something to bump up against, a running commentary on who we think we are. At the other end of the scale are the machines, which have such short lives that they can be fitted closely to their purpose and, unlike buildings, be truly useful.

Another student, also called John, has looked up *machine* in the encyclopedia and come up with the five simple machines: lever, wheel, pulley, screw, and wedge. Interesting, but not much use, I think. Where's the dynamic? He brings up the subject of the inclined plane. He says he guesses that's a wedge. He points to the enormous ramp up which the stones for the great pyramid were elevated and says he thinks that such an inclined plane is at the same time a landscape, a building and a machine. This John is a good Texan who is going to marry his fiancée, a minister's daughter, upon graduation and take her to live in his hometown of Lubbock, where the land is so flat an inclined plane would indeed be a significant matter. But still, I press him, where's the dynamic? I ask everyone to make a human condition statement. I may be naive but I know that every philosopher has to start with a human condition statement. It's what turns *a posteriori* into a picture of the world.

If you keep these seminar discussions open enough, if you make a policy of entertaining every single utterance, however daft, and allow the class to mull it over like a bunch of beachcombers examining a strange new find, you pretty soon arrive at a state where ideas seem to spring from the air itself. The people around the table shed their painstakingly built pecking orders and elaborately configured self-consciousness and become mediums for the transport of inventions. So it was that a simple observation from a third student—also, for heaven's sake, called John—suddenly solved this question of the dynamic. For the first four sessions he had sat there in his golfing clothes and his Eddie Bauer cap without saying a word.

"One second I was crossing the road," he said, "and the next, bam! I'm lying in the emergency room with tubes up my nose!" He said that nobody knows what the next second will bring. We're all on the edge of a wave, surfing into the unknown. "We're like surfing time, that's what life is. That's what evolution is. That's what the Big Bang is!" Everything is dynamic, all moving forward through different scales of time, but all we can know about is the point called right now.

"Bam! There goes another one!" says John. He is standing up, holding his arms out like Jesus, miming a man leaning forward into time. He is trying to illustrate each passing moment, each split second, as it forms the present and instantly slips off to become the past. "Bam! There goes another one!" He means that it is the future itself that keeps erupting into the present, as though water were boiling backward, the nothing of the bubbles perpetually coming into being; and it is all implemented by our own being alive, for without that none of it would be perceived.

Is this Can-Can philosophy? A human condition based on gossip and rumors and the uproar of now? There are three histories in this moment of right now—three time journeys—three *progresses*. The first is the current position of the expanding universe, some fourteen billion years into its progress from its mysterious origin to its mysterious end. Second is the story of life on earth, the expansion here being the steady complexification of the last two and a half billion years of evolution, and the current "now" being your own species, *Homo sapiens.* Third is your own self, you at the age you are now—bam! Now—bam! Now—getting older every second, with your burgeoning memory filling up your brain as though it too were an expanding universe, as you race through your life. These are your three frontiers. The universe, the other people, yourself. This is your condition.

By the time we finish the seminar four months later, 1999 is almost with us and the bent architectures of the Deleuzians are on every other page of every other magazine. *He will be folding in his grave,* cracks my stout friend Jeff, because philosophy is philosophy and nothing else, according to D&G's own testimony in *What Is Philosophy?* But we are still just inside the twentieth century and the story of architecture—read *buildings*—all the way through that century has been to try to be something other than what it is. That is why machines seem so effortlessly architectural to me, as though architecture really is happening somewhere other than in the buildings. Not least this big fat bus of a Boeing that is flying me to Stockholm. In the next seat is a Finnish engineer from Nokia who has been quality-assessing their San Francisco outfit. He tells me that it has just snowed in Stockholm, which is lucky, he says, because at this time of year this far north the days are as short as elves and snow on the ground brightens the afternoons out of their suicidal gloom.

We land in a dawn as grey as the Luftwaffe, and I discover it is St. Lucia's day; a choir of school children all dressed in white robes is already caroling at the head of the escalators. One of the singers has been chosen to be St. Lucia. She has a golden halo and a blood red choker, with two red ribbons hanging down across her chest.

"Some muzak, huh?" says the man from Nokia. "Do you know the story of St. Lucia? She was a virgin—persecuted by the Romans. They put her eyes out with sharp sticks. See the red ribbons? Get it?" I look back at the fifteen-year-old St. Lucia whose Scandinavian-green eyes were not at all put out and reflect on the unlikelihood of her being a virgin.

That evening my hosts took me to a restaurant in Stockholm that they said is very chic. The meal was an interesting complex of fish and herbs chased by aquavit. At one point the lights dimmed and another St. Lucia procession came in and sang carols by the light of candles and then left again for the next restaurant. It was all so warm and foreign and strange I thought I could have been Marco Polo in Xanadu—and then suddenly the whole place froze. A couple had just entered and all eyes were on them. The woman looked like a photo in a magazine. Every part of her except her breasts and her buttocks was hard muscle. Her lips were stuffed so full of collagen she couldn't close her mouth. Her hair bounced with a million shades of blonde. She was as gorgeous as a palace. But it was not she whom everyone else was looking at. My companions hissed to me that the man was a hot young movie director—they called him *Sweden's Tarantino.* Everyone wanted to catch his eye, to have a piece of him. He went round the tables shaking hands with his chosen ones, towing his babe behind him like a trophy on wheels. It was the strangest thing, to experience the electric effect of celebrity on the people around without feeling it at all inside myself. This ordinary guy, just another guy on the street to me, had the whole place spellbound. It was Xanadu with bells on. It was like being cast back to the beginning and finding myself in among a strange tribe, perhaps even another species, whose customs, from their beautiful ice-bound city of a hundred islands, to their processions of tortured virgins and this celebration of the unknown living totem, were utterly strange to me.

So to my human condition of the history of the universe, the history of life on earth and the history of yourself I want to add a fourth progress. It is the history of your tribe. I mean to distinguish between the people you know and interact with and the great mass of humanity that is unknown to you. You are inside a *Homo sapiens* body, but your interactions are with the people around you, the people of your tribe. There's a difference between people and humanity, and the difference is a material one. The bodies versus the ideas. It's why going to war has been so effective.

The whole business is complicated by the interwoven histories of the different human tribes. We may have all come from the same tiny pack of individuals that separated from the other hominids a hundred thousand years ago—but the spreading out across the globe, the determination to differentiate between different peoples, that is the fourth progress, the fourth frontier. Globalization is, as furious European philosophers point out, a ballooning of North American culture rather than a real inclusive worldwide thing. But there are other observers, the deeply phlegmatic internet watchers, who say that that is all about to change. *Six billion people on the planet, and how many do you know?* they say. *You'd better watch out. Pretty soon you're going to be face to face with all of them!* And what will happen to our tribal frontiers then?

. . . full of accelerations and crash stops and the brazen postures of being human . . . Carmen Amaya, June 26, 1941. © Hulton-Deutsch Collection / Corbis.

1

INFANT

THE CHIMPANZEE'S
FALL FROM GRACE

I love my little boy Chimp. He is just short of one year old.
Sometimes he looks like a lump of lard, a human roughly
formed by clumsy thumbs, head too big, arms too short, ankles
made of dough. I love him then: and I love him also when he
is beautiful, with his fragrant hair shining gold in the sun and
his eyes the color of the Pacific.

Chimp had a brutal birth. Maybe I love him so because of that.
He set out on his journey from the womb chin first and got
stuck. B was racked by enormous spasms from dawn to dusk,
refusing help for the pain, on her feet all the time because she
couldn't sit or kneel or lie down without causing him distress.
She was connected by wire-pads to a heartbeat monitor that
slowed like death every time she tried to take the pressure off
her feet. We were surrounded by machinery. We were in London, in the delivery room of a huge old Victorian hospital that
played host to its infestation of modern medical robots like an
ancient grandmother surrounded by rug-rats—and there was
little Chimp buried deep inside B stuck chin-first into the top
of the birth canal, his head bent back and his umbilical cord
wound round his neck; and all the time the contractions were
crashing through her like waves breaking, trying to turn her

inside out, engulfing Chimp over and over again and squeez-
ing him ever more tightly into his predicament.

The whole long day dragged by like this, and we saw noon
and dusk come and go, suffering every breath she took. Until
at last the doctors and midwives who had been whispering
in the corridors declared a state of emergency. They filled B's
veins with oxytocin to strengthen the vigor of her contractions—which were already as big as mountains—and they
called up an anaesthetist to deaden the pain of what they had
just done. The double-strike of their chemical invasion scared
me. How risky is it? It happens all the time, but how risky is it?
I waited for B to be released from her pain as ashen faced as an
execution victim. Anaesthetizing a woman in childbirth is not
as common as the launching of airliners into the sky—but is it
as difficult as that?

———————————

The anaesthetist arrives. He is courteous, careful, and nattily
dressed. Maybe Italian. He says his name is Alberto. He out-
lines his plan. He has to take his two-inch Tuohy needle and
insert it between two of the vertebrae in her back. He has to
push steadily on the needle until it punctures the strong ligament that attaches her muscles to her backbones: as soon as
he feels the ligament pop, he must stop the pressure, because
there are only a couple of millimeters to spare before he'll hit
the spinal cord itself. He has to take his syringe and socket into
the back of the needle, whose sharp slanted little hole is resting inside her spinal column, and then slowly pump in the
exact dose of lethal juice. She has to lie perfectly still for the

procedure, so the thing is to time it between contractions—but by the time we've got around to it they are coming every three seconds and the whole thing has to be expanded out to fill two measures of time.

"Okay—here we go," he says. He rolls up his sleeves. In the first three seconds he deftly places the needle—then there is one of these volcanic tremors a full three minutes long, during which I am a human strap holding her as still as I can with all my weight applied and Alberto hangs on to the butt of the needle keeping it perfectly perpendicular to her spine and not too far in or out and Chimp's amplified heartbeat grinds away in the background like a freight train on a steep incline and the noises in B's throat as she struggles not to move sound like the muted howling of wild beasts: then another three seconds pause for him to connect up his syringe and introduce the miracle of painlessness. Alberto and I are working close together, practically intertwined, over B's suffering body. His face is steely with the concentration of the craftsman at work, and sweat is breaking from every pore.

"Ready to rock!" He suddenly says. "The thing is done! Ready to roll!" He is grinning like a monkey. He clasps my arms. "You want to go into business with me? We'll make a fortune!" He picks up B's limp hand and kisses it operatically. "Cara! You are the bravest woman I've ever seen!"

———————

B and I had discussed the possible existence of Chimp for three years. It was not like mounting an expedition to find Bigfoot; we were engaged in future planning. We were behaving like product engineers. At least I was. B was engaged in an act of will. I was the one with pages of cost calculations and lists of pros and cons, trusting to the architecture of prophylactics to buy myself some extra deadline while I tried to get used to the idea of another child. In the chimp-pack condition I guess babies are the result of having sex. None of this deliberation, or second mortgaging, or the putting of careers on hold that our liberation from pack life has led us to. No calculations—just the urgent requirement of sex. Procreation by the seat of your pants. But as B cradled in her arms the latest offspring to emerge from her circle of friends and showed me how gorgeous it was—*look at this crease around his wrists! The open directness of his gaze! His sublime neediness!*—I found myself behaving like an engineer trying to formulate a new product. Wasn't I too old for this? I started consulting anyone I came across who had done the same thing, accosting grizzled men pushing babies in prams to ask, "How has going round a second time changed your life?" In the end it was clinched by this observation, surrendered from the unshaven jaw of the fifty-five-year-old father of twins who tore at his clothes and scattered themselves all over the place while he stood stock still looking like a scarecrow in a wind-tunnel: "It's already decided. If she wants a child and you won't give it to her, she'll leave you and find someone else who will."

Simple. I would rather have my hands and feet cut off than lose B. I gave our unfinished packet of condoms to twelve-year-old John, and she was pregnant, I swear it, before his friends had time to explain to him what they were for and how they worked. He wouldn't believe me when I tried to tell him.

I have never seen such calm radiate from a human face as B's in that postepidural moment. As exhausted as she was, the euphoria of her relief was so strong I felt it myself. I turned to thank Alberto: "Hey, man, it's my job!" he said, just as his pager bleeped. "That's me again," he said, shrugging his shoulders. "No rest for the nasty!" And he disappeared off to deal with some other crisis in another part of this vast brick ship of endangered souls, leaving the swing doors of the delivery room banging behind him. The midwives gathered round and hooked B up to a whole different set of monitors and drips, and we found a position that worked for Chimp and locked her senseless legs and trunk into it and arranged the basket of wires and tubes around her. A continuous record of the birth started spooling out of the machinery on a thermal paper roll, her now painless contractions and Chimp's now steady heart rate represented in the same jagged tracelines with which they record seismic movements.

She is a planet riven by earthquakes, I reflected, with a poetry induced by deep anxiety. And then collapsing into an equally anxious prose: *It's still stuck in there. How is it going to get out?* At that stage none of us knew whether Chimp was a boy or a girl.

A hundred years ago, they both would have died. Chimp remained jammed in his crevice like some puppy lost down a well as midnight came and went and the cusp of Sagittarius slipped past and he turned into a Capricorn. And at last, in the dead of the night, the grim-faced doctors decided to get out their knives and cut him out.

Six miles away, the city of London sailed on through space, perched on its piece of earth crust, notching up another day in its two-thousand-year life. In the orange gloom of the night the palace guards were standing to attention, facing the gilded statue of Victoria, empress of an empire now lost: at her feet were the big black bronze empire trophy statues of Britannia surrounded by spears and shields and sleeping lions and allegories of the continents. And that's what B looked like, riding on top of a pile of medical machinery and peripherals, feeling nothing from her diaphragm downward, whistling through the dingy corridors of the old hospital. Into an operating theater lit as bright as day and full of people all loosely dressed in green wraps and cotton hats and facemasks. It felt as though we had been captured by aliens and ushered into their inspection chamber. They dressed me up like them and stationed me by B's ear and gave me her hand to hold and erected a screen so I would not panic at the horrors of the surgery going on behind it. My job was to whisper *okay, it'll soon be over* into her ears. Alberto was there too, sitting up at the head end on a high stool so he could look over the curtain. He looked like the engineer on a three-man flight deck surrounded by switches and plastic tubes of fluids and cathode ray screens full of information, the current stock prices on B's blood chemistry. He was winking and exchanging jokes with the two surgeons who were going to extract Chimp from his confinement. They sliced through B's skin and parted the yellow jelly of fat that had made her beautiful pre-pregnant belly swell, as she used to say, like Marilyn Monroe's—and they cut through the muscles at the base of it and on through her uterine walls, which they peeled carefully apart: and suddenly there he was! Little

Chimp! Held up in the air for us to see, slick with amniotic fluid, cerise in color, perfect: his huge testicles as plain as a bull in a slaughterhouse. Good enough to eat. They evacuated his lungs on one machine, and sluiced him down with another and quality-checked him and put him into an incubator while they stitched poor old B back up again. They took their time, an hour, at least, so she would be minimally scarred—and all that while I stared at Chimp through the Plexiglas walls of the incubator while he grizzled and growled for his first meal, looking just like a newborn chimpanzee, all compressed by his traumas and looking at least one hundred years old.

———————

"Oh, Life! It's bigger! Bigger than you and you are not me!" thumps through my head while I gaze at him. A snatch of post-modern lyrics. And then comes a memory of reading an account of the first days of our species. The idea is that *Homo sapiens* were not alone, that there was not a slender chain of evolutionary links that culminated in Us, but rather an explosion of different hominid species that lived side by side much as the half dozen species of pigeons do today. All these hominids had the brain capacity for speech, but it was only *Homo sapiens* who discovered how to talk to each other— about sixty thousand years ago—and when they did, the first thing they said to each other was, *Let's kill all the others.*

It was the first great cultivation of the world, I think, an event to match the agricultural revolution—a vision of a landscape free of competition. *It may even be the original sin,* I find myself musing as I contemplate my newborn son, who lies there clenching his fists on the floor of the incubator. He is square shouldered, looks like a boxer, looks ready for anything. He has survived his ordeal.

When everything was completed and all the paperwork signed off, and the lights and the machinery were all shut down, Chimp and B were reunited together in the glimmer of the recovery ward. Mouth to nipple and skin to skin. Released from the machinery, simple mammals again, their hearts beating in counterpoint. Hers as slow as sleep and his as fast as a runner's. They could have been in a grass hut in the middle of the forest fifty thousand years ago with a fire dance being stamped out in the dust outside to the sound of drums and the chant of the shaman. Except that instead of the wind it was the giant compressors in the hospital plant room that rumbled in the background, and instead of moonlight it was the glimmer of fluorescents that crept in under the door, and the sound of the dance was the whisper of technicians in conference. I thought again—they could have been in a spaceship hurtling through Andromeda galaxy in fifty thousand years time.

I tiptoed out of the room and made my way slowly up to the entrance hall of the hospital feeling like the father of every baby in the world. A responsibility as deep as the ocean. And there, sitting in the lurid bonhomie of a drinks machine sat Alberto, his hair and clothes as dishevelled as mine after this long and busy shift.

"You want a Coke?" he said.

"I want therapy," I said. "Something for new fathers."

"I got one for you," he said. "Alternative therapy. Like aromatherapy. Me and a friend going to start up an alternative health business. Linguatherapy. Maybe we call it *Lick Your Wounds*. We hire young women and the idea is, they lick you till you're better." I was too tired to argue with him.

"You got any children yourself?" I asked.

"Hell no! No way." he said. "I couldn't put a woman through all that." I guess it's an occupational hazard for anaesthetists. But like I said, I was too tired to argue. I drove home as the new day dawned with all the windows wide open, thinking of the shuddering apocalypse of birth. The hatching of crows that smash their way out of their eggs with the same beaks they use in adult life for smashing their way into other bird's eggs; cuckoo chicks, who have a reflex wing-flip action if a spot on their back is touched, which eventually heaves all the other nestlings out onto the forest floor far below. And that dreadful lowing of the cows in October when all the young males of the herd are suddenly spirited away to be eaten by humans. It goes on without pause for several days and nights, this lament: *Where have all the boys gone? They've stolen all the boys!* By the time I got home and listened to *Good Queen Jane* by the Bothy Band, the sad tale of a medieval caesarean, I was in floods of tears. I crawled into the empty bed and dreamed of Chimp and his generation—and every single one of B's friends has had a boy, not a girl in sight among them—losing their teenage lives in the trenches in 2017. It has happened before.

In the afternoon when I showed up at the maternity ward I found B, smiling and fit and well and as excited as a lottery winner, looking plump as a mother in the voluminous pink dressing gown her own mother had lent her. She had the Chimp cradled in her arms, sucking away at her breast, an expert already in the only thing he knew how to do. And with huge and elaborate care she levered him off her nipple and handed him to me, this twenty-first-century boy, born into a world of machines. Who was neither beaked nor ejected to the ground nor kidnapped nor fighting world war three. Who just wanted to be held tight and to look around him at the strange light of the world and to listen to the sound of his father's voice.

———————

Chimp's *falling from grace* has been the coming into being of the animal Chimp out of the desire for Chimp. He is safe, we have caught him, and now the little one is sharing the same world as my own father and me. He of the seventh age—the old man—is both bald and grey at the same time and as chock full of memory as a hard drive. The memories are starting to be random-accessed, however, because the old man has had his own falling. Twigged by a stroke into a wheelchair. He ruminates on the state of the world from what he calls his dungeon-on-wheels. He is given to poetics: "Look at me! This fantastic invention, this spinning axle that mobilizes everything from the compressors in jetliners to the drive motors spinning inside our computers, has here been pressed into use as a crutch!"

My father is an old man. My son is a little baby. They stare at each other over the gulf of time that separates them. The old one was born at the beginning of the last century and the little one at the start of this new one. I am in the middle. In *The Seven Ages of Man*, Chimp is the *mewling infant;* my father *sans teeth, sans eyes;* and I am the *Justice,* gently paunched, wine lined, *dispensing wise saws and modern instances.* We are three men. We love watching things fly. We love the big old owl that flaps across the shadows in the garden at dusk, and we love the roar of camouflaged fighters as they stream their vapors fast and level over the fields. What else do we love? Of course: we all marvel at the stone buttocks of the *Three Graces.* There is a fifteen-inch-high copy of Canova's statue of the three naked women caressing each other standing on my father's piano, and we love it. We marvel at the quality of their breasts. Especially the little one. What about the time when B and Chimp and I were cruising the mall and B decided to purchase some new breast management technology? We all crammed into the changing cubicle and Chimp and I sat in the corner while she tried on a series of exotic contraptions and as soon as he saw her nipples Chimp flipped, yelling and straining to get at them and feed. It was still all he really knew how to do—and he did it there in the mall—he is the paradigm of the consumer, with his childish lusts. It made me think that our culture of consumption keeps us all childlike, in the way our pet cats never grow out of being kittens. But that's what I mean. My father, Chimp, and I are three men, living in an obsolete patriarchy, and preoccupied with the same things.

This afternoon the house in Houston rings with flamenco music. My heavy-duty sister Liberty and her forget-me-not daughter Juliet are teaching B to dance in the Spanish style. They stand in a line flicking fingers over their heads and stamping on the polished floor and clap in that staccato eight-time beat that makes flamenco so assertive. It is like life, this dancing, full of accelerations and crash stops and the brazen postures of being human. There is a place for youth and a place for age in it. The women, all three, pull faces of dense concentration, frowning like eagles and hollering along to the singing that arises from the loudspeakers like smoke from campfires. It is the wail of Islam compounded with the stamping of Celts, plus virtuosic flurries of guitarism and the rustle of twirling silks. It is furious, bloody and sweet. And then it stops: suddenly the dance ends. The women rest standing, doubled over with their legs apart and their elbows supported on their knees, gasping for breath and sweat pouring off them. Not at all like the Three Graces, it occurs to me: more like beasts of burden. *The women are holding up the house.*

"You are holding up the house," I tell them. I mean it as a compliment.

"Damn you." says Liberty. She says she is nervous about Ex coming for Thanksgiving. Nervous about Duke and Juliet being in the same house with him. She is holding in her hand the remote control to the CD player. She hits the play button and the room fills up with gypsy music again, and she and B and Juliet are off stamping and shouting and clapping, grandly defiant of the multiplying complications of life.

Ever since she arrived, Liberty has been carrying the remote control around with her like a cowpoke with a six-shooter, and she's been zapping the stereo into life any time she feels her emotions need a lift. The remote is hooked up to a 32-bit sampler, a machine that was revealed to Liberty with biblical impact as I demonstrated to her what it could do. I played her an English disc of choral music, Stanford's "The Bluebird," which is as precise and moistly phrased as a lover's whisper. It was recorded in the Lady Chapel of Ely Cathedral, Cambridgeshire, a place of the utmost calm. The chapel is a big room the size of a barn with huge plain leaded windows that flood light all over walls covered with small stone figures. The sounds inside it are immaculate. When you step in there your heartbeat and your breathing are taken from you and gently amplified and, replete with echoes, issued back into your ears. They recorded "The Bluebird" acoustically, with just two hyperquality microphones suspended five feet from the floor and six feet apart, duplicating the ears of a giant's head resting its chin on the paved floor—and so the subtleties of the chapel's sounds have been converted to disc and transported eight thousand miles across the Atlantic and the North American continent and played back on a stereo that cost as much as the Cadillac—I admit, it is an obsession with me, and this is why. Liberty was stunned by the complex aura of that mediaeval chapel in misty England recreated here in Houston. She immediately stacked the changer with the gutsiest music she could find on my shelves and holstered the remote in her jeans pocket. All day the music has been pounding the walls: Coltrane's reedy futurisms, a piece of house with trumpet riffs that sound like the collapse of Jericho, the evacuating apocalypse of Sibelius number two. It is wonderful to have the house filled up in this way.

And now *Los Malaguenos* crashes into the room again and the women get stuck into stamping again and Chimp is born aloft and swung round and even John is caught up in the mood; and by virtue of machinery we are transported back to the flamboyant actuality of seventeenth-century Spain, when life was lived without the technology that has bought this family to this particular climax; when people knew they were alive because of all the other people around them, and not because of their hegemony over the power switches.

. . . what's the difference between a blender and a race car? . . .
Skid testing Boeing 747 prototype at Everett, Washington, circa
1969. Boeing Company photograph.

2
SCHOOLBOY

Next day, early morning. Something woke me. A house full of guests has a slightly changed rhythm. I could hear Juliet snoring in the far distance. B and Chimp were sleeping in their usual dawn tangle of arms and legs and pieces of coverlet. I eased out of bed and abluted in our complex bathroom. The electric toothbrushes sat in their little trickle charger stand winking at me, and Liberty's absurd gift to B, a battery-powered soap dispenser, lay next to them, still boxed. The motorized hair clippers were there, too, which I had planned to use on John; but shorn heads went out of style between the time I purchased them and the time I got them home. These gadgets are the froth of our mechanized society. What do they mean? What does this petty assistance with the easy things of life add up to? Can you imagine van Gogh metering his paint with an electric tube squeezer? Or Napoleon waking to an alarm clock/radio?

———————————

In the kitchen I found John dismantling the differential on his radio-controlled car. He said one of the pinions had been locking up and flipping the car on its back in tight left turns. So the kitchen table was covered with the delicious sight of close mating components. I have taught him always to replace fixing screws in the holes they came from so as not to lose track, and even at this bleary hour, with the kitchen fluorescents buzzing their supermarket light at us, he was doing it. Strange neat boy.

"You know submarines? Deep in the ocean?" he said to me. "Patty says they have ship-to-shore connections specially for the crew with love letters in code." Patty is she whom we call his girlfriend, but really she's just one of his gang. She wears jeans that are fully thirty inches round the cuffs. They make her look like a chess piece. "She says on Valentine's day the sea is full of low-frequency Burma messages, like whales mating." I closed the coffee machine lid and looked at him— *she says what?* "What's a Burma message?" he asked me. And I thought, *and how do whales mate?* The hippie poet, that one who discovered that people who don't wash eventually achieve an ecology of body bacteria, which means they don't smell—apart from their feet, he says, which is why Jesus was always washing people's feet—tells us also that the whales mate face to face, like humans. Personally I think that no one would ever get conceived if humans mated exclusively face to face, and also that given the shape of whales' heads, shouldn't that be *chin to chin?*

"A Burma message is a B.U.R.M.A. message. It's a wartime code that soldiers used to send to their sweethearts when getting ready to go on leave: *Be Undressed and Ready My Angel.*" He looked at me, wondering whether I was telling him the truth. "It's like snafu and fubar and naafi. A five-word acronym. A fad engendered by wartime coding."

"Yeah, see, that's what Patty said, but I don't get it. She said the messages had to be forty words long."

"So you'd have to send eight Burma messages in your valentine. Sounds intense." The mind boggles at what you could suggest.

"She says forty words is the exact length a personal message should take up."

This was all news to me. I hadn't heard about the Navy's forty-word thing before. It sounded as if they had invented a machine-age poetic scansion. At last: something to succeed metric pentameters that is not symbolically modern, like free verse was, but communication technology related. This forty-word thing must be one of those pulse sets they use in encrypted transmissions. They call the time gaps between the pulses, mere nanoseconds in duration, *Epochs*.

"How does Patty know all this?"

"Her brother's in the Navy."

"Let's try it out. Let's write a forty-word valentine to Patty." And this is what we got:

Dear Patty, how are you darling? I dream of you at night, and think of you by day. The guys all tease me but I don't mind telling the world I'm in love. I'm in love with you, Patty. Burma.

The *guys all tease me* part was John's idea. So was *Burma*. And the limit of forty words did indeed make it like writing poetry. The same languor, the same acceleration. But should there be punctuation in an encrypted message? Doesn't punctuation have information value? So we tried it without:

dear patty how are you darling i dream of you at night and think of you by day the guys all tease me but i don't mind telling the world im in love im in love with you patty burma.

It has good points and bad points. Start again:

patty meeting you changed my life and when i think of you

i hear angels singing in the ether i smell roses i feel the blood pumping in my body—

Luxury. We still had ten words to go with this one. "*I long to see you,*" I said. We needed another five.

"*Burma?*" said John, again. He's right, it is a five-letter acronym, but *be undressed and ready my darling* is six words long. Literature, even in its rules, is a flexible art. An abbreviating medium. But this is technology here, and therefore conclusive; we needed five words exactly.

"What about INDIA?" I said. "I long to see you *If Not Dead In Action.*"

"Gruesome," said John.

———————————

The erudite exercise of these Patty Valentines, coupled with the meditative distraction of car repair and coffee making, coupled with the early hour, made a very comfortable vehicle for me and my twelve-year-old son to be in. In three years' time he will discover his teenage hatchet and sever the ties between us; but at that moment I could not have wished for anything better. He looked up, screwdriver in one hand, rear axle subassembly in the other, and indicated the table top covered in parts. "Dad, are all these pieces machines? Or is it only a machine when they're bolted together?"

I said I thought that the pieces on their own are tools. A screw is a tool. A clock face on its own, without the rest of the clock, is a tool.

"Isn't this a tool?" he said, waving the screwdriver.

I said that while he was working with it, the screwdriver had the same status as the pieces of the car.

"So what do you call this?" he said, holding up the completed rear axle—differential gearbox, springs, shocks, wheels, tyres and all the bolts holding them together. He zoomed it across the table making engine noises.

I said that it was a subassembly, but an interesting thing about subassemblies is that if you give them power of some kind, if you can energize them, they turn into what used to be called automata. An automaton is a discrete collection of components that carries out some specific action. More than a tool, but not yet a machine. A clock is an automaton. And that solenoid that locks the car doors, as well. And computers: the brilliance of the computer is that it abstracts the automaton from the machine into the hardware and lets the software define what sort of machine it is.

Just then the air-cooling fan switched off and we were plunged into quietness, in which we could hear the pleasant burble of coolant coming to rest as the pump ran down.

"What about that thing that switches the air on and off? The thermostat? Is that an automaton?" I had to stop and think. A thermostat is not powered. It is an assembly of smaller parts, but it operates inside its own physics.

———————

Old Duke shuffled into the kitchen, wrapped in a robe made of blanket material tied with a tasseled cord and sliding his slippers across the floor like a polishing machine. He smiled a weak early-morning smile and went about getting himself his orange juice. I told him we were busy defining machines, and filled in the idea that machines are made of collections of automata and each automaton is made of assemblages of tools.

"Machines, automata, and tools." I said. All the while he was watching my mouth intently and fiddling with his hearing aids, which screeched and whined with the feedback, making him wince. "So what do you reckon, Duke? What's a thermostat?"

"Perhaps it's a complex tool," he said, casually inserting a subcategory into my neat trinity. He picked up the car's radio control from the table and flipped a switch and made the servo-motors, lying disconnected in the chassis, twitch from side to side. "They didn't have toys like this when I was a boy."

"It's not a toy," said John, taking the radio from Duke's old liver-spotted hands and pointedly switching it off again. Duke just sat and grinned at us both, a gentle whistle emanating from his hearing aid, enjoying how much he was managing to wind us both up. And the day barely begun.

He started telling us about an automaton he'd seen in China on some aerospace shindig back in a temporary warming of the Cold War. "A clockwork toy," he said, cocking his old crew-cut head at John, "dating from the seventeenth century, immaculate in every detail, all the lines of expression on the faces of the people painted in, all the folds of the Jesuit's robe moulded for real, and when the executioner swung his sword, whack! off came the priest's head and rolled on the floor and"—he imitated the expression of surprise with his own face—"pop! the decapitated head opened its eyes and stuck out its tongue!" I knew what would happen next; any expression of the macabre had the same effect on the boy.

"Guns! What about guns!" John said. "What kind of machines are they?" In spite of B's attempts to stem the tide, John is busy working his way through an obsession with guns. He is not the only young lad who feels this way. His obsession is catered to. Last night we sat up watching *Die Hard* for the millionth time, in which all the characters carry guns appropriate to their character. The long-haired blond assassin carries a Sigg-Steyrh assault rifle, Austrian and cold hearted: Alan Rickman, head baddie, has—as far as we can tell, having freeze-framed a thousand times with *Small Arms of the World,* a big book, thick as a dictionary, open on the floor in front of the television—a satin stainless Smith and Wesson 40 caliber automatic. It has a slightly heavier bullet than the standard 9mm, and was put into production after an FBI shoot-out that left the feds feeling in need of more stopping power. I guess you can see what B is worried about, and why she has banned all combat clothing from the house on school days, but myself, I think he'll grow out of it. Sex is more interesting than guns, I tell her, and music is more diverting than the sound of explosions.

However, *what is a machine gun?* is a nice question in the context of our discussion of *what is a machine?* so I attempted an answer.

"The bullets must be tools." I said.

"Complex tools," pointed out Duke.

"Right. Complex tools made of powder and detonator and case and head—almost, but not quite, automata."

"Say automatons for Pete's sake! You're speaking English, not Latin!" interrupted Duke. I looked at him, sitting there all skinny and advanced in years, and savored the Eisenhower-age simplicity of what he'd just said.

"Okay: the subassemblies, like the bolt mechanism and the magazine, are true *automatons.* The bolt is powered by the gas from the explosion and the magazine by the energy stored up in the spring when you load it." While I spoke, John was miming the actions, making clicking noises as each round pressed home. "The whole collection of automatons—which are made up of the tool pieces—when arranged to work in concert, is the machine."

"Phalanx!" said John. He and I have discussed such things before: for example, the symbiotic way that Hawkeye handles his musket in *The Last of the Mohicans*. We call it "the human in the machine." Phalanx is the gun that the Navy uses to cut down cruise missiles as they complete their last few seconds run in toward a ship. Humans are not fast enough to do it. A rapid-fire cannon is linked to radar via a computer, in a system that can both locate and destroy a missile in a couple of seconds.

"So where is the human in Phalanx?" I said. "He is a ghost. His intention is encoded in the program. He is both there and not there."

"Patty says they have women in the Navy, now, too," said John.

"So he or she is both there and not there," I said.

We all went silent for a few moments and I sipped coffee and Duke scratched his head methodically from ears to crown—does he do this instead of washing?—and the sky outside got a little brighter. Then John looked up. He had it figured out.

"Me, plus this screwdriver, plus these subassemblies are a machine!" he said. "A machine that makes cars."

Is this the foundation of a machine ethics? It says a *machine* is only *machinic* when it's running. Perhaps when he completed the car John would initiate a new symbiosis between him and the car and the control box. We speculated on the possibility of automating the car completely, like the Phalanx gun, so it could run races without him.

"What would be the point of a race-car race without anyone watching or driving?" said Duke, and it stopped me dead. The image of an abandoned racetrack, with the machinery belting round it in an emotionless, pointless effort to be first, was eerily desolate. We had stumbled across a deep materialism, which goes like this: the machine is a metaphor for creation, but it is a metaphor that does not include the worship of the creator—unlike that of the Father in the holy books.

"What would be the point," I asked Duke in return, "of making machines whose function was to worship us?"

———————

In the silence that followed, as we all tried to work out the next step in the sequence, Juliet suddenly appeared at the door. She was sucking her thumb and holding her doll and wearing her little rag of a nightie—she looked as if you could blow her back to bed with one puff.

"Hi, Juliet," I said, and she held up her doll. "Hi Juliet," I said. She advanced into the kitchen without a word and crossed over to the refrigerator, while Duke and John and I followed her every move. She opened the door and the light from inside floodlit her like an actress. She took out a banana, closed the door, and walked across the kitchen and put it on the counter. Back to the fridge, opened the door, this time took out a quart of milk almost too heavy for her to lift, closed the door, returned to the counter and put that there too. The refrigerator's compressor started up, to recool the interior. It's developing a sigh when it does so, like an old person getting up out of a chair.

"Want some help?" I asked her. She shook her head, still sucking her thumb. Back to the fridge, this time to take out a tub of ice cream. When she pulled open the freezer drawer, the steam of evaporation mixed with the floodlights like dry ice. She closed the door, came back to the counter and heaved the tub of ice cream onto it beside the banana and the milk. Then, watching us out of one eye, she took one of the kitchen chairs and dragged it across to the counter and climbed up on it and reached over for the blender and pulled it toward her. She needed a spoon now, so she precariously knelt on one knee and with tremulous precision pulled open the drawer and took one out, and stood up again. She took the banana and peeled it strip by strip and dropped it into the blender. This was followed by a swoosh of milk and a glop of ice cream. It seemed to take her forever; and it was all done with such care that she reminded me of a tower-crane picking up three-ton pallets of bricks and swinging them across the heads of workers on a building site far below. Duke, too: "The giant constructs her milkshake," he said. When at last she flipped the switch, the sudden cacophony of the blender ripped apart this impression. The tension of her own silence broke, too, and she started to giggle, and since the collapse of her composure threatened the whole enterprise, I took a glass and dumped the frothy liquid into it for her, and stuck a straw in it that bobbed like a fishing float, which made her giggle even more. She tried to take a sip and giggled at the wrong moment and splattered milkshake all over her face, which made her giggle yet again. Trying not to giggle made her giggle. She grabbed her doll, and clutching the heavy glass full of shake, made her snorting way out of the kitchen.

John looked ready to spit. "She's only four," I said. "Give her a break." I cleared up the mess and put the stuff back in the fridge. "Tell me now, John: what's the difference between a blender and a race-car?"

Blender and race-car? One question too many, too early in the morning. John gathered up his completed machine and made his way out into the yard to test the repair.

"Look at that lucky kid," said Duke, and then surprised me by waxing philosophical, the gist being that when you're a child, the problem of the self is solved by growing: you are always becoming new. When you've grown up, however, growth becomes internal. First you have to learn to love, then to act on the world, and finally to make judgments.

I could hear Plato: this was Diotima's advice to Socrates in the *Symposium;* and, I realized then, it was also Shakespeare's *Seven Ages of Man.* After the baby and the boy comes the lover, then the soldier, and then the justice.

"What Age of Man does that make me?" said Duke

"The sixth," I said: "*The lean and slippered pantaloon.* The retired man. Shakespeare says he's a man who's grown too small for his socks."

"You want to know the best way an old man can die?" he said. His pathetic look fitted the description of pantaloon perfectly. "I've thought about it a lot. But don't tell Liberty," he added in a whisper. "It freaks her out when I talk about this kind of thing." The best way for an old man to die, he said, is to throw himself off a cliff. "That way his entire life will flash before his eyes as he falls, and his head will be full of everything he's ever done by the time he hits the rocks."

Hits the rocks? Hits rock bottom. I imagined myself wheeling my old father's wheelchair along the edge of the white cliffs at Beachy Head, England, with the coast of France visible in the distance and the gray North Sea three hundred feet below. We stop to admire the view right on the cliff's edge, with the wind whistling past so strongly it makes our clothes flap like flags. I maneuver the chair to the top of a sloping path that disappears over the edge. I kiss the top of the old man's head.

i take my father in his wheelchair to the top of a cliff from where we can see the whole world we say goodbye we kiss we hug he says okay im ready and i give the chair a shove

"Gruesome," I said.

. . . the Society for the Repatriation of Enchanted Rubble . . . The top of the Acropolis, Athens, Greece, looking west. Photograph by the author.

WHAT DID THEY DO
WITH MY FUTURE?

The continent of Australia is full. It is a huge desert, with a fringe of habitable land where eighteen million people live. "The place is full right up to bursting," say ecologists. "The ecosystem cannot support any more human activity." The problem is water. There is nothing like the Mississippi, no Rocky Mountain rainsheds. Just this huge ocean of orange sand. The sliver of land that has all the people on it might as well be an island archipelago in the middle of the Pacific, and—*Hold it!*, say the Australian ecologists. *The place is full right up to bursting!* Australian racist bigots agree with them. They have nightmares of rusting hulks wallowing outside the Great Barrier Reef bulging with Indonesians. *Sorry mate, we're full right up to bursting,* they say. The rest of the world thinks that the Pacific Rim phenomenon is the logic of Australia's future. *Wrong,* say the ecologists, taking up the batten again in this strange relay: *Globalization is an American plot to rape the world.*

It is 1999. I am spending six weeks in Brisbane, capitol of Queensland, a city famous in Australia for being boring. All the cities in Australia have these one-word epithets, applied by the people in the other cities. Sydney *superficial,* Melbourne *pompous,* Adelaide *rusty,* Perth *provincial.* They are all perfectly good places, with pros and cons just like anywhere else, but the Australians are very acerbic with each other. Every time someone sticks his head above the parapet and says something that hasn't been said before, a fusillade of abuse rings out. "Who does he think he is?" They shout. "Off with his head!" They call it the "tall poppy" syndrome. They say they're "cutting the heads off the tall poppies." Why? Because it's democratic. You've heard of the levelers, circa English civil war? They were a bunch of head loppers, too. "In a democracy," they say, "everyone should operate at the same level."

When the desk clerk at my hotel discovered I was teaching architecture he said he had a question that he'd wanted to ask an architect for twenty years. He said that as a boy he had read science fiction comics, nothing hairy, just wholesome next millennium adventure stories about guys who flew dumpy dark green spaceships for an intergalactic airforce. The cities in these comics were full of fabulous buildings, all colors of the rainbow and with wonderful curvy shapes towering into blood-red skies. He said as a boy looking at these pictures and living in Brisbane he could not wait to grow up and be there in the future. He waved out of the window at Brisbane's motley collection of glass and concrete towers. "What happened?" He said, fuming earnestly. "What did they do with my future?"

Now, this book is not about the future. Sometimes it's about machines, sometimes about technology, but it's not about the future. It's about right—bam—now! And here is this character whinging about his never-happened dream of Tomorrow's

World. I tell him: dreams of the future are like debt repayment schedules. They are projections of the present. I take him to the window and point at all the Toyota Camrys streaming down Coronation Drive. "A ride so soft and quiet it is like driving a marshmallow," I said, "but there is your modern architecture. And there!" Pointing up at a Singapore Airlines 777 that was shafting through the sky toward its cruising altitude on a bed of jet thrust that boomed out across the city like a fanfare.

"Hey!" he said. "I'm not stupid. I know you get Camrys in Ho Chi Min City and Acapulco as well as here in Brisbane. You want this fist in your face? I know you get microchips in every crevice of the modern world."

"And does the Nokia care whether it's in the pocket of a Prada or a Versace?" I teased him.

"Look, you blockhead," he said to me. "I know what you're saying about machines and globalism. But buildings are architecture too." He pointed across the city to a green glass tower that had a rooftop plant room camouflaged with brick arches. It had the word *Samsung* pinned to it like a Purple Heart. "Okay, so the machines are stylish and particular and go everywhere—but why do the buildings look like casualties? The Victorians were technology minded too—so was Napoleon. So were the Venetians. And so were the Plantagenets, for Pete's sake! And yet their buildings all run deep. Why don't ours?"

———

I am in Brisbane as a visiting professor, a six-week post. Architecture school. At first the students are so pugnacious it feels more like a six-week tour of duty in the war zone and I start to think of myself as a grunt. A visiting grunt. The fantasy is clinched by the journey I make every other day from my hotel to the Uni on the Rivercat. This is a catamaran with powerful water jets that pushes up the meandering Brisbane River like that gunboat in *Apocalypse Now;* winding through the jungle with god knows what aberration around the next bend. In my case, a class of thirty students who doubt everything I say.

"We don't want to hear your Eurocentric crap. You come here all full of North America and England and we don't wanna know! We want to hear about Australia!" They told me on day one.

The ebullient rainforest flora of Brisbane and the green parrots flitting through the trees along the riverbank smooth everything out, however, and the rush of warm wind on the front deck of the Rivercat fills my heart with optimism. As do the swallows, just like those back home in England, who flirt with the surface of the water chasing flies and flash Prussian-blue at us as they zip past. Sometimes disappearing between the twin hulls of the boat and shooting clear under and out of the back where the water churns in its wake.

████████

The project we are doing is a maternity hospital. I want to explore the idea of machine buildings. Airports, hospitals, and factories; they are so process-driven, it's as though a human body had been reduced to skin and skeleton and alimentary canal. Where's the verve? Where's the muscle? And what do these emaciated programs do to the people who use them?

Hey-presto, one of the students suggests a fully automated birthing ward with robot midwives clicking about, extracting babies from rows of puce-faced laboring mothers. I tell him there are procedural problems inherent in that interface. He comes back the following day saying he's managed to get rid of the mothers, too. Now he has a bank of soft thermos flasks, inside which fertilized eggs and their placental beds are being brought on hydroponically. He shows me drawings of a five-storey metal-clad shed with an automated wall of artificial wombs and one of those computer-driven forklift access systems they use in warehouses.

"I'm not so sure about this," I say, treading carefully, "machine nurturing. It sounds—" I wonder what it does sound like—"expensive. And how do you fertilize the eggs?"

"If I gotta tell you that, I gotta tell you, man, I feel sorry for your wife!" he says. "You never heard of the birds and the bees?" See what I mean? Pugilistic!

———

After three weeks, the dust settles a little. We still argue a lot. Teaching has never been so emotional for me. I dream vividly every night and the students tell me it is the heart of the continent speaking. They say I am hearing the songs that the aborigine heard and made sense of. They are infatuated with aboriginal life, and consequently most of them maintain that health is a cultural issue, not a technical one. But they are willing to speculate on the human condition, and are okay with my four frontiers: expanding universe, evolving life, exploring tribes and growing self. They are behind me on the distinction between the tribe and the species because, they say, out there in the great Australian central desert a hundred different tribal affiliations are intertwined with the landscape with a profundity that is beyond thinking. People call it the "songlines." It is a tradition of oral history that places the story of each tribe inside an eternal present. They walk for endless miles between their sacred sites reciting litanies as they go, and so maintain continuity with their origins.

My students sit me down for a songlines talking-to. Starting with the great big red rock in the middle of the middle that used to be called Ayers Rock, but is now called by its ancient name, Uluru. It forms a huge knot in this aboriginal scheme of sacred tracks, an island singularity jutting out of the ocean of sand. Even for world-weary atheists the place is stunning; for the people who live here it is a holy place. An Enchanted Rock. Suddenly, *Enchanted rock—Smart rock!,* I think—I can't stop myself; and you can imagine the reaction as they show me pictures of this fabulous place and I start talking about Star Wars—the American intercontinental nuclear defense strategy. Incoming warheads are to be destroyed not by explosives, but by kinetic energy in the shape of inert guided missiles that the U.S. Air Force call 'smart rocks'! The room heaves with disapproval when I utter the words "Uluru" and "U.S. Air Force" in the same breath. But I am becoming immune to it. *Enchanted Rock—Smart Rock.* It's a link between the landscape and the machines. The raw material of the world animated by the human imagination.

I decide to give them a little Eurocentric crap: I tell them how I once stood for three hours in a queue in Paris, waiting to get into the Louvre to see the headless, winged statue of the goddess Nike that came from the Greek island of Samothrace. She is voluptuous stone. She stands at the top of the Daru staircase in her windswept peplos ticking like a bomb. She was carried off to Paris in 1863, like Helen was carried off to Troy, and held the nineteenth century spellbound like Helen did the Trojans. As did the *Venus de Milo*, the subject of another archaeological raid. They are made of marble, these statues—are they also Enchanted Rocks?

The cult complex of Nike at Samothrace is one of those Greek holy sites where the landforms themselves were enchanted. The landscape of the Aegean was as thick with narratives of its origins as the Australian desert and, as in Australia, the stories are the stories of the gods and giants who made it. The charged void of the ancient Aegean, I tell the students, was a European songlines. Why doesn't the pressure for the return of the Elgin Marbles from the Parthenon frieze on the Acroplis extend to the Nike and the *Venus de Milo?* Why not to every piece of stone in every museum in the world?

"That's it!" someone says. "The Society for the Repatriation of Enchanted Rubble." Empty Paris! Empty London! They all break into song: "First we take Manhattan! Then we take Berlin!"

Enchanted Rubble, they say! They never let up teasing me. But I know the words to their song—and this fact unexpectedly and suddenly releases me from my stereotype. And when they discover I can name all four Metallica personnel, and have actually witnessed Machine Head live on stage they are ready to grant me a permanent visa.

My hotel room in Brisbane is arranged round a big brown bed. It has a '60s *Playboy*-magazine-style console at the head of it to control the lights and the radio and the air conditioning, covered in brown melamine. There is a brown carpet, a brown chair with brown upholstery at a brown desk, a little brown refrigerated mini-bar and brown woven grass wall coverings. The adjoining bathroom has brown floor tiles and brown wall tiles and brown sanitary fittings. The view through the picture window of downtown Brisbane and the Brisbane River can be shut out with a full-length brown curtain. What else is there? A big television set in Fujitsu black. It's astonishing how this glassy blank thing lends color to my life.

I am teaching two days a week and the rest of the time working hard on my manuscript, describing my sons who are far away in England: my first son's love of guns and my second son's turbulent entry into the world. Every morning at eleven I am interrupted by the chambermaid who comes to clear up. She is enchanting. She is deaf and dumb and communicates with sign language and little notes scribbled on a pad she wears on a string round her waist. My other regular visitor is one of the students, James, who has taken pity on my lonely state and does me the honor of drinking with me down in the bar in the evenings. He explains to me, in language full of tough guy expletives, how architecture is his ticket out of a working-class, fatherless background. It's this or cutting sugar cane in the fields up the coast, he says: and he has figured out how to do well. He works harder than anyone else. It's so simple. He explains it in words full of bruised stars. "You find out who works hardest, and you work f*****g harder than him," he says. And it's probably because of this attitude that I find we are not just having a drink together: we construct as the days go by a schematic of architecture.

It goes like this: *architecture is rearranging material for human purposes.* The single-sentence clarity of it appeals to James, because it's like an incantation to repeat on his treadmill: *Help me Jesus.* I like it because it includes sculpture and machines in architecture as well as landscape and buildings. But when I try it on the other faculty out here on the edge of the blue Pacific they tell me it has no character. No *formation of masses in light,* or *new materials for a new age.* No vision, in other words. How can I explain what it has instead?

"Rearranging material for human purposes" is a string of four interrelated propositions about architecture. The first, *rearranging,* refers to the 'architectonic', its systematic organization. The difference between the post and lintel organization of the Parthenon and the frame and skin organization of the Bilbao Guggenheim. *Material* includes what people call materiality, but also everything else that constitutes something's physical presence in the world: where it is on the globe, how it possesses and configures its site, what its shape—its xyz coordinates—is, as well as what stuff it's made from and the fingerprints of the artisans. In other words, its unique character. The corresponding word to 'architectonic' is 'stereotonic'—a word not in the dictionaries and in fact the result of a clumsy mishearing of the word "stereotomic" on my part, which opened up this whole idea by giving me something to compare to the previously—also on my part—hazy inclusiveness of "architectonic." Look at the Parthenon and the Bilbao Guggenheim again: their stereotonics have some coincidence, because they are both ultimately shaped by cutting-edge curvilinear precision.

Human and *Purposes* are intertwined in the way that "architectonic" and "stereotonic" are. This time the words are "chronotonic" and "tachytronic." The 'chronotonic' is what's usually called "program," or what something's function is, but the two words declare that function and use are not the same thing. 'Chronotonic' refers to time and 'tachytronic' to speed. The idea is that architecture comes into existence in response to specific human lives, whose time is measured as a duration—'chronotonic'—but that it continues in the world—is used—in a state of constant renewal, 'tachytronic'. One of the things that sculpture and machines have in common, though machines become obsolete and sculptures become timeless, is a close correspondence to their tachytronic. Buildings and landscapes do not engage in their futures in the same way. Except, of course, for the Parthenon, say James and I, raising another toast. It is all these things simultaneously, landscape, building, sculpture, and machine. Landscape because of its integration into the origin myth of Athens. Building because it's a roofed program. Sculpture because of its exquisite hand-carved entasis, in which there are no straight lines. Machine because of its instrumentality in the Pan-Athenian annual procession. *It is the best piece of architecture,* say James and I, me lifting my glass, he his bottle, *on the whole fucking planet.*

███████████

Toward the end of the semester, one of the other students brings a book to show me that contains another four-part scheme, this time of technology. He came across it while searching "technology" and "health" in the library computer. It is called *Technologies of the Self.* The cover photo shows a bug-eyed bald man pushing sixty: Michel Foucault. He is surrounded by shining-haired youths with deadpan faces, the better to mask any doubt or incomprehension they might feel. "It's called *A Seminar with Michel Fookwar,*" he says. And the shock of his mispronunciation is so liberating I resist correcting him: a rose by any other name would smell as sweet.

Technologies of the self, the book says, are the means by which we know ourselves, and also by which we take care of ourselves. Prayer and meditation are examples, and good health is the outcome of the care we take. But there is more—technologies of the self are one kind of four technologies. They are a vast correlation of everything that humans do—to the world, to each other and to themselves. And what is action? He says we do what we do in order to understand ourselves.

"I reckon what you've been calling the human condition is really the human predicament," says the student, turning to page eighteen and thrusting it under my nose. Besides technologies of the self, the other three types are: technologies of production, with which we interact with the material world; technologies of sign systems, through which we mediate the rest of the species; and technologies of power, by which societies dominate the individuals within them. "Technologies of domination," my student says enthusiastically. "That's what the Uni is. Trying to hammer brain-shaped pegs into degree-shaped holes." He looks at me with eyes honest as a dog's and I find myself raising my eyebrows and squinting at him over a pair of nonexistent glasses like a bony old magistrate. Like a pantaloon. But, my god, this boy has a point. *What you've been calling the human condition is really the human pre-dicament,* he says. Then he shows me "technology" raised to be a description of everything humans do. The human condition is not what humans are, he suggests: it is what humans do. And what humans do is technology. Technology is the human condition.

That evening, as the Rivercat rumbled back down river under a brilliant moon and a universe of stars and the city shone with its own pale fire of neon and sodium, I reflected on one piece of Fookwar's quadriga, the part that deals with species and tribe. *Homo sapiens* is one species, but in its course of a hundred thousand years has made itself so diverse in its tribal separations that it no longer has one language. That's the paradox of the "technologies of sign systems." The "technologies of power" describes what these separated tribes do to the people within them. The pejoratives that emerge—the *normalization* of society, the *domination* of individuals, the *subjectification* of the person—could be other words for what tribal custom, tribal taboo, and tribal ritual do. The tribes have got bigger and have taken on national and multicultural flavors. They have grown into the monstrous state complexes that demand our loyalties in spite of ourselves; when once they were our protection, our family and our whole interwoven reason for being.

"O what a piece of work are we!" I exclaimed aloud to the rush of night-time wind. "Now we glimpse Us whole for the first time, and the wonder of it eclipses everything!"

Back in the hotel bar I get stoked with the desk clerk and commiserate with him over his confusion about the future. The vodka comes in tiny shot glasses that magnify the troubles of the world with their thick glass bottoms. Before long the woman behind the bar says we remind her of a couple of hospital cases being drip-fed with volatile liquids.

"Look at us—we can put a man on the moon but we can't even get the traffic jams sorted out!" he says. "We can grow babies in test tubes but we still fight each other like savages." But who is this we? I ask him. I don't put men on the moon. I don't grow babies in tubes, either. Do you? What he means by technology is the accumulation of human action, but it's not the action of *Homo sapiens* working together. Most of it comes from other people. From other tribes. It is not under our control.

"We are humans, you and I"—I raise my glass and he clinks his up against it looking as gloomy as a child with a deflated balloon—"but we are not *humanity*. That will always be a collection of strangers. Nobodies. The components of humanity are creatures on another plane."

"You know something?" he says, suddenly smiling all over his face. "That could be a really depressing thought." He stands up unsteadily and goes on: "but it's not." He swivels his smile onto the woman behind the bar. "He makes technology sound like a force of nature." She shrugs. He points out of the window at the river of cars. "Why get upset? It's like gravity. It's like the gravitational field." And wham!—he succumbs to gravity right then and there.

Does insight strike like thunderbolts, or is it lying everywhere, thickly pasted over everything all the time, and visible only when the lightening flashes? My friend here sure has hit the nail on the head. Technology is the human condition, but most of it is made by other people. So it behaves like a force of nature, and we live in its field like we live with gravity. All we can do is respond to it—we must adjust our lives and update our understandings to accommodate the changes it forces on us. When we yearn for the clarity of past times we are wishing for the clarity of people who have managed to make such an adjustment; and then we find that what they did is no use to us, because the field has changed.

. . . you are released from evolution's clutches into your life and fall through it as the bomber departs . . . B52H unloading 750lb M117 bombs. U.S. Air Force photograph by Master Sergeant Ralph Hallmon.

3
LOVER

Here is Jaques zipping down the freeway in his Lumina, with the big tires slapping against the expansion joints in the concrete. He signals left to pull out past a huge truck whose articulated trailer gently sways from side to side as it hurtles along in the center lane, pulling 75. He presses *acc* on the cruise control stalk and the Lumina gently pulls away from the truck; he presses *set* and resumes cruise at 78. This car has its thigh bone connected to its hip bone. Can't get the key out 'til the gearshift's in park. Can't get out of park till you depress the footbrake. Door locks clunk locked when you shift into drive. Lights come on after dark when the parking brake comes off. It toots if you open the door with the engine running and pings if you forget the safety belt. The living car, remember? Its backbone connected to its headbone.

Maria is sitting next to him sprawled out like a dead thing, head back, eyes shut, mouth open. Asleep at last. She had been on his case all morning. She had told him the first task for his *Field Guide to the Machines* is coming to grips with the names we already use for them. We give them names as if they were human. Family names first, like Chinese humans. *Chevrolet Lumina.*

"There goes Lumina's sister, Impala," she had said, pointing out of the window at a feisty blue sedan. And then, looking up at the sky and seeing a passing plane, "and there's one of the Boeing boys! 767? 757?" It was a 737, Jaques told her. It was one of those tan and scarlet Southwest Airlines Boeings flown by ex-Navy pilots who treat airports as though they were aircraft carriers pitching in the swell of the ocean.

"*707* and *727* are old boys," he said. "Obsolete. Past it. They'll soon be as extinct as the Red Baron's Fokker triplane." So *history* has to be added to names and Jaques will have to come to grips with that, too, said Maria—and now look here, she said: imagine Howling Wolf in a purple silk suit, backed by silver horns, all lit up by magenta floodlights. *I got my Mojo working!* he yells over the throb of his tremolo chords, his big wet lips sucking the microphone, as though he is a huge, real sweat, real skin, real spunk, vibrator.

"Now how does a Mojo do what it does?" said Maria, poker faced: "How does it *function?*" She said Jaques must add that to the list of things to consider, and now it's names, and history, and function. And then there is the whole subject of *assembly,* the subject of parts and components and their definitive interfaces by which machines purchase their special character of particularity, which is one of the things that gives them the aura of life. So she says perhaps in place of animal families and morphologies and habitat and habits in his field guide to machines, Jaques'll have names and history and function and assembly. Before settling back and sinking into sleep she had leaned across and planted a kiss on his cheek.

"And that's just to start with."

———————

The phenomenon of machines—of anything human made—is complicated by our inside knowledge of them. Unlike the beasts of nature, humans made them, so humans know them inside out. You could say: their breakdowns are always immanent. We can take them apart and change them and put them back together again, and because of this they have an objective certainty we cannot find in the rest of the world. They are so obvious, and they have such a complex evolutionary history, that they challenge the very idea of classification. What would you do?

The two-name classification of animals and plants into the *genus* and *species* of their Latin names was invented by Linnaeus in the middle of the eighteenth century. It was built on his minute observations of the apparent differences in the structure and arrangement of the flowers of flowering plants—in other words, of their sex organs. Next time you are faced with the deep luxury of a flowering meadow, or speed past the springtime miracle of the blue bonnets, or wander with your lover in a moonlit rose garden, remember—it is the sight of genitals waving in the wind.

Linnaeus' invention was a simpler thing than it has become. The demands of a dynamic natural history—the evolution and the genetics and the molecular biology—have inserted the *families* and *phylums* and *domains*—and even *subphylums* and *suborders* and *superfamilies*—into his original pile of *kingdom, order, class, genus,* and *species.* Underneath, it is as simple as *general* and *special* are: the distinction of the two terms is the dividing line of successful reproduction. The species is the ultimate grouping, of organisms that can have sex with each other and reproduce themselves.

Last night Jaques activated his information technology and sifted through thousands of pictures of airplanes. Starting with the order *Combat*. He was trying to construct a binomial classification of his own. He started making lists of type, on a hunch that machine *types* would correspond to biological *families*. He flipped the pages of his spotter books, looking at their funny purposeful shapes. The plain naivete of the prototypes compared to the later marques all bristling with extras like pike-struck bulls in a Spanish stadium. The mean looking interceptors and interdictors. The big grey bombers. The converted airliners they use as fuel bowsers and radar platforms. And those strange new little things they call *UCAVs*—unmanned combat aerial vehicles—that look like armed frisbees. These are today's types, and Jaques may be getting somewhere. And yes, these types are like the families of the biological world. So, where the family *Discoglossodae* includes the fire-bellied and midwife toads and the painted frogs, as opposed to the *Bufonidae*, which includes the proper toads such as *Bufo calamita*, the natterjack—and all are within the order *Anura* of the class *Lissamphibia*, subphylum *Vertebrata*, phylum *Chordata*—then the airplane family group *Interceptoridae* would include the *tornado*, the *eagle*, and the *foxbat*, though all are as different from each other as beasts of the field.

You can imagine Jaques immersed in these Linnaean pains, undertaking the aviation equivalent of measuring stamens and examining hairs under the microscope. These interceptors are of the order *Combat Aircraft* of the class *Airplane:* okay, Jaques, but what is their phylum? The taco he put together six hours ago was going black at the edges, and still he was only plane-spotting. Maria's opinion had been that machine animals would be more interesting. She waved in front of his nose a picture of an eighteenth-century mechanical lapdog who could sit up and blink its eyes, but who never defecated. And another of a leather-covered artificial mare for use on stud farms. It looked like the horse he vaulted in high school.

Another late night. Jaques yawned and heaved the uneaten taco into the waste disposal—order *Kitchen Gadgets,* family *Water-Connected Appliances,* genus *Waste-side,* species *enough already!*—and flipped on his television, his late-night sleeping partner. He was in luck. There, dressed in a toga, was Richard Gere, Jaques's favorite actor, walking his funny gigolo's walk along the peristyle of some shattered Greek temple, with the azure of the Mediterranean sky dancing between the columns. Gere was pretending to be the Greek writer Plutarch and was reciting some words taken from Plutarch's *Life of Theseus.* The subject was the boat in which Theseus sailed to Crete to kill the Minotaur. It is the ancient question of growth and change. The actor half closed his eyes and took a small, sharp intake of breath, as he always does, to indicate emotion. He started to speak.

"The thirty-oared galley in which Theseus sailed with the youths and returned safely was preserved by the Athenians for a thousand years." He paused and looked straight at the camera, brutally deadpan, his grey eyes tied in a knot. "At intervals they removed the old timbers and replaced them with sound ones, so that the ship was gradually entirely renewed. It became a classic illustration for the philosophers of the dispute about growth and change: some of them argued that it remained the same, and others that it became a different vessel."

Jaques was already asleep again. Slumped in his vibrating chair and silently aging like the rest of us do, his metabolisms busy replacing worn-out cells with new ones. Some argue that we stay the same as we get older: and some that we become different vessels.

———————

And now, Jaques and Maria are zooming toward the Gulf of Mexico to have a day by the sea. She sleeps beside him in the car, her eyelashes resting on her cheeks like mink pelts. No CD. No radio. No sound in the car save that of smooth progress. He does not want to wake this sleeping beauty beside him. Ever since his late-night encounter with Plutarch on the television Jaques has been imagining himself as the protagonist of some ancient Roman love story. They are snares, entanglements, these stories: brushes with divinity. The gods stalk the landscape interfering with human lives as humans interfere with the lives of midges. The humans are riven by desire. It shoots through their bodies and their genitals like electricity and forces them to be ecstatic. To have been one of the first humans, and to have lived before the great pile of information got too big for the unaided brain to handle, that is Jaques's fantasy. To have lived at a time when love was the prime technology, the thing that made all else possible—now that's what he would call authentic. He is *the Lover.* So he grips the wheel and drives on in silence, thinking up his own food-of-love music, a silent opera with an audience of one called *Cupid and Psyche,* hardly daring to breathe, thinking that he must not wake Maria up. The feeling is as strong as a magic spell. Each passing moment seems to fragment from the one before it and hang in the air as delicate as a wisp and as definite as a smack on the head.

Cupid and Psyche? Psyche was the most beautiful human ever, and Aphrodite resolved to punish her for it: she sent her son Cupid to make the girl fall in love with an ass. There is a ribald scene in Jaques's opera as she describes the beast's monstrous phallus—that is the punishment. One look at Psyche's face, however, and Cupid decides to have her for himself. He bewitches her into agreeing to an affair of exclusively nighttime assignations, so that she will never see him. She must not know who he is, because what they were doing muddled the mortal with immortality. But she was making love to the god of love—how could she not want to know the source of such huge potency? In act 3 she takes a candle and examines his sleeping face, and plunges into an abyss of emotion at seeing a god close up. She cannot contain herself. The heat of the passion drips like the hot wax of the candle onto his chest and wakes him, and his fury goes off like an atom bomb. The veil is drawn over what he does to her, but her screams reach all the way to Olympus. She appeals to Zeus himself to save her. And as with Cupid one look at her perfect face is enough: Zeus saves her.

The singers all crowd on the stage to take their applause, and the woman sleeping on the Lumina's bench seat beside Jaques opens her eyes and looks at him. He is astonished; the spell is not broken. Far from it. It magnifies and fills the car with clamorous gongs. He braces himself for the crash.

"God!" says Maria. "God, what a dream!" sitting up straight

and slapping the dashboard. "We were in free fall!" Then she grabs on to the door handle with both hands. "Whoo! Vertigo!" she yells. "Still falling!"

———————

They were getting close to the coast, driving through little one-street oil towns hardly changed since they were founded back in the 1920s. The sick-sweet smell of crude oil is sucked into the car by the air-cooler. Through the windshield it looks like a stage set—the sun beats down, illuminating the scenery. It has the ring of Shakespeare to it, of him gathering himself up into his immensity to declare *All the world's a stage and all the people on it merely players.* A sixteenth-century realization that the earth goes round the sun and that we are bathed in the light of the sun as actors are bathed in floodlight. From now on, it goes, we will raise our arms not only to pray or to warm ourselves but also to display our exquisite human forms in the glow.

And then along came something else; an explanation of what goes on behind the scenery. The theory of evolution. Organic life forms copy themselves on to their offspring, but in the copying minute and random variations occur, so that over long periods of time profound differences can accumulate. At first it was held that humans were the culmination of it all, thus maintaining a little divinity in the origins. But now evolutionists prefer to view each species as a dynamic assemblage, optimized, for sure, which tends to correct divergences from the general pattern, but by no means permanent.

It is this dynamic, this accumulated history, which has stalled Jaques's ambition to write his *Field Guide to the Ma-*

chines. Nature seems to stand still, he thinks to his sorry self, as we hurry past it in human time, but to the machines, we are the wilderness. We are slow nature and they have the speed. How can we keep up? A proposition to make a *Field Guide to the Fishes of the Great Barrier Reef* is do-able. You put on your scuba suit and get stuck in. Waterproof notepad, waterproof camera. But machines! By the time the color plates of all the Chevrolets are finished, with all their colors and trim options cataloged, and put together with the pages of pictures of Walkmans and intercontinental ballistic missiles and those little hand-held hummers that strip the hair off women's legs, the whole lot will have moved on to another phase of development, and edition two will be fast going out of date before it can be written.

"I was in a falling elevator," says Maria. She is talking about her dream. She says she was trapped inside a falling elevator, cables twanging way above her, all safety devices malfunctioning as the car plunged down the lift shaft toward the bedrock. One second making her way to the top of the Empire State building for a romantic rendezvous, the next plunging into an unknown future. As the car fell, so did she; her feet left the floor and she found herself floating. She was weightless. That's what weightless is, she says. Weightless is falling inside a falling object.

"Then I turned into a bomb," she says. She was "Little Boy" falling slowly to earth on her way to collide with the city of Hiroshima. Falling by parachute to give the airplane that dropped her time to get away. A big iron bomb, dumpy, lethal, the first atom bomb ever to be set free into the world. "Happy Holiday Hirohito" chalked on her camouflage green flanks. This is the moment that the new worldview of invisible particles comes of age.

"Everything is falling, all the time," she says. The universe is all falling. Spaceships fall toward the nearest planet and everything inside them falls as well. A space shuttle in orbit round the earth is falling round the earth, and the people inside it are falling with it, weightless. Gravity and falling is the same thing. As the shuttle orbits the earth, so the earth orbits the sun, and so the sun orbits the center of the galaxy. The sun is falling round the galaxy and the earth is falling round the sun.

"So what does that make us?" she says. "We are falling round the sun along with the earth." Her question is—are we weightless or falling? And also, she wants to know—is this the way it is with evolution, too? She says that she thinks being conceived is your species moment, and that's it: your life itself is a duration of gathering commitment, as you fall, rather than a process of change. *You are released from evolution's clutches into your own life, and you fall through it while the bomber departs* is Maria's interpretation of her dream. She's exhilarated at the thought of it. Poor old Jaques, doesn't get it, looks like he's going to implode. She unclips her safety belt, and slides across the Lumina's sofa of a front seat to sit up close to him.

———————

They arrive in the early afternoon on the white sands of Padre Island, a long spit of dune land that hugs the Texas shore of the Gulf of Mexico, flat and featureless and empty. The parking lot is full of miscellaneous concrete structures that look like the end of the world. There are squadrons of cormorants flying in formation close to the water and strange little short-legged waders that accelerate up and down the beach chasing the waves in and out, snapping at crabs. The detachment that made Maria so excited has brought Jaques to a level with those crabs. He is all washed up. *No man is an island,* he thinks, *he is an asteroid.* There are millions of others out there, but they are all out of reach. Maria walks beside him on the sea-slick sand, full of the vigor of her dream; but Jaques, left behind, has become vapid.

"Hey, tell me a story," she says. "Forget about the machines. You know what I think about the machines? Their origins don't matter. All airplanes are bastards," she says. "They may look the same but they're all unique, just like you and me." She punches his arm. "Hey, cheer up! Tell me one of those ancient love stories."

"You still believe in love?" says Jaques.

"What else is there?" she says. "Falling in love isn't falling into some deluded foolish fantasy," says the new expert on falling. "It's falling into the real world."

The stories seeped out of him as they made their way arm in arm alongside the slowly lapping waters of the Gulf. He did Cupid and Psyche for her; and he told her about Daphnis and Chloe, his favorites, a pair of foundling babies, boy and girl, who grew up together in pastoral innocence, and who eventually discovered as teenagers one day how different their bodies were. They had no clue what to do about it, until the woodcutter's wife got hold of Daphnis and showed him.

They walked along the shore for a couple of miles, and his

mood improved as the unchanging horizon of sea and sky gradually sank into his consciousness and promulgated its image of a simple world. The beach got wider as they walked toward the south, and the grassy dunes that flanked it retreated inland; and eventually they came to an expanse where the fishermen drove their camper vans across the sand, right down to the sea's edge. Impromptu communities were forming, made of groups of Winnebagos: a sort of suburban version of those wagon train circles from the pioneering days. They passed smoking barbecues and men and women drinking beers at collapsible tables with televisions flickering inside the vans. Is this it? Is this the machinic future already? All along the shore fishing rods stood unattended on tripods, their lines disappearing into the water a hundred feet out. As dusk came on and the blue sky started to burn orange at the horizon they could see the lights of this strange city of machines stretching out along the edge of the shore for miles. A perfect gulf-side day.

———————————

They end up in a shore-side shack eating prawns the size of thumbs out of greasy plastic bowls and drinking Mexican beer out of bottles that come to the table with slices of lime crammed into their necks. The music is modern mode country, rocking the place with its augmented human voices, its electric fiddles and drum machines and its heartfelt stories; the emotion of it pitches Jaques back into his asteroidal frame of mind and he is pretty soon getting sentimental about the "family of man," in which all our human differences, and all our ethnicities, disappear. Maria, pacing him bottle for bottle, likewise returns to her tales from the dreamtime. She calls the idea of the family of man an "antigravity machine." She describes how NASA simulates weightlessness by taking people up in an airliner fitted out like a padded cell and flying it along a parabolic trajectory. When they throttle back the engines as the plane goes over the top of the arch the people start to fall inside it and as the dive steepens along the parabola the illusion of weightlessness is maintained. At the center of the illusion is an antigravity machine, the airplane itself; the pilot pulls the stick back and pulls out of the dive, and everyone settles back on the floor.

If he let it crash, if he switched off the antigravity machine and just let the plane keep on diving into the ground, there would have been no illusion, and the weightlessness would have been actual, is what Maria thinks. "Maybe that'll happen to the family of man someday." Such a nightmare has been articulated by Virilio. It is a techno-sex anxiety he calls "teledildonics." He anticipates a globalized future in which we forsake all personal ties, having sex with people on the other side of the world via machine. Because there will be no babies arising from this cybersex, *Homo sapiens* will gradually die out.

Jaques groans, imagining a planet full of nonagenarians straining under the obligation of their digital orgasms.

"It won't happen," says Maria. "It's just a nightmare coming out of a bigger nightmare, which is what the family of man is." She says never mind granny and grandpa—what about sibling rivalry? Can you imagine what accommodating the whims and feuds of six billion relatives would be like?

If Jaques had bigger ears he might hear in Maria's words a sliver of assistance for his field guide project. Darwin's proposition—and biological taxonomists still use it—was that all of organic life springs from the same ancestor. All of it. The humans, the ash trees, the sharks, the seaweed, the bacteria. The continual splitting and divergence of lines of genetic material is what has produced the 1.7 million known species from this single source, as well as the putative 30 million unrecorded and even the possibly 400 million bacterial and archaeal species that might exist and then, on top of this, all those that may have come and gone extinct, perhaps 4 thousand billion in total over the 4 billion years of planet earth's existence. The people struggling to classify organic life call their taxonomy "cladistics," after the Greek word for *branch*. The current conception of the biodiversity tree has this vast thicket of twigs at the ends of its branches. And Jaques thinks there are too many machines to keep track of?

Machines are not organic life. They don't spring from a single source. They well out of necessity and desire, continuously firing off new lines of development from new circumstances. Their cladistics is an odd looking tree, whose roots are multifarious and whose branches cross and recross and regrow together like a pleached lime: it will take a lover to unravel it.

Jaques is the lover—so what's love got to do with it? Here's a thought. Perhaps this is all a question of emotion and passion. Entymology says that *passion* means "suffering"—the passive—while *emotion* means "excited to action." But the two are conceptually intertwined—we even use the words synonymously. Is that because we still think we are the clay of God?

Machines might be alive, might be nonorganic life, as Maria says, but they don't cry. That is an organic prerogative, like fear and laughing and anxiety. You could say that organic life is active—it has an emotional presentation, an emotional interface with the world. Dogs do it, the fleas on the tails of the dogs do it—and so do the trees.

Machines don't have fear and laughing, and they don't have ambition, either—when the *Challenger* space shuttle blew up in 1987, the faulty O-ring that had caused the accident was to the machine not a fault but simply a rearranged parameter. Blowing up was as valid to the machine as pursuing on course—it suffered an explosion. So now you could say that nonorganic life has a passive interface with the world. Is this the difference? That organic life is emotional, and nonorganic life is passionate? And could this distinction be helpful in putting together that field guide of Jaques's? It could describe two different evolutionary modes. Evolution by accumulation—the passive life of machines—and evolution by mutation—the active life of organic genes.

To Maria, love is the human condition. "The four frontiers," Maria says. She counts them off on her outstretched hand. First, the material universe in which we find our space and time—the love of the pursuit of truth. Second, the current evolutionary state of the species we belong to—the love of life. Third, the tribes we still affiliate to in spite of our enlightenment—brotherly love. And fourth? "Our own sweet selves."

When they finally stumble outside, the sky has turned black. Spots of turquoise efflorescence glow in the huge dark ocean. Maria takes charge and hauls Jaques all the way back to the car, and his feet drag in the sand and make deep tracks like a sea turtle. But she's not finished yet; she wants answers, too. She wants an answer to the selfish question: how do you love yourself? Jaques the evolved particle, alone in the universe, his tribe all scattered across the valleys that used to define it, hangs drunkenly to Maria as though he were the stricken craft and she were the rescue module and murmurs his don't knows wetly into her armpit.

How do you love yourself? It's not so hard, though these young lovers might not understand. Loving yourself is a long-term relationship. After the initial excitement has died down, there you are together, you and yourself. Physical attraction is no longer enough. You must build on trust and a mutual sense of care.

. . . so interesting, this typification of the generic . . . Image from *Ridge Racer.* © Namco Limited.

4

SOLDIER

Ex has arrived. He has come in on American Airlines via London, hubbing through O'Hare, and is raving about it already. He just drove up in a beaten-up goose-egg green cab and disembarked to hoots of laughter from the driver. They slapped hands together through the open window of the cab as it sped off. He stands on the driveway with his nuclear submarine of a suitcase at his feet, holding his arms wide in welcome. He is dressed in powder-blue linens. Twenty-four hours of jet-lag and he's looking good. His face is the color of rainforest teak, his hair's as black as outer space, his eyes are full of a thousand and one sights. "Chicago!" he says. "That's my kind of town!" He stands outside the triple garage of my Houston home talking about the deep viridian of Lake Michigan, and the shadow of the Hancock Building on the water with its TV masts looking like owl's ears, and the dramatic banking descent they made—miming with his arms outstretched like a kid—while he watched the horizon drop down behind the crust of tall buildings at the water's edge.

"Chicago, that's my kind of town." Ants'-nest urbanity swings back into view. Coming back from Australia my jumbo flew over ancient territory, over the Ganges delta and Afghanistan and the Caspian Sea, and I got to see Delhi from the air. That's where Ex went to live on the rebound from Liberty and her declaration of independence. The city looked like scratches on the ground. It was impossible at cruising altitude to make out individual buildings. It was just a cluster of marks, as though some giant had scoured the landscape with sandpaper. You need tall buildings to see the ants' nest from the sky. You need Kuala Lumpur, with its twin termite nest blips, and Toronto, with its space needle like a stick stuck in mud and the smudge of Niagara in the background. You need Paris, too—which looks white from the air, like a sugar cake, with the tiny but exquisite black prong of the Eiffel tower just visible. And you need Chicago, with its contenders for world's tallest all lined up like skittles. Yes, that's what I thought at that moment. And this is what I like about Ex—he says one simple thing and your head floods with thoughts.

All of a sudden the door bursts open behind us and Juliet comes shooting out, yelling "Daddy! Daddy!" and leaps into Ex's arms. They whirl round in a temporary private paradise, and her little face next to his suddenly shows its adult self. Long eyes, full mouth, fine chin. The sudden burst of gravity puts years on her, she could pass for a cool eight; but pretty soon she is screeching and giggling fit to burst as usual. And now here is Liberty, striding out into the sunshine to give him a guarded kiss and Duke, too, sidling out like a crocodile to check him out. B follows up with a tray of margaritas and Ex is all smiles and says now he really feels he is in America and raises the glass and so do we. Happy day before Thanksgiving!

"Of course, he's only saying that to ingratiate himself," said Liberty behind his back. "His politics won't accept what we're about to subject him to." She meant Anglo, middle class, high energy, and Western. "I don't know why he came here. I mean, margaritas on the patio," she said. "You might as well hang him by his thumbs from the basketball hoop." Liberty's still as bitter as a lemon. "You know what he did when he left for India? He set up a Web site for Juliet—she was two, for God's sake—called *My Digital Dad.* If she programmed it right, it said goodnight to her, but of course she couldn't. There was his self-satisfied mug staring out at her all night long going goodnight, sweetie, goodnight sweetie. Night after night. She wouldn't let me turn it off." Bitter as a lemon. But I have no problem with Ex. Our postcard exchanges since he became not-one-of-us have been some of my most engaging reading. He is as honest as Bede, and he understands America from the outside better than Liberty does from inside it.

Sometimes I feel like a child on the Mayflower, *headed for the New World but surrounded by Puritans,* he wrote once. Think of it—the child, the only free-thinking future American on the boat, surrounded by the prejudices—dissident maybe, but still English—of his traveling companions. Ex used the image to describe his Delhi days, when he was attempting to interject Web business into the throng of India. It is the perfect place for computer programmers and code writers, he explained—there is an educated English speaking young professional class, fun-loving and progressive, all into cars and cocktails and cruising, who want only a fraction of the salary of their Californian equivalents. And all the import-export traffic can be beamed out paperwork-free to the other continents at the speed of light via satellite. But it was still no good. India's balloon of poverty, the petty graft he met at every turn, and most of all the flak he had to take for having been raised a

Muslim, all conspired against him. Hence his metaphorical child on the *Mayflower*.

"So what are you doing now?" he says. We are cruising down San Jacinto on our way to the liquor store, and the sky bounces back at us off the mirror-glass towers like huge waterfalls. Did I say that I love Houston? It's my kind of town. It's full of strangers and this gorgeous rearranged natural light.

What am I doing now? I don't want to tell him—I don't want him stealing my ideas. So I say, oh, Ex, the same as ever—reading and writing, talking and thinking: just now I'm busy with an *Anatomy of Architecture,* I tell him. Oh yes, he says, "Landscape, Buildings, and Machines." Ex always had a problem with architecture. "A nit-picker's pursuit" he calls it. He thinks architects sit around like baboons picking problems out of each other's projects and getting into hilarious spats about nothing at all. He may be right about that, but a life without nit-picking is an itchy life, is my opinion. "So have you figured out the difference between buildings and machines yet?" he asks.

I try to describe the complex of function and use that my student James and I uncovered in Australia. The difference between the *chronotonic,* the program a building's maker uses to set the thing up, and the *tachytronic,* its continuing use. Two different things. It's as though architects make buildings according to a function, and then abandon them, empty and full of promise, to the world of use. Ex ruminates for a split second and then comes up with this: if a machine compromises with time—risks obsolescence—to bring its chrono and tachy into confluence, how does that compare to a highly stylized building, which is so acutely pitched in time that it becomes dated? Would that mean that style is some sort of function too? We pull up at a stoplight.

"Here, take a look at this," he says. He pulls out his cellphone and flicks it and clicks it and it winks at us as it boots up and connects itself to Ex's Web site. "Here we go," he says, all tech-junkie happy at the fruitfulness of his machinery. "It's from the Renaissance Society up at Illinois Institute. They call it the Loaf House." It is a strange building project, Webbound, but with complete suites of functional spaces so tightly packed together its occupants cannot squeeze into them. It looks like the engine bay of a Mercedes Benz. It's astonishing: an architecture so packed with function that it has to come alive, turn machinic. It cannot house us, so it has to join us in the world, as Maria says of machines, as a cousin.

"What else have you got in there?" I ask him as the light turns green.

"Everything," he says. And he means it. He is building a memory theater that he says will have everything in it. The technology to do it is here at last: what Giordano Bruno set out to do five hundred years ago is finally possible. Bruno was a Renaissance magus, a sort of high-tech magician, a baroque modern thinker looking through the lens of medieval cosmology. His memory theater was an attempt to frame the entire knowledge of the world—a sixteenth-century desire for twenty-first-century miniaturization. He was so spookily ahead of his time they burned him at the stake.

"I'm calling it *pictureit*," says Ex. "It's going to be the complete picture of the world." Picture it? That's *www.picture.it.*

He got an Italian server to get an English name, he says. He waves his cell-phone like a wand and says that in Bruno's time, they had to build cathedrals to house the kind of complexity he was holding in his hand. "Or a city: ever thought how much like Web sites cities are?"—no I haven't, in fact I start to dispute it, because even in an indeterminate city like Houston the interconnectedness is a spatial necessity, not an option—but Ex won't let me finish. I tried to tell him that the point of a memory theater is to hold everything in your head. That's why you need the magic. But he held up the luminous *picture.it* again and shook it at me and said, "You're getting old, man. This is where the magic is." Just then a dark blue sports car wafted swiftly past us, the bald head of its driver shining in the Houston light. "Look at that old guy in the Viper!" laughed Ex. "You work hard all your life to afford it, and then you're too old to enjoy it! He's just like you!"

"You know nothing," I said back. "Ex, you're just a kid."

"Come on, try it. You have one wish. I will grant you one wish. What do you want to see?"

"Progress" I said. "Show me what progress is."

––––––––––

Imagine us stopped there in the parking lot of the liquor store, in the ruby-red upholstered interior of my gorgeous car, our faces illuminated by the little screen like two people staring into a crystal ball. The cursor arrow darted round the screen at Ex's bidding, bringing up the little pointing finger of the Web-link's hand all over the place. It was as dense as the rainforest in there.

He showed me a movie clip of a saltwater-battered trawler ploughing through heavy seas, its radar shoal detector spinning lazily on the poop. In the background was a floating factory ship, where the catch would be canned and shipped off to Japan. It was a picture of how progress does not improve the world, does not even shift it toward a simple, enlightened state. On the contrary, it works to make it more complex. The prehistoric act of fishing—man with spear—has been organized and bankrolled and industrialized and automated over hundreds of years to bring it to this pass.

New technologies don't eliminate old ones, they simply add another layer. Everything that there ever was survives in an altered complexity. Machines go obsolete all right, not as in a species extinction, but rather as sacrificial victims of the herd, like Jaques's TV-trapped wildebeest. They reincarnate, in the way my typewriter has become my laptop's keyboard—still qwertyuiop—or in the way young lovers manage digital and analog sound, sweating for hours in split-second precision performances over their twin deck systems, and being able to say at the end of it the same thing Huddie Ledbetter might have said out there in his cotton field honky-tonk about the repetition implicit in the invention of the phonograph: "I never played the same thing the same way twice." In the presence of Xerox, people still print love poems on handmade paper using Gutenberg presses; and out there in the Czech Republic they manufacture high-tech biplanes for aerobatic purposes.

These are not humanist examples, but humanoid ones. Machines implicate humans in their operations, and the technological world has become slowly more complex with each invention, in direct analogy with the steadily enlarging human population of the world. Every baby born begins by screaming its head off about the specific proposition of being alive, and slowly, as it grows, begins to contribute to the general circumstance of there being so many of us: I guess it was always so. How did Liberty's lament go? *Anglo, middle class, high energy and Western?* It is an understanding of someone who knows without experience. Ask yourself if you know the answer to this: in the middle of a famine, do people wish for more food or fewer people?

Ex's vision of progress is wide-angle, strategic. It is a progress without end or destination, a continually expanding complexity. Technology is a force of nature—it is the force of the human presence in the world. It has proceeded by a series of accelerations, waves in the human force field, which reincarnate what went before and spawn new complexities in ever larger clouds. I could imagine the architecture—the landscapes, buildings, and machines—as solidified events in this complexity, whirling through the gas clouds like planets in a galaxy. Complexity is an ever burgeoning condition that arises from the continual transformations forced by individual technologies.

"Now then," he says, clicking his little machine to bring up a new image. He replaces the fishing boat with the original pack of human beings, deep in history, living as chimpanzees do, so interdependent in the pack that they have no individuality outside it. Except for the complication of speech: and the first great acceleration—the human Big Bang—is when they eliminated all the other hominids and sprang into the unique relationship with the world that we still occupy. You could think it a feat of clarity, not complexity, to kill all the others—but immediately now the complexity of the difference between each member of the tribe was upon them.

He carried on, bringing up image after image on the tiny screen: the totems of chiefdom that turn pack into tribe; the great masonry mounds of the first cities; the domestication of animals and plants—"the first slavery," he calls it. The meteor of Christ and the clash of the faith wars; the Portuguese and Spanish exploration and the discovery of the New World—all of them accelerations, which pitched humanity into ever more complex understandings of the world, of each other and of themselves. It is as if the force of the human presence in the world had started like the universe, with a Big Bang, and had been expanding ever since, a huge dense cloud of solidifying material.

Outside, the rapid low-latitude dusk that affects this part of the world was descending. It was dramatically altering the mood inside the car, as I sat entranced by what I was seeing. His dark face felt so ripe with knowing, it seemed that I could press it with my fingers and answers would come seeping out. These virtual solidities of Ex's reminded me of a block of fluorite I once saw in the geological museum. It was a single crystal about the size of a human head, and when you looked through it you could see hundreds of tiny flaws transfixed like stars in the density of the solid, all glowing with the property of the fluorescence. If you moved your head the scene changed; a whole different set of cracks and scratches and a whole different rainbow of reflections caught the light. Ex's *picture.it* was constructed out of blocks of related thoughts that were not held together by lines of analysis like an argument. They were built, like solid artifacts, using the possibilities latent in his machinery. It felt alchemical. It felt like the philosopher's stone.

"What do you think?" he said. And "magic" was the word I had to use. I had a sudden image of Giordano Bruno standing in the middle of the flames, his flesh coming off the bone. "Okay, magic," he said. "Take a look at this." And he double-clicked again and up came a flickering movie clip taken by some Mussolini blackshirt in Abbysinia in the 1930s. It showed a group of bewildered tribespersons, themselves all watching a movie projection screen set up in the center of their grass-hut compound. They know what a real chicken is: but when the filmed chicken exits, screen right, they all get to their feet and look behind the screen to see where it went.

———————

Inside the liquor store we find three young men with scratchy beards and Blue Note T-shirts bopping their heads in unison to Charlie Parker. Everything seems touched by the enchantment I've just experienced. Everything from this miracle of recorded sound—bringing Bird back from the dead—to the cleverness of the automated billing machinery that clatters its way around my credit card, and the strangeness of the wine we're buying having been shipped all the way from New Zealand. Even the little location map on the bottle label bearing its colonial names is haunted by the memory of the subjugation of the Maori people.

"One day wine-bottle labels will be film clips showing their place of origin," says Ex, in that easy future prediction mode that IT geeks affect, and the boys behind the bar all say "Yeah, cool man." One of them tells us how in the future you will be able to change the color of your bedroom walls by saying "yellow" and hey presto—and I think, what would be the point of that?

"The limbs of the Walking City are full of the crushed bodies of children who've fallen through rips in the gaskets," I tell them.

"Cool," they say, and all of them, even Ex, look at me as if I was Mussolini, and they were members of that Abbysinian tribe.

On the way back Ex reclined his seat and shut his eyes and went to sleep. Jet-lagged. Driving down the sodium-lit parkway with the live oaks gently billowing in the breeze, I reflected on the web–city analogy he had come up with. *When you say Paris,* he said, *you don't mean a bunch of stone structures laid out in boulevards on the banks of the Seine, you mean everything about it, all the art and the style and the sex, all gathered up!* He had held up his clenched fist and kissed it, like a boxer. His idea was that the web's like that too, full of clenched solidities. Complexity, he said, that's what it all is—forget process.

What if he's right? What if Paris *is* a web? Are web surfers information tourists—who experience knowledge without knowing it, like tourists do with places? I started to talk out loud to the other cars on the road, saying that this material–immaterial confusion spawned by virtuality rests on our all having different world pictures. We have no collective certainty. We can't have it if we want to live free thinking and geared up for constant change—those Abbysinian tribespersons had collective certainty, but what good did it do them? The lack of consensus in our splintered democracy is what allows us to see the mechanisms that maintain certainty—the conventions, the regulations, the enforcement of normality—as negatives.

My god how I did go on. And as if to point up the mystery, suddenly two cars ahead of us there at the stop light, was the old coot in the dark blue Viper. I said Houston was full of strangers; but here was a stranger I knew!

———————

When we get back to the house Jaques's Lumina is outside, ticking quietly as it cools down. He and Maria are delivering pecan and pumpkin pies for tomorrow's meal. It feels like Thanksgiving already, with B̂ and Juliet and Liberty and Jaques and Maria all accumulated in the hall, being loud and affirmative, Jaques and Maria still in outerwear. When Ex and I walk in hefting bags of bottles everyone feels the acceleration; Ex and Maria, meeting for the first time, set off collision sparks that have a secondary affect on Liberty and Jaques. It's like the break in a pool game when all the balls shoot off in different directions save those at the point of impact. Liberty hauling Juliet off up to the bathroom, B taking bags through to the kitchen, Jaques outside to start the car, Ex and Maria stuck looking at each other like rabbits caught in each other's headlights.

I go outside to get the rest of the stuff in the trunk of the Cadillac and find Jaques sitting at the wheel of his Lumina, engine idling, his face lit up like a spook by his dashboard lights. I tell him about Ex's memory theater. It could help him with his project, I say. I remind him that the problem with his cladistic taxonomy is its trunk and branch assumption of a single source of origin. Ex's Big Bang has that, too, but the galactic model can track cross-currents and movements and forces of influence. Hey—I think to myself—look at the effect he had on your girlfriend. I can't tell if he's listening or not. The expression on his face is the same a horse has when it puts back its ears. Maria emerges from the house and raises her eyebrows at me and gets in the car, and off they go without a word, two red lights disappearing into the dark.

Back inside I find John and Ex taking refuge in front of Ex's laptop, playing a video race-car game called Ridge Racer. It is entrancing to watch the game's generic view of the world unfold. The races take place in generic cities, with wired-off courts and weed-strewn sidewalks, and huge blank gray beige buildings festooned with cellphone aerials. The generic cars pitch and drift and flash their brake lights on corners not like real things, but like the real thing. There is even—or perhaps this is the whole point—a generic female game icon, a girl-next-door type with a grippingly realistic way of shaking her hair away from her face. Her—should I say "its"?—jaws are too small to chew food and her eyes are as big as a bug's but she is uncannily cute. She looks like a cross between *Runway*-era Janet Jackson and Lucy, the first ever homonid female. It is so interesting, this typification of the generic that our young ones are inheriting. The world landscape in this Ridge Racer game is like Theme Park Earth. It is powerfully recognizable as the place in which we live, but I am reminded yet again of the arbitrariness of the oriental Caliphates, complex and fateful and historical.

———————

Eventually, my agitated household relaxes and starts finding equilibrium. Liberty busies herself laying up the table, Juliet follows from room to room behind B like a cloud of gnats stuck to her odor, and Duke carooms from place to place looking like an old Kirk Douglas in his blue tweed sport coat and his mock serious expression. Supper is a huge carp on a plate, surrounded by an ocean of parsley. It is seeping white drool from its lips, its dead eye, glazed by heat, staring at the ceiling. We all sit down to our meal and I tell Ex what I told Jaques and how I think he could help out with the field guide project. I reiterate this problem of the single source. The original human-made thing. And then Ex says that such a thing might indeed exist; and he tells us all to sit quiet and listen, because he's going to tell us a story. And he starts to relate the origins of the Islamic holy of holies, the black cube in Mecca called the Ka'aba, and of Adam: human number one.

When Adam fell from paradise he landed somewhere in India. He was so tall that his head, which still wore the wreath of stars of the constellation Iklil, "the Crown," almost reached the sky. He stood listening to the faint echo of celestial music, and the sight of him standing alone was so dreadful that the angels prayed to God to remove it from their eyes. So he shrank Adam down to the size we are today. The wreath of stars shriveled and fell off his head, and he set off in misery across the world in search of his soul. He wandered for years until he came at last to Mecca. It was a barren place, but he knew he had found the center, the axis around which the planet had spun when it came into being. And before him appeared a vision of the throne of God, a giant ruby supported by emerald columns under which a luminous stone shone so brightly that it lit up the whole place. The stone was his soul. He set about tearing rocks from the desert ground and built walls all round it, to reclaim it and bind it to the earth.

"That building that he made was the first human-made thing on the planet," says Ex. Everyone at the table is listening in silence, wrapped in the strange security of hope given off by origin stories. "Adam's son Seth guarded it after his father's death, hiding the stone of his soul in the grave, but because of the iniquity of men one day the vision suddenly vanished," says Ex. "It was all washed away by Noah's flood, along with everything else." He pauses for three long seconds. "And then, a thousand years later, a cloud appeared in the Mecca sky in the shape of two dragons, and Abraham and his son Ishmael saw it and dug out the shape of it on the ground and there— and it was a sight that bought them both to their knees—they uncovered the ruins of Adam's temple." So Abraham and Ishmael rebuilt the thing, retrieving and cementing into one corner the miraculous stone. The Ka'aba that's the center of the Islamic pilgrimage today has been rebuilt more than once— "but the point is," says Ex, "those are still Adam's own foundations right there in the ground. The first human made thing on earth."

"Is this Adam's house in paradise?" I ask—there is a book of that name. But no, says Ex—the Ka'aba isn't in that book. This is Adam's house here on earth.

We are replete and at peace. The carp has been way too much for us, and everyone gets up to clear the table except for me and Juliet. She sits staring at the unfinished carcass stretched out across its huge plate. "I suppose we're going to have to eat the rest of this fish all by ourselves," I say. She looks miserable and turns her pleading eyes toward me. "Don't worry," I said, "I'll eat the head."

. . . *riding his four-horse chariot across the sky* . . . The Apollo quadriga on the roof of the Grand Palais, Paris, France (Georges Recipon, 1860–1920). Photograph by the author.

SEMINAR THREE

The Artist Currently Known As Dan—which is how my English sculptor friend Dan styles himself—says that the postmodern condition is simple to explain. He says that today we concern ourselves not with the ownership of the means of production, but of the means of consumption. We know that everything is fabricated out of our own perceptions. Hence the ironies with which his generation face the world. He is thirty-four and it is the year 2000, first of the third millennium. His current project is a full-size velveteen sofa floating in a canal in East London, its soft bulk just breaking the surface of the water like a maroon hippopotamus.

We are talking during the coffee break of a bidding competition for grant aid in which all the bidders are free to interrogate each other. You can imagine the atmosphere. Ridicule and character assassination are the order of the day. More than once I find myself wondering what the difference is between a "heavyweight" argument and one that is "obese." I am up next, looking for money to make a study of Michel Serres's three objects of desire. They are an anthropological speculation about the origins of technology in primitive societies, and they seem like a promising way in to the idea that technology is the human condition. The three objects are the fetish, the weapon, and the thing of value; Serres calls them *quasi objects* because they are not exactly material things, but are made of the desire in us to have their qualities manifest. The weapon, for instance, is not so much a killing machine as it is the glint of spears across the desert that announces the presence of another tribe. The three objects are universal to human social groups—our glinting spears are the nuclear deterrent—so we are in the murky land of structure. Serres says they correspond to Georges Dumézil's ancient archetypes of priest, warrior, and chief. And because this notion is all so exquisitely French, I am planning to start with that story about Jean Cocteau, the modernist dramatist and poet, being asked by a journalist to imagine that his house is on fire. All the living creatures in it having been saved, which one thing, M. Cocteau, would you take from the house?

The great man ruminates a while on the question, apparently wondering whether to say "The portrait of my lover" or "my gardening boots"; but then, throwing his head back and shaking his white hair, he cries, "Why, I would take the fire!"

The point of using this story is to assert that the inflammatory excitement of the modernists about their changing times was more important than their iconoclasm; but an interruption from a voice at the back of the room brings me up cold.

"By taking the fire, Cocteau would extinguish it, and so save the house and all his possessions," said the voice. "Twentieth-century iconoclasm isn't the issue. Twentieth-century dematerialism is."

We were all gathered in the Alcock and Brown Conference Room of a spanking new airport hotel somewhere in England. The carpet had a pattern that looked like discarded snack packets and the chairs were red polyester velvet on gold fake bamboo frames. The ceiling was grimly modular. It was wretched. The drapes were drawn against an incandescent summer sky and every so often the presentations were punctuated by the distant roar of an airliner taking off, provoking a universal longing in the whole gathering to be up and away. And now here was this torpedo speeding toward me across the room. I had no room to duck. I disintegrated.

"Never mind!" said Dan afterwards. "These things always turn into hair-splitting factories. You'll get your own back. You can split a hair with your bare hands."

But did I want to? I thought that my tormentor was almost right. The gradual trend toward nothingness of the last century, which left us with the capacity to evaporate all life with our bombs and an art so full of the everyday it makes you want to yawn: that was my concern, too. Our worldview is one of invisible particles—how do we go from Nothing to Something? At lunchtime I sought him out and we sat eating coronation chicken and sweet corn salad at a table that overlooked the parking lot through a world-eschewing, sound-attenuating glazing system.

"Art is dead," he said. "Experience no longer matters." In the future everyone will communicate via the Internet, he said, and there will be no need for roads—cocking his head at the Beemers and Mercs outside—or airports—raising an eyebrow at the Airbus that was even then ascending into the sky—because physical movement will be obsolete. He foresaw a planet so choked with traffic congestion that archipelagos of concrete bunkers will spring up and become the new nonplace global civilization. "Everyone hooked up by modems. We won't need experience, we'll be communicating the raw material of thought." And because of that, art is dead!

A disillusioned materialist is a hard nut, as hard as a sulking child. You don't speak to them, you speak at them. I said that if everyone sat in their bunkers hooked up by modems, then there'd be no congestion, it would be easy to move around, so why would those people be staying at home? And I said he was wrong about technology. New technologies don't replace old ones; they just add a new layer, which is what has made human life progressively more complicated as the centuries have rolled by. At which point he went Hollywood on me and invoked the polluted haze that will linger for thousands of years after the present age experiences its big bust up. That's why people won't go outside—they'll be too scared. I called him an old-fashioned fire and brimstone catastrophist. A Jeremiah. He said that progress should have solved the problems of the world but could not because of too much greed. And that I could go and jump in the lake. The unpleasantness of it all lingered for the rest of the day.

It was a relief to climb into Dan's old Volvo and motor back to town in the evening sun. It was wonderful to see the long shadows of the other cars slipping over the hood and the huge tires of the eighteen-wheeler trucks spinning only an arm's length away as we hurtled past.

"Slow down, Dan!" say his two young musician friends who are sitting in the back. They both have jet-black dyed hair and grey eyes and Omega Speedmasters and they look like teen movie heartthrobs. It is their music we're listening to; Barcelona-inflected Deep House at one hundred thirty beats per minute. You can hardly hear it above the throb of the tires and the roar of the wind. "The car is way too old for this!" says Ramon, and they both laugh and slap their thighs. "Dan Schumacher!" says Juan, and they crack up all over again.

"Typical technos," hisses Dan. "Show them a machine more than two years old and all they can see is a junk heap." He bangs on the steering wheel with the flat of his hand. "Volvo!" He shouts: "Forté!" Suddenly an acrid smell fills the car followed by a mighty clattering from the gearbox and clouds of blue smoke streaming out behind us like a contrail. Dan's face goes white and he tugs the car over to the side of the road where it jams to a stop, quiet as the forest, smoking furiously, all hopes of future lost. It is a classic Heideggerian breakdown. One minute the car is part of the dynamic presence of our teeming lives and the next it is nothing but a forlorn object, a useless pile of steel and plastic and glass. We are suddenly pitched into another universe. From four urbanites enjoying the rolling cultivation of modern times to four human pieces under the sunset with only their feet to carry them.

Luckily we are only half a mile from a rest stop, and leaving the defunct Volvo behind us, we set off for it. Dan wonders whether he should remove the license plates and prize off the identification badge on the scuttle under the bonnet so he'll be untraceable and won't have to pay the removal costs.

"Now look! Typical English," says Juan, "always talking about money."

"'Three pounds twenty five! For a hot dog!'" says Ramon, and they start to laugh all over again.

And so, although the bid was a washout, I got my seminar

on technology and Michel Serres's quasi objects sitting in the rest-stop café with The Artist Currently Known As Dan and Ramon and Juan the digiphile Catalans. I wanted to talk out the possibility of the three objects of desire as a sorting system for the complexities of the idea of machines and architecture. Michel Serres himself cautions against classification, saying— in different words than this—that the moment you manage to describe the world is the moment you lose sight of it. But here's what I think—this is one lesson of Maria's free fall. Your life expands as a commitment, not a dispersal. That career movement you can sense is the ground coming up to meet you, fast.

■

On the roof of the Grand Palais in Paris, and at the head of this chapter, is a sculpture of Apollo riding his four-horsed chariot across the sky. You can see these big metal sculptures of four-horsed chariots in all the capitals of Europe. There are two of them on top of the Victor Emmanuel monument in Rome, and a flamboyant Nike, the winged goddess of victory, rides hers across the top of the Wellington monument in London.

A chariot drawn by two horses is called a "biga." One drawn by three is called a "triga"; one like this is called a "quadriga." *Quadrigas* is almost an alternative title for this book so far, composed as it is of attempts to produce four-part descriptions of the world of architecture. In seminar one I introduced the four frontiers of the human condition. The expanding universe, the evolving species, the exploring tribe, and the aging self. In seminar two there were two quadrigas: Foucault's four technologies—of production, signs, domination, and self—and the

Australian scheme of architectural qualities, the architectonic, stereotonic, chronotonic, and tachytronic. Then Maria bought up four questions of love. Love of the pursuit of truth, love of life, brotherly love, and self-love. All these quadrigas are replete with mutual correspondences, so what, in this stampede of horses, am I doing now with three objects of desire? Where is the missing animal? Could it be the philosopher's stone of Ex's memory theater—everything? Or is it his Ka'aba, the first thing made by a human being—one thing?

"I don't know," says Dan, suspiciously. "Maybe I'm too fast for all of this."

"Okay, we vote," says Ramon. "Hands up to continue. Or over to Burger King for food." It's like nursery school. I put my hand up and so do Juan and Ramon. But Dan excuses himself and disappears toward the games arcade. We decide to continue the seminar in the fast food line anyway.

███████

As we stand there in the queue shuffling toward the counter, it seems the most important thing is to get the others on board with the idea of technological accumulation.

"Whopper, large fries and a Coke," says Juan, and the everyday utility of that sentence makes me think that the three objects of desire may seem a little flaky, but the idea of accumulation is not so strange. Everyone knows about the age of exploration, about colonial expansion, about the industrial revolution—the point of accumulation is to see all these different accelerations folded into one increasingly complex event. How to describe it? Analogizing cosmologies is difficult because they are themselves analogies—so I try this version first. Technology is not a flow, it's a force field. The force of the human presence in the world. Events—technological happenings—accumulate in the field bit by bit and coalesce, and gradually warp it so that it becomes like one of those Einsteinian motion and gravity diagrams where planetary solids drag their way through huge fishing nets of space-time. How does that sound?

My two companions laugh like hyenas and slap their hands together. They are cracking up again right there under the baleful gaze of the Burger King. "Hey, look!" says Ramon, taking a penknife with a rabbit's-foot key ring out of his pocket. "The weapon and the fetish! All I need now is a goat!" He is snickering so hard he can hardly get out the words: "Whopper, large fries and a Coke."

"Try again," says Juan. Okay: here's a geological analogy. Technological events are like the eruptions and folding that make mountains in the earth's crust, changing the landscape forever; but which are then overlaid by new events, like vegetation overlays the rocks, and then overlaid again by still further events, like the Ice Age glaciers, each phase altering everything but keeping everything, too, in altered form; a continuous and gradual complexifying of the surface of the earth.

"I've fixed up a tow truck," says Dan, rematerializing in front of me. "Whopper, large fries, Coke for me please. What's up?"

I decide to try describing one of the technological accelerations in detail, one that might throw some light on the three objects. The mainstream assumption is that the great masonry cities of antiquity grew out of the agricultural revolution—that having discovered a way out of the nomadic confines of primitive life humankind was ready to move on to permanent settlement. But an alternative proposition is that it was the other way around—indeed, that the three objects themselves were a sort of prototypical city organization, and that it was that organization that made it possible to develop the chance outbreaks of domestication in plants and animals that would occur in permanent settlement.

"See that!" says Ramon, his eyes popping. Suddenly he's convinced. Suddenly he's an apostle. "Did you see that? The objects of desire are still there! Weapon, fetish, and thing of value, right, but now we have a city, made of those objects, the fort and the temple and the palace!" This is what seminars are for. Fort, temple, palace, okay! We could call it the masonic era. But what about those pyramids and ziggurats, those ancient tombs? Are they the fourth horse? Are they the way a human social group, falling together as it were, accommodates itself toward the up-rushing ground? And now it's my turn: I get a Whopper, hash browns, and a chocolate shake.

"You hedonist," says Juan.

———

We sit down to eat and transform into the elaborate litter-machine that fast food dining is. My analogizing has set Juan thinking, and we munch our burgers to the sound of his accelerating concern. At what? It sounds to me like he's lost his tribe. Listen: what is it that holds us humans together? he asks. Is community some sort of machine? Some intricate system of levers and springs all bolted up to the proper torque? There are moments in the dismantling of machine assemblies under repair, he says, when, if care's not taken, the whole thing will suddenly fly apart, and disperse to all four corners of the workshop. The thing to do, if that happens, is to sit tight and watch where all the pieces go. If you try to grab at the springs and washers as they shoot off in their little Big Bang, they will be lost, befuddled in the dust, never to be found again.

"That's what's happened to us," says Juan, "We live botched lives: whole communities losing contact with their boys, who rampage through the sodium-lit nights stealing cars and using spray-cans full of shit to scrawl slogans of defiance on the filthy walls." What a picture! *"The boys are alienated,* the people say," sneers Juan. *"Their families are dysfunctional.* As if the machine had broken! As if the protest and homelessness were something other than desire! And as if we wouldn't all benefit from being free of the clockwork!" See how exclamatory he gets. He must be talking about himself.

People have used machine analogies to describe human society ever since we discovered the earth goes around the sun. The idea has woven itself in and out of the crashing dominoes of belief as each new wave of thinking bullies out the last and a new host of images is erected among the rubble of the old. But what are these waves of thinking? Where do they come from? Are they really a complex dynamic of shifts and breaks, or could it just be that each generation stamps on the ground and says, *we will think the opposite of what went before!?*

I wanted to get into detail. I wanted them to help me with the intricate complexities that accompany each billow of the technology cloud. But the tow truck had arrived for the stricken Volvo and we were all going to ride back to London in it. The others climbed in the back seat and fell asleep, and I sat up front with the driver. Her belly slumped over the safety belt like a satchel of fat and her poor back curved to fit her seat. Her whole life was rescuing stranded cars. Already that day she had been up to Doncaster, down to Exeter, back up to Birmingham and now, to pick us up, down to Sevenoaks. Up and down all day long, for six hundred miles. I kept expecting her to fall asleep, too, but she drove like an automaton, pointing out the location of every speed-limit enforcement camera along the way. I was wide awake. I was so full of the subject that I couldn't resist the captive audience. As we cruised steadily toward the luminous yellow horizon of the city I explained the acceleration of exploration to her.

"Jerusalem having been lost to Islam," I say, "the keepers of the Christian faith in Portugal and Spain decided to send out ships round the African coast to try and discover a back way into the Promised Land. To maybe even find the Garden of Eden. So the Holy Roman masonic transformed and found itself exploring, sending pieces of itself across the seas, and they ended up discovering the New World! It was land not mentioned in the ancient Books—a challenge to the very authorities they had fought Islam for."

"Amazing," she says. "And I suppose the technologies of printing and banking and ships that could sail into the wind were techniques of the exploration?"

Well, no she didn't say that. But if she had I would have agreed with her. Each new acceleration brings new techniques that clatter round the world like gremlins at a wake, frightening the pantaloons and waking up the guard dogs. But people themselves are the same as they always were. We entered Trafalgar Square at four o'clock in the morning, Sunday morning, and the place was jam-packed with lovers out partying and clubbing. It was wonderful to see them laughing and dancing and kissing and carrying on as though nothing had changed for fifteen thousand years. Young Londoners do it all night long. At one hundred and thirty beats per minute.

... *at Delphi they bound a meteorite with chains to keep it from flying away again* ... Hellenistic replica of the Omphalos in the Museum at Delphi, Greece. Photograph by the author.

5
JUSTICE

It is the end of an up and down day. I have squeezed away from my strife-torn house and its disgruntled crew of exes and steps and am sitting in the dark in my studio. Tomorrow it will get more up and down, perhaps. Tomorrow it is Thanksgiving Day. We will be joined for our customary Thanksgiving brunch by Jaques and his Maria—though whether she is his, he never seems to know; young men are forever rainchecking their lives in case something better comes up—and later on for the big meal, the turkey, yams, and pumpkin pie, by my ancient father in his wheelchair. I tried to persuade the old man to visit electronically this year. I said we could have a video-conferencing Thanksgiving, because I fear for his heart in these bumpy Houston thunderstorm-season landings. He told me his heart has had plenty of exercise, he is ninety for god's sake. "It ought to be strong enough to do England to America by now!" he said. The reasoning of oldsters never fails to startle me. He's coming in on a British Airways flight in the afternoon.

Now I am sitting in the dark in my studio trying to remember the past. I am trying to regain the steadiness an artist needs. The impassioned delirium of the poet Shelley careering disheveled through the streets at dawn tearing at the fresh bread he had just bought, howling its virtues to the rising sun, is not for me. I need steadiness.

My studio was once a fireproof packing shed, a perfect rectangle of plain bricks forty by eighty feet and twenty feet high. It has wonderful phosphor bronze locks on big cast-iron doors that look as though they could keep out the Hulk. The floor is made of polished cement. All the light comes in from the top through skylights that double up their shading devices as security screens. They are as elaborate as Tuscan shutters, with chain-operated baffles to give shadow screening, insect screening, through ventilation, daylight in six degrees of darkness and total blackout. It reminds me of Alberti churches, this shed, because, like them, it packs more punch than a building this size should. I was so impressed by the mechanical togetherness of the place that I signed for it at first sight. I needed somewhere to put my statues. I am not a collector of art, I am a sculptor. I want to do stuff for NASA.

If only life were that simple! Our individual human lives accumulate complication just as evolved life and tribal life have done. Children and wives, debts and failures, triumphs and ecstasies: they all add up to more than "I am a sculptor." My academic life here in Texas, my life as a writer and my life as a father all steal time from the simple statement. Life is supposed to be like this, because in the seven ages of man I am the Justice. But at the bottom line, I am a sculptor.

One Good Friday back in my own Lover days I watched a Hawker Seafury, the last one flying in the Royal Navy, charging around a cloud-filled summer sky like a ballet dancer. It was painted a beautiful chalky green on the undersides and a storm dark sea blue on the top. Heraldic flashes of white and yellow adorned its tail and wings, and it had a bright red spinner like a joke nose. Against the neutral profundity of the sky's grays it seemed to be alive. It had a huge eighteen-cylinder engine that ripped it through the sky almost as fast as a jet. And what a sky it was! The blue was there, plentiful and sunlit and rich with the summer, but it was way up on high. Between it and me were alpine heaps of powder-white cumulus struck by black chasms of summer rain and billows of blue-gray, all backlit and silver-lined and laced with rainbows. The pilot threw his growling pretty-colored airplane in and out of this scenery, rolling under hanging drifts of white, and plunging into the blackness, then swooping out into the distant blue, almost invisible except for the flash of sunlight reflected off its wings. I stood there with my mouth hanging open, and the whole expanse of England, the whole of tiny, historic England, seemed to ring with the sound of the engine and shine with the spectacular colors of the machine against those grays.

That was on Good Friday. On Easter Sunday I had a visit, with portfolio, from my photographer friend Carol. She had emigrated to the Ivy League and made her home in the cold, calamitous, centuries-old city of Philadelphia.

"I used to take photographs of nudes," she said. Showing me a portrait of two naked knock-kneed twins sitting on a sofa. They were tall, lanky women and they had make up and big hair-dos, and the walls of the room they were in, and the sofa they sat on too, were covered in Native-American blankets. "I used to take photographs of nudes. Now I photograph people with no clothes on."

Until that moment I had not known what artists did. I knew that Donatello yelled at his sculptures in an attempt to bring them to life; "Speak to me you piece of shit! Speak to me!" he shouted at them. I knew about the toils of old Michelangelo Buonarotti, dressed in goatskin gaiters caked on to his legs with unwashed sweat and carving his sublime marbles at the dead of night with candles strapped to his head; and I had stood in the Santa Maria della Vittoria in Rome and witnessed the effrontery of Bernini's brilliance. But Carol's art was something else. Her pictures were as revealing as a first kiss. A change as subtle as her "nude" and "no-clothes" is similar to shifting down a gear and stepping on the gas.

Oh Carol! I will always want you for my sweetheart. Because then you showed me Gerome's painting of *Pygmalion and Galatea.* It's a neoclassical fantasy; the story of the sculptor who finds his statue coming to life right there under his hands, and as he kisses her stone lips they become flesh. Another parable about the passion of the artist. Another *artificial love* story.

The fable became an obsession with me. I found that I too was falling in love with statues. In Italian museums I could not keep my hands off them. In Paris I was bewitched by the Second Empire nymphs and satyrs that dance in the streets. Their sculptors had tried to capture the sublimity of the *Venus de Milo,* but instead they conveyed the fevered erotogenics of their own time. The figures they made writhed and pouted and stuck out their breasts. They had exquisite patinated metal skins. They flirted and propositioned me. I could hardly bear it. I coined a name for the feeling—I called it *Voluptuous*

Bronze. And from there it was a short step to what I'm doing now: the lumps of smart bronze I'm calling *Enchanted Rocks.*

One of the things I do every morning in the quiet of my studio is sweep up the carcasses of the creatures that have died in the night. Today there were four of them. Two roaches, a small black spider that had curled up in death like a tiny flower, and one of those creepy long-shanked crickets that flop about in the hot Texas nights like Mexican jumping beans. I maintain the floor surface at a continuous toxic level with insecticide sprays. I think of it as a tabula rasa, a hyper-clean surface on which nothing can take place but my ideas. Does that remind you of St. Cuthbert, waging spiritual warfare on the devil in his lanolin-covered hide hut, out there on a rock island in the middle of the cold North Sea? No? It does me.

Except that this is Houston, Texas, home of NASA, who commission satellites so full of the complexities of fabrication, so packed with subassemblies, that they are almost solid things. Solid lumps of complexity. Ex's clenched fist comes to mind. Forget it, the entire human body comes to mind—the juicy sac of membranes and chemical processes strung together by muscle and bone that our imaginations cruise around in. The origin of the exquisite sensations that sluice through us continuously in bursts of organic electricity. The fabulous symbiosis of ourselves. The satellites are like that, as solid as clenched fists. Remember Ex's complexity? And what about Jaques's asteroids? Think of the difference between those huge black lumps of iron hurtling through space and the delicately bleeping Comsats transmitting *honey, I love you so much* across the continents. *Call it a million and we have a deal.* The asteroid and the satellite are not solid and void: they are two different sorts of solid.

This is what I'm doing: I am engaged on a project to hurl solid metal sculptures out into low earth orbit, which will be visible as points of light in the sky, like artificial constellations. I think of them as asteroids, with rocket motors carefully inserted up their backsides. The dullard uniform metals that have aroused such passion in me may have been eclipsed by new heterogeneous materials, stuff that's not cast or wrought but grown like crystals and woven like hard cloths. But I am insisting on bronze because I have a fundamentalist burn going. I think sculpture is carrying the survival of the entire real world on its back. I want to cast it in dumb chunks because any strategy more complex than that will let in a deluge of narratives. Let the painters do Internet art. I want to do things so full of space that they are solid, like rocks. *Enchanted Rocks.*

Here are two questions for sculptors: what? And why? The "where" and "when" of more complex architectures are resolved in sculpture with right here! and right now! That's part of its exquisite simplicity. My "what" is those bronze asteroids. But what's my "why"? Why do we rearrange the material of the world? Why does NASA? Why should I?

I think the question is the same now as it was for the ancient Greeks. Up there in the fresh air on top of the Acropolis in Athens, with the twenty-first century swirling smoggily around the base of the hill, there is a clarity as convincing as my studio floor. I am an Anglo, and the Acropolis is my place of cultural origin. The landlords of this building here in Houston are a bunch of beaming, middle-aged African-Americans. They wear charcoal suits and cream silk shirts like Swiss bankers. They told me how they had taken a vacation to their roots in the Gambia and found themselves visiting the relics of slave transit depots on the coast. They had tears in their eyes when they described them; colonial-age brick warehouses of the kind you see lined up alongside docks all over the world, from Antwerp to Boston to Sydney, warehouses for grain and cotton and manufactured goods; but used there in Africa for human stock. "We are eighth-generation Texans," they tell me. "Our families have been here longer than anyone else except the Indians." *Indians,* they call them! But their hearts and lungs are somewhere else. That's how they say it, *hearts and lungs.* They still breathe Africa, they say. They still breathe the charge of the Gambian rainforest.

That is how I look at Athens. I am an Anglo, my own eighth generation was immured in English farmland, my fortieth I guess came over in boats from Saxony or Denmark and took the land by force, but my cultural breath is all Athens. I breathe the charge of ancient Greece.

And here is my Acropolis origins fantasy. On top of the rock a tribe of people gather around a pool, by which a single olive tree grows. They think the pool and the tree are remnants of a battle between Athena and Poseidon for possession of this place. They have come to stare at the sun rising over the mountains in the distance. They have made a huge discovery; they have found a way to live without kings. They say they are a people woven together like a cloth, and that authority is nothing but the pattern in the weave. If there are some who articulate better than others the collective consciousness, there are others who are better in the heat of battle and others yet who are better at judging the best time to plant a crop; they have found a way to share it all.

In the evening, as the sky starts to go pink, they stitch themselves together by linking their elbows in a circle on the top of the rock, all four hundred of them, and they watch each other turning to stone. They become human columns. Their bodies are fluted with muscle tone, their heads are capitals. They look like B and Juliet and Liberty did in the aftermath of the flamenco dance. They look like Caryatids.

When Pericles reconstructed the war-blasted rock-top six hundred years later, the tribe of Athens had billowed into a rich and complex event. The top of the Acropolis was still their ritual embodiment, but now they had philosophers and scientists and artists as well as farmers and orators and warriors; people so perspicacious and accomplished I blush for us. Their sculptors made buildings and statues on top of the rock to stand in for their own bodies. Petrified Athenians, I call them. Buildings and statues that shared their world as if they were part of the family. *Enchanted Rocks.*

So what is our Acropolis? What is our own ritual embodiment? As we cruise into the fully automated era of the technological field, as we disperse onto our individual asteroids, I am asking what our own social space is. I remember the chunk of moonrock bought back by Apollo 17, sitting in a glass case in the Smithsonian. It's just a chunk of rock in the raw, a scientific sample, a piece of geology. The ancient Greeks had space rocks too, but they thought they were gods. And they knew just what to do. The first statue of Artemis was a meteorite carved with a nose and two eyes. And at Delphi they bound a meteorite with chains, to keep it from flying away again—and later made statues of it, with the chains carved right there into the stone. So, I ask, what shape should our space rocks be? A Buzz Aldrin figure? A Saturn Five rocket? Who knows?

But I also remember this: *There's scarcely a thing in my house that doesn't have swarms of identical partners located elsewhere on the planet.* How did it go? That computer by Dell, that toy airliner by Shabak—*I may live in the space they configure but there are parallel universes, other homes, in which the same things are permutated differently.* These artifacts and machines, with their talent for describing a partial life in a general world are the sculpture now. And the means by which we know about them and construct their value, the stream of images and lies that drive the pantaloons wild, are the ritual of the charged air we breathe.

———————

West Texas: a sculptors' meet at Marfa. Judd's place. Donald Judd the minimalist, who constructed empty things as silent as rocks and put them down in a landscape so empty it makes Texans think the two emptinesses are related. Myself, I think that the pink-painted hegemony he constructed down there was to insulate him from the cacophony of the New York art world: which is now all here, on his place, having a party. The joint is heaving. It feels like the middle of SoHo on a Saturday night.

It's ten hours out of Houston, this place, and Jaques, the lover of machines, persuaded me to drive. We went beating up the interstate in the Cadillac all day long with scarcely a word, the silence broken only as we passed through Fort Stockton by me trying to tell him to close on Maria.

"She's not a business deal," he says. Mr. High and Mighty—"I don't have to define myself by a relationship"—his exact words—"and neither does she." As a good relativist, I have to remind him that we are all defined by our relationships. Everything is. There's a lot of people playing this game, I reminded him, and they don't all play by your rules. "She's not some ballpark," he said. "Maria can have whatever she wants. Whenever." As if he had all the time in the world. As if passion is not the most precarious of a man's ecologies. "Get off my case, will you?" He said.

So I did. I guess I was bullying him to get myself in the mood for the party. Judd's descendants throw it every fall and everyone turns up in the most cubic of moods and tries to be just like Judd.

"If ever you disagreed with him too loud, he'd take offense," one of them says to me. "Tell you to get up on your feet. When he had you standing, he'd tell you to apologize. Veins popping in his forehead like a snake skinned alive. If you didn't he'd take a swing at you. And you never did apologize. Only way you'd ever get respect from Don was, never apologize. Hell of a guy."

I find myself being a satellite in the orbit of a big bearded man wearing a bootlace tie and a Hopi belt buckle and a Dunhill blazer. He is surrounded by groupies, arselickers, and acolytes. He was the other beneficiary of the foundation that helped Judd; he got a pile of dollars to buy an extinct volcano in Arizona and is attacking it with backhoes and bulldozers, sculpting it into a profundity that has all the presence and clout of Machu Piccu. I mean it—this is the real thing. It's Architecture with a capital "A." But more interesting to me is his statement that he's going into cattle ranching. He says that he has five hundred head grazing on the slopes of his mountain. Suddenly we are face to face.

"Sounds great!" I say, sycophantically. I imagine the exotic genetic distortions he must be perpetrating on this herd of cattle—think what a sculptor could do with selective breeding! Cows with legs so short their bellies graze the ground. Horns ten feet across. Banana-yellow hides! "Sounds great. Is that part of the project?"

"Hell no," he says, puffing his cigar, "In Arizona, if you ranch cattle, you get a tax break on the fenced-off land. And the fences keep the photographers out of the place." I am as disappointed as a cockroach caught in one of my killer sprays. But I guess it's logical for land artists to turn into landlords.

Outside there is a black sky studded with stars. I walk out from the crowd toward the lovely blackness, and come across a white-faced man standing with his head craned back, gazing at the universe. He has big boots and work clothes and one of those chintz-lined welder's caps you wear sideways, with a big peak to protect the side of your face from the flame. He's slugging a bottle of single malt flown in from the isle of Islay.

"I've been standing here looking at the stars and thinking 'til my hat's ready to blow off," he said, handing me the bottle. "And you wanna know what minimalism is? I'll tell you what, man. It's not like abstract like Braque and Pollock and all that shit. It's figurative." Figurative of what? "It's figurative of Nothing."

Oh boy. I told him I think that *Nothing* is another word for how the twentieth century tried to come to terms with invisible, automated, universal, global culture. I tell him about the First World War battlefields in northern France. They looked like that sort of nothing. Bombarded into oblivion by the machinery.

"Hey, that'll work," he said. "That's the twentieth century, Nothing, so what we have next is Everything, right?" He paused, and then grinned at me. "Dubbya dubbya dubbya dot everything dot com," he said. You can never tell if a Texan is making fun of you. The odds are against it, but you never can tell. "We used to talk about getting to the edge, remember that?" he went on. I did, too; it was a '70s thing. Early multiculturalist: *all the action happens at the edge.* "I guess we were looking for the edge of nothing. All the time, here's this guy Judd, man. Staring nothing right in the face. Right dead center."

I tell him about those giants who made the Ancient Greek landscape, and the gods who fought them for possession of it. I say that the Greek myths are like those Australian aborigine songlines. I am guessing he will start to shiver at the sheer profundity of it, but I'm wrong.

"You believe that?" He says, looking at me with his eyebrows raised and the Scotch halted halfway to his lips. "I mean, it's a nice story, but you really believe that?"

"What's your point?" I say, warily—the other thing you can't tell about a Texan is how soon he's going to thump you.

"Shit, man, those gods and those giants. It's a nice story but look at what we've got." He gives me the bottle and holds up his big welders' hands and starts to tick off his fingers. "We got *Big Bang,* we got *evolution,* we got *continental drift*—" he looks straight at me and draws the last word out of his mouth like an eight-syllable piece of bubblegum: "we got *uniformitarianism.* Now, you gonna tell me that isn't a whole heck of lot better of a story than what those old Greeks had?"

No way am I gonna say that. I agree with him. With the sounds of the party in the background, blasts of Judd's bagpipe music, smashing bottles, gunshots and all, we stand there watching the deep magnitude of the night sky. One day it will have an extra constellation of artificial asteroids held in formation by rocket motors inserted into their beautiful bronze bodies. My work. I think they are figurative of the partial response to everything, but until they are safely up there, I don't want to talk about them. Not because discussion contaminates creativity—I just don't want anyone stealing the idea.

. . . Pardon? . . . Display at the Royal Air Force Museum, London, England. Photograph by the author.

6
PANTALOON

Here's a room half full of men who look like a bunch of cement block buildings. Flat tops and crew cuts. Short-sleeve shirts, some blue, some white, all with their ties tucked in beneath the second button, all in dark gray slacks, some shoes brown, some black. It is not a uniform. The uniforms are worn by the other half of the men in the room. Their green and blue drab serges look, in contrast to the cement blocks, like vegetation. Complete with a hundred newly shined chrome buttons glinting like the eyes of animals in the jungle.

It is the year 1958. We are in a preparation room at Enewetak Island, a coral reef just barely peeping above sea level in the vast expanse of the Pacific. Not that these men can see the sea—or the sky, or the white sand of the beach or the fringe of coconut palms that wave in the breeze like holiday heaven. The room is in a sealed-shut hut made of steel and siding like an industrial shed. There are no windows. They could be in the middle of Pittsburgh, except that they are getting ready to destroy the place with a thermonuclear device.

We are here because Duke's here. He is one of the cement block guys. Third row from the back, looking as serious as everyone else. He is on extension from his California base observing how you get a place ready to be destroyed. There has been a surprising amount to do, from the transfer of the couple-hundred grass-skirted inhabitants to other islands to the calculation of the best bearing for the attack, and the placing of sensor devices all round the atoll, some of which have to have little concrete bunkers built specially for them. It is all in pursuit of the Cold War activity of transglobal saber rattling, something that is new to the world, and something that Duke and his colleagues find viscerally exciting. The global stakes are what is so exciting to them; the prospect of vast swathes of blackened enemy territory peopled only by stumbling mutations unable to resist has been stared in the face and taken on board. They all still believe in God, which is what makes it possible to ethicize such a thing. The world has not yet become ecologically balanced to them. Reality is still a question of truth, rather than material: what you might, indeed, call virtual reality, had the term not been previously used by the processors and then appropriated by the simulators.

By nightfall everything that was to be done has been done and they embark on a series of small boats and ferry across to the task group waiting for them out at sea. There is a rumor on Duke's boat that some of the islanders have absconded from their new location and returned to the island. Their headman will not negotiate with anyone but the admiral, who has already left for Washington. No one else has authority to stop the test outside of the established abort parameters. Whispers race across the ship: *the islanders are gonna get toasted!*

"The story was invented to spice up the event for the guys," says Duke, laughing at the memory. "They wanted something to think about while they watched the explosion." He is telling us about his Cold War days on this brilliant November Houston afternoon, out back of the house on the patio. We are having Thanksgiving Day brunch barbecue. Maria and Jaques are both here. Ex has been dancing around Maria like a bee on a geranium, to Liberty's great discomfort. Talking about the Spanish language, for example, which is spoken by a majority of the population of the southwestern United States, Maria says, "What's so complicated about an ethnic group demanding equal rights for its language?" And Ex says, "Spanish is not an ethnic language, honey. Spanish is the language of the conquistadors." And Maria says, "So what?" And Ex says, "They did to Mexicans what the English did to Native Americans." And Maria says, "I'm not your honey," and swats him over the head. And so on. It was like watching television, I thought to myself, as the stoically disinterested Jaques got up out of his chair and went inside to help B with the baby.

This barbecue is Duke and Liberty's show. B is organizing a huge Thanksgiving meal scheduled to hit the table at seven o'clock tonight, but we don't want to wait that long. Smoke wreaths up from the brisket roasting on the grill. Duke, deaf as a post, is in an ebullient mood. He is enjoying talking about hydrogen bombs. He calls them *super bombs.* They use an ordinary atom bomb to compress and ignite a core of massively inert deuterium; hence *thermo-nuclear.* The men who led the Manhattan Project, appalled by the destruction they had made available to the world, attempted to veto the development. Except for one Edward Teller, who was somewhat of a hero to guys like Duke, and who would not let the idea go. In the end his work was stolen by spies and sold to the Russians, and so the U.S. government declared it had no choice but to go ahead. "What I'm saying is," says Duke, "this all happened with maximum security and no information exchange allowed—look at you people with your information explosion! Don't worry about it. Those hydrogen bombs, those huge twenty-megaton boys that could have wiped out the whole of New Jersey in one swipe, they came out of no information exchange at all!"

It was the requirement for mathematical models of these apocalypse machines, which were needed to get a handle on how to build them, that spawned the development of high-speed computers. "The computers we had back then were the size of great white sharks," says Duke. "They were like captive animals." In his memory, those bombs were needed to pacify the world, so that we could concentrate on setting everyone free: and what happened? The damn computers got free!

He is pacing up and down in his cook's apron and huge heat-proof mitts, holding a pair of hickory-handled tweezers for turning the meat. Old Duke is not a redneck, but there he stands in his cook's outfit chuntering on about the world all going to hell and being the very figure of the pantaloon: a man at the height of his perceptive powers who suddenly discovers that the world doesn't care about what he knows anymore. When I try to maintain that the social program is alive and well, but machine-dependent and therefore out of our direct control, he says that's not a social program, a social program is solving the problem of poverty. Why is that not an issue anymore? He wants to know. What use is an information explosion if it doesn't blow away the poverty?

Ex is right there with an answer. He says that Americans talk up globalization as a universal application of the Bill of Rights at the same time as their finance capitalists are reinforcing the differences between people.

"See what I mean?" says Liberty.

"Seimen's?" Says Duke. "Fujitsu? Bayer? American companies?"

"Okay," says Ex, exaggerating his exasperation by opening his face up wide. "But it's all one big Western hegemony. People complain about American culture neutralizing the differences around the world, but have they got that wrong!"

I decide to stick my oar in: hegemony is a fact of human life, I say. Some version of it has always been there—it's what serves as stability. Would he rather have hegemony or a world full of warlords?

"Just imagine I'm holding a globe," says Ex, stretching out his fingers like a basketball player ready to shoot. "Planet Earth. Now I'm going to skin it," he says, miming the action. "I've changed my mind. It's not a globe, it's a bear." He makes a careful imaginary slit with an imaginary knife down its imaginary belly. He kneels and flattens out both hands on the patio. "There," he says, "We have a map. If you took the Earth and skinned it like a bear and laid the skin on the floor, you'd have a map. Is that one thing?" He says. "Look closer," he says. Look closer at the globe-skin rug. Get down on your hands and knees and you'll see the wriggling exotica that fill its every follicle. "Globalization is an illusion. That is not 'one thing' down there. That is 'everything.'"

"It's everything," says Maria.

And now here comes B with that magic tray of margaritas again to stop us bickering. Jaques appears behind her, carrying Chimp—they look so sweet together. "We had the baby monitor on," says B. "We could hear you all out here. You sounded like a bunch of chimpanzees." She goes round passing out the long cool glasses like she's kissing us all in turn. "You want to know what I think?" she says. "When we do all get globally hooked up the thing that's going to change isn't poverty, it's women and men." Liberty and Maria suddenly stand up: high fives.

"Hey man," says Ex to me. "This is just like watching television."

———————

A little later Duke and I are left sitting by the pool in the shade of a big umbrella. Huge cascade of Houston sky above as usual. A telephone sitting on a small onyx table flashes gently at us in a state of readiness. We look like two old Mafia guys in a movie. All we need is babes in bikinis—but the women have all gone to meet my father at the airport. Ex is visible through the glass walls in the gloom of the house, showing *picture.it* to Jaques.

"The thing about that Ex is he's so slippery!" says Duke. "What he and all the other wired-up guys have got to realize is that the world's still in trouble. There are things to get done. This great new technology of theirs is taking everybody's mind off that." He means ending poverty, housing the homeless, educating the ignorant, and eliminating tyranny. "The standard program," he calls it: he is too ossified to see the catch that my generation has seen, that the first two parts of the program are pollution generators and the second two are projections of the Western enlightenment. I keep that to myself, because my generation came up with no alternative but protest. Ex's so far has only come up with an anticipation of global complexity, but it's a step in the right direction. And what about Jaques's generation? I recently watched an architect the same age as Duke, a full-on unreconstructed modernist, lecturing a crowd of twenty-year-olds. He had made his name building chic steel houses in California, but his political thrust was to use factory-made buildings to solve the problem of the population explosion. "Come on you guys!" he implored them, waving his arms about, "this is your job! It's up to you! If you don't do it, Boeing will!"—and they all sat there thinking, thank Christ for Boeing. Because we want to go work for Disney and do Imagineering. We want to do theme parks. I tell all this to Duke, hacking my way word by word through the ice block of his deafness.

"Jaques is young, yet," says Duke. "He will mature. He will realize the world is not a plaything. He will come face to face with that reality that Ex says will change the politics, but which has in fact always been there." This is such a shiveringly pantaloonic observation that I have to turn to my future Duke-aged self and humbly plead: *Please don't let me ever hear you say something like that.*

I'm not the only one who thinks that that this theme park thing, these Edge Cities, this Las Vegas, is not the nadir of Western civilization but the first expression of a desire to remake the world into an exciting place. As exciting as the cathedrals must have been to medieval peasants, or the Acropolis to ancient Athenians. Were those not theme parks in the very sense of the words? I sat there listening to Duke's jets and bombs and Great-Grand-Coolie-Dam's-eye view of the world of machines, a world that could be solved by democracy plus technology—if only we'd get down to it—and thought to myself that the desire for excitement is not the same as solving the problem. The problems will always be there, like the stars and the planets; and this new desire is standing on the back of a fully automated world, where there is nothing else to do but explore experience. Art is not only not dead, it is becoming everything. With the management of our affairs shouldered by machinery, we revert to childhood, and spend our emotional lives playing and fighting.

So I dig at Duke and try to undermine his surety. I say this is people, not humanity. I say what we need is narrow band, not wide band. The local in the global. I say we're on a joyride, not a railroad track. I tell him he should wise up! I do it because I am aghast at the lost hundred years of the twentieth century, when people stared at their resultant, machine-made landscapes, their concentration camps and battle-wasted fields and speculated on the terror of human nature, and let their faith in themselves go cold.

"You're a self-righteous bastard, sometimes," says Duke. "I suppose you think that being an atheist is a question of feeling, not reason." And he's right! I do!

While Duke droned on about the great crash of 1929 and the Cuban missile crisis and the possibility of colonizing Mars my mind drifted back to Ancient Greece, where those petrified people stand on the hill reminding us that democracy is not the same for us as it was for them. Democracy, as an ancient model of action, is an imitation of life, positioned in a universe stricken by the arbitrariness of the gods. It is a way for human societies to sustain themselves through commitment in times of change, acting like an immune system in a body. But it all depends on a society seeing itself as organically whole. The difficulty now, as we struggle to be multicultural, is that democracy is not a vehicle for representing minorities. Democracy is a majority thing. In our automated condition our problem is not just how to distribute equality, but also how not to trip each other up when we do it. How do we enable our clumsy, representational, remotely activated version of democracy to handle the continuous ocean of automation technologies? What do you say about that, old man? *Old man* is what Ex calls me, and no doubt what Jaques calls Ex.

But Duke had veered off on a tangent and was talking about the beauty of Switzerland in the summertime. I had stopped listening for long enough to miss the connection—perhaps it was that Switzerland is the oldest democracy in the world. Duke described the little brown marmots frolicking in the grass. The cows bearing their great bells with the patience of nuns. The red and white electricity pylons charged by crashing clean waterfalls of melted snow standing proudly in the green valleys, the mountainsides sprinkled with Edelweiss. And it did, indeed, sound wonderful. We were in agreement again.

B's pickup and Maria's Golf docked simultaneously on the concrete apron in front of the garage. The women were back from the airport. Duke and I stood to watch the three of them, plus Juliet, levering the old man onto the ground and into his wheelchair, which unfolded to receive his crippled form like a throne. He looked like the Great Khan, he of Xanadu, who was attended by five courtesans wherever he went, buffered by a female cloud of mercy, assistance, and sex on demand. I imagined his bodyguards, trained in some martial art that rendered them invisible, surrounding the group like a force field.

Ex and Jaques and John all came out of the house and joined us looking across the front lawn at this regal party making its way toward us in slow procession. Little Chimp was riding in the wheelchair too, planted on his grandfather's lap, with the old man's good arm clamped round him like a safety belt. I almost wept. Maria, B, and Liberty looked like three Amazons bearing their battle trophies of innocence and experience, the Great Khan and the Golden Child. It was a glorious sight. They looked like a Hellenistic statuary group in living color.

I know—first caryatids and now Amazons. I am objectifying like a babe magazine. But I do it because I have sculptor's eyes. And you should have seen Duke. As the procession reached us, and passed through us like a Jupiter-bound mission traversing the asteroid belt, Duke stood slack-jawed and horrified. "What's happened to them, for crying out loud!" He was affecting irony, but pantaloons can't do irony. Their end is too close. "They look like a bunch of androids! How we gonna turn them off?" he said. "Does anybody know where the damn off-switch is?"

And then Maria held out her hand and took Jaques in tow. And broke the spell at last.

. . . The plane of hegemony . . . Newark airport, New Jersey, April 2001. Photograph by the author.

T H E   F I E L D S   O F   V I S I O N

It is the fall of 2001. A month ago nineteen terrorists attacked the United States by taking one piece of its machinery and turning it against another. It was spectacular. At first, watching the impact and the explosion over and over on Fox 7's loop that morning, it seemed biblical, a strike against hegemony like Samson's in the temple, an ancient thing to do—but then there was the insult of the puerile joke. The coincidence of the date and the emergency number—nine one one—was the sort of thing Batman's Joker would have done. It made me think of John putting his boot into the ants' nest in order to watch the ensuing panic. If that was their intention, I have to say it nearly worked. The whole country felt the shock wave through to its fingertips. I was all set to fly to Rome with twelve students to see some big architecture, and one by one they came to me saying that their families had been calling, asking them not to risk it. I discovered that Italy was flagged on the Department of State's Web site as a problem location for American tourists. I was told that the University of Virginia had already canceled their field trip. "But we do not give in to terrorists," I said. "Life must go on."

"Sure," one of them said, all of twenty-six years old and the closest to Christ of them all: "we've all got to die sometime."

So here we are, sitting on an empty American Airlines 777 being buffeted by some nasty clear air turbulence thirty-nine thousand feet above Greenland. I watch the wings flex and the trim tabs twitch and recall the opening sequence of *The Satanic Verses.* On the little video screen set into the seat in front of me the beautiful Ashley Judd is walking through nighttime New York, and there in the skyline are the twin towers of the World Trade Center. They look like ghosts. You get so used to seeing pictures of the old days looking emptier than today that this once-upon-a-time fullness seems haunted. In the seat across the aisle, Jaques—signed up for my class this year—is by coincidence watching *Gladiator* with its computer-generated reconstruction of ancient Rome, full of people and buildings and comings and goings. Soon he will see the ruins of the real thing, and vigorously try to imagine that same once-upon-a-time fullness. The prows of captured battle fleets hacked off and hung on the Rostra. The sacred fire, never extinguished since Romulus lit it seven centuries ago, burning inside its temple. Marc Antony on the steps of the Curia addressing the crowd. Why are we going to Rome? First because it's full of big things, and second because it's full of us. It is one of our songlines: "Senators, Congressmen, lend me your ears! There is no past or future. Everything exists in the Right-Bam-Now!"

This big buildings class has so far been a hoot. The project is "Design a Big Building." It's simple, but it's tough—What? Where? Why? And when? All have to be worked out. So far, "big" turns out to mean wide, long, capacious and tall; it even means heavy. The capacious guys are all into NASA's one hundred and seventy-five million cubic feet final-assembly shed at

Cape Kennedy. The heavy guys like the great pyramid on the Nile—all five and three quarter million tons of it. They say the assembly shed is just so much air, while the capacious guys say they can fit the pyramid inside with ease. It's like rock/paper/scissors. The tall guys—in fact the only two women in the class, Sandy and Nina—are looking at Norman Foster's half-mile-high thing in Tokyo Bay. Except that their scissors idea is to fit the tower out with that Phalanx rapid-reaction area-defense system I've told them about, to shoot down incoming airliners. It reminds me of the palmy days of 1980s ironic high-tech, post-Archigram, in which machine-building hybrid projects had aero-engines in them to respond to wind loads, and tethered zeppelins to help out their enormous cantilevers.

This is all right up Jaques's lover-of-machines street, I think—but in this class he is taking "big" to mean "ground cover." To put it another way: landscapes. He has a machines-landscapes hybrid going. He says that one day it is going to solve *A Field Guide to the Machines.* I guess the landscapes would be the fields? He shows us airports, and his take is a lot more vigorous than the airport and hospital comparison I was using in Australia. He turns "Airside" and "Landside" into a metaphor for our mechanized world. He says that Landside is all flat floors and Muzak and shopping. That's where we think we live, in the land of Landside. It's a simulated reality. But Airside is full of dynamics and fuel burn and control systems and machines—that's our actual life. That's our dependence on technology.

At Leonardo da Vinci Airport, while we wait to disembark, he points out of the window at the expansive concrete apron—big architecture—littered with its panoply of service vehicles.

They are exquisitely shaped by their various tasks. Luggage loaders, galley servers, fuel bowsers. Push-out tractors with tires as big as themselves. They look as exotic as the creatures of the deep ocean beds.

━━━━━━━

Our hotel is up on the Via Veneto, away from the feces-strewn streets of the station precinct, but in among Dolce Vita cafés we can't afford to eat at. In Texas drinking alcohol in public is forbidden, so that is what the students want to do here. We spend the days looking at the sites of Rome and the midnight hours careering from one place to another, from the Spanish Steps to the Trevi Fountain, down to the Pantheon and up to the Piazza Popolo, all the time swigging red wine from plastic cups and debating architecture in furious tones. Big architecture: the Coliseum, the Baths of Caracalla, and the Basilica of Constantine. The Aurelian Wall. Not as capacious or as tall or as heavy as other things we could mention, but big in time. At the Teatro Marcellus, which is a Roman theater down by the river converted into apartments way back in the Renaissance and, when we visit, under a comprehensive archaeological regimen of scaffolding and polyethylene sheets, we stare astonished at a human skeleton exposed to view by the dig, skull and teeth and all, like bloody Yorick himself. It's three A.M., and it's all I can do to keep my Shakespeare down, let alone the eight glasses of Bardolino.

But Jaques is happy: he has found landscape number two. Damned if he isn't calling it the ants' nest. "This is the landscape of the ants' nest," he says. He means the accumulated effect of all our attempts to tame nature. He calls it an "artificial wilderness." He is being deliberate. He says he is superseding my lazy analogy for contemporary urbanism with something more useful—a potential origin landscape for machines that will accommodate their growth as well as their decay. The airports are his landscape number one, the Landside–Airside of modern life—the ants' nest is the artificial wilderness in which it is set.

Our first two days in Rome have been spent looking for Bernini—whose sculptures have a strange machinic quality we can't pin down. His curves are not the sinuous continuities of Michelangelo, but seem to be made up of a series of infinitely small straight lines. Sandy compares it to digital and analog, and then explains the difference in quality of the vinyl and compact disc as being a result of the forty-thousandth of a second gaps that separate the cd's bits of digitized sound. "You can hear it, if you listen—you can hear the gaps!" she says.

It is not difficult to find Bernini in Rome. He is everywhere. But best of all is his statue of Apollo and Daphne up in the Villa Borghese. The statue stands in the same room it was made for nearly four hundred years ago, so powerful but so delicate that no one has ever dared remove it. The story here is that the rapacious Apollo has pursued Daphne without remorse. She is a priestess of Mother Earth, and just as Apollo is about to catch her she appeals to the goddess to turn her into something less appealing than the huge beauty she is. She obliges by turning Daphne into a laurel bush: and Bernini's sculpture shows the moment of transformation. Just as Apollo's hand is circling her waist, her skin is turning to bark and her head and hands and feet are sprouting hundreds of leaves. All carved from a single block of marble, life-size, both bodies caught in violent motion, every leaf as thin as a leaf, every hair as thin as a hair. He was twenty-six when he made this thing. It is as astonishing as a newborn baby. Every toenail, every muscle, every pore is there.

Maybe it is also as astonishing as a piece of high technology. I find myself suggesting to Jaques that Bernini's studio was the "skunk works" of his time, that the sixteenth- and seventeenth-century Spanish hegemony of the European world used Rome as its medium of authority and art as its power base, in the way that the current American hegemony of the Western world uses individual freedom and aerospace technologies. I think that to his airports and ants' nests he has to add another landscape that machines emerge from, which is the plane of the hegemonic. At any time in the process of our species—at least since the coming of cities—one or another of its tribes has been ascendant, expanding way beyond itself and distorting life for everyone else on the planet.

━━━━━━

Every afternoon, five of us—Sandy, Nina, Dan, Michael, and I—make a trip down to *easyEverything* to check our e-mail. Today I have incoming from the Dean of Architecture at the University of Texas. He wants us to go and fly the Lone Star flag at the American Academy in Rome, who are throwing a party that night for their exhibit of Stephen Holl drawings and models. Dan is right there—he clicks a button on his digital camera and shows me the little screen—it is a picture of the

EUR, Mussolini's new Rome to the south—where Stephen Holl lectured the day before. None of the rest of us knew anything about it but somehow Dan was in the vicinity and just got included. He found himself in a long, thin, fascist assembly room, listening to Holl's complicated positions on architecture. "I don't know," says Dan, "I really like his buildings, you know, I'm just not so sure about what he says about them." Then he clicks again and shows me a picture of one of Holl's slides. A dim blue rectangle impossible to read: apparently it is a picture of something Holl referred to as the "tesseract." "I don't know about this kind of thing," says Dan. "He said the square is to the cube as the cube is to the tesseract."

"That's not quite it," says Michael. Sandy and Nina pull faces and cover their ears. "Here it comes!" they say—and sure enough, Michael delivers: "the square is to the cube as the cube is to the hypercube." "Oh!" They say, fleeing up the Via Barberini and out of sight. "Save us from the fourth dimension!"

That night in the hotel lobby, all of them travel-stained and weary from trying to keep up with the sweet life, sit my twelve students. They are downloading the day's digital images. Dan's four-million pixel camera has an astounding capability. Watching him cruising through the streets of Rome is like watching someone tugged along by a little hand-held jet engine. His camera seems to suck in Rome like a jet engine sucks in air, compressing it into images and spewing them out behind in a trail of efflux. He doesn't use a laptop to store these images, but a pocket-sized hard drive that he carries in his fanny-pack. He has spare capacity, so Sandy and Nina are docking in it too. They all sit slotting their flash cards into the little machine like surgeons sterilizing knives. Every so often they fall back pealing with laughter and hand around their cameras, which show on their stamp-sized glowing screens the images of the previous night. Nina sallow faced and propped up against Sant Andrea al Quirinale. Michael sallow faced and lying flat out in the middle of the Piazza Navona. Jaques sallow faced and looking like Marcello Mastroianni in *La Dolce Vita.*

When Jaques and Nina go out to forage for wine for the night's travels, a conversation runs up about Jaques's landscapes and whether such flat, idealistic parcels can even be considered big buildings. I explain that he is hoping to use them to define a series of habitats for machines. Dan explains it better by saying they are more like the spawning grounds of new kinds of machines than habitats: that's what Jaques is looking for. It could be a way of organizing families of machines together by their origins in certain landscapes. He points to these landscapes' similarity to the idea of plateaus, which are, Dan says, quoting John Marks—an explicator of Deleuze—an invention the anthropologist Gregory Bateson minted to describe "complexes of social intensity within cultures that are not organized around a point of culmination." Not to be outdone Michael reminds us of the "fitness landscapes" evolutionists use to describe the space within which things evolve. He quotes Greg Lynn, who uses virtual versions of such landscapes to grow his computer models: "a landscape is a system where a point change is distributed smoothly across a surface so that its influence cannot be localized at any point." Sandy and Dan cover their ears and howl like dogs. "What's the big deal?" says Michael.

The big deal is using this para-language to describe such vital ideas. I have a problem that way myself. The other day someone told me that my characters reminded him of fashion victims, staggering around in Gallianos of metaphor. But I'd rather have that than a surfeit of shortcuts. Whatever—this idea of the evolution landscape is just what Jaques is looking for. They contain as a potential everything that will shape the machines as they move across them, expressed in abstracts—ambitions, necessities, economies, and probabilities.

"Did someone mention me?" says a voice—we all turn to see Jaques in the doorway dressed in a white suit he's just bought at a boutique round the corner. Nina, standing behind him, raises her palms in the air and shrugs.

"This is my friend Marcello," she says.

The American Academy in Rome occupies a palace up on the hill behind Trastevere, and when we arrive a throng of people is pushing at the gate as if it were a guest-list-only nightclub. But no problem—it is just that this is a fragment of America. They are checking photo-IDs as a response to the raised security threat. When we get inside we find a terrace that looks right out across the lights of the eternal city, a decorous patio with wine waiters cruising with silver trays and nachos in little white dishes and a room full of Stephen Holl's drawings and models.

And over there, by god, is Holl himself. Dan points him out as excited as a kid spotting Captain Hook in the Disney Hotel lounge. The man is surrounded by groupies. They look like a litter of piglets sucking at his charisma, and when Dan says we must go and join in I express my most serious doubts. "But we've got to find out the truth about the tesseract!" he says. And I'm glad he made us do it. The answer turned out to be extremely useful.

Piglets gain access to a nipple by pushing in through the others. That's just what we did. Holl turned to survey his new admirers, as hopped up by his own celebrity as everyone else. "Alright!" I said, straight at him. "Now, how does it go—the square is to the cube as the cube is to the—"

"Tesseract!" he said—happy, I guess, to feel the warmth of architectural theory in among the cold world of fame. "It's a way of calculating the modulation of an irregular ellipsoid," he says, "how they figure out the deflections in the geoid."

This was far more than we expected to get. But before we got any further, a woman not much less elegant than Vogue itself came up and took him by the arm. "I'm so sorry," she said to me, "But we have to go now. The table is waiting." And off he was led into the Roman night.

━━━━━

The "geoid" is the name given to the surface of the earth's gravitational field, which can be expressed as a hypothetical ocean surface. Water finds its level as a perpendicular to the gravity of the earth: that's how spirit levels work. What Holl was referring to was the fact that the earth's crust and core vary in thickness and density, and that this mass variation causes differences in the pull of gravity at different points on the surface. The sphere of gravity of the earth—the geoid—is not a constant smooth plane but a subtly undulating surface. Satellites when they orbit are constantly fluctuating slightly out of the true path in response to it. Why does it matter? Globalization is why. Mapping the world is achieved through triangulation between vertical poles located by reference to the stars, and if the verticals are deflected, the whole picture is distorted. You can make a map of Spain or of England or of the United States without geoid corrections, but you can't make a map of the whole world and get it to join up. And what is the geoid doing here in this discussion of machines and architecture and artificial life? It is a metaphor for the plane of hegemony—a globe-wide landscape in which deep and invisible distortions influence the actions of the rest of the world.

Jaques and Dan and Michael and Sandy and I talked it out as we walked in the garden of the Villa d'Este on the hills outside Rome. The garden is laid out like a carpet on a steeply sloping site. It is one of those baroque gardens in which the grid of paths, and the statues and fountains on point duty, remind some people of military encampments—ancient Rome—and others of paradise—the four-square Eden of the Old Testament. It is a rational formality set inside the turbulent formality of the wilderness.

In one corner of the garden is a statue of the classical goddess Artemis, with her feet of rock and her chest with its thirteen breasts. We come across it just as a woman is posing beside it for her lover's camera. She plants her hands on her waist and sticks her own two breasts out like battleships. She sees us watching and laughs; what she doesn't see is that Dan has fired off a couple of shots himself. With his camera's rotating screen he can shoot from the hip without anyone knowing.

"I just love to see people doing this stuff," he says. Sandy tells him his camera is turning him into a monster.

We are in Italy, but this baroque that's all around us is part of the Spanish hegemony that ruled Italy and dominated the Western world from the time of their occupation of the American continents until the end of the long seventeenth-century wars against Protestantism. Hegemonies are tribal events. They seem too huge to be parochial in that way, but that's my suggestion. Look at America now: a daisy-cutter in one hand and a self-help book in the other. Or at England back in the time of Dickens: a coterie of one hundred families playing out their fantasy of born-to-rule. As tribal events—and this is the second part of the idea—hegemonies incorporate the three tribal objects of desire as landscape strategies that generate their material domination. They have a landscape of the fetish, which is their songlines, and which describes their moral authority. They have a landscape of the thing of value, which is ultimately some abstraction of the land itself, as money is. And they have a landscape of the weapon, which is how they maintain their physical power.

"The Spanish rode to dominance upon the acceleration of exploration," I say, in full pontificator mode. The thing of value for Spain was treasure, hauled back from the New World in big heavy ships made of New World teak and turned into art—the weapon—for the glory of Holy Rome—the fetish.

When I say this I get a round of dissent. Somehow away from Texas the students can forget my status, and the teaching becomes as two-way as a coot fight. How can art be a weapon? They say. And I have to explain the character of a speculation. There are no proofs, just little sparks in the atmosphere. I remind them of the flamboyantly carved Spanish mission churches back in Texas, set down in the wilderness and used for capturing human souls. And of the gorgeous, baroque trompe l'oeil apartments of Ignatius Loyola by the church of Il Gesu we were astonished by only yesterday. He founded the Jesuits as the Counter Reformation's army—as soldiers of Christ.

Okay—temporary truce—when the hegemony passed to England in the nineteenth century, I continue, the thing of value had become not the treasure but the land in which the treasure was located. Their fetish was blood and honor, their weapon was the sea. Their thing of value was rent. The acceleration they rode was colonization.

"I guess that's what the English natural landscape garden is," says Sandy. She is standing in full sunlight, her back to the swooping horizon beyond the garden wall, the glittering splash of fountains all around. "The English colonized their own land, they enclosed it systematically, turned it into scientific farming"—and turned Scotland, Wales, and Ireland into little Africas, adds Michael. "Which meant that they had turned their wilderness into gardens," she ignores him. So? Say all of us. "So they grubbed out all their treasure chest gardens, all those parterres and box knots, and replaced them with mock wilderness. They turned their fields into gardens, and their gardens into fields." Beautiful. If it were not expressly forbidden in my contract, I would give her a hug.

These landscapes are what Jaques will use to construct *A Field Guide To the Machines.* They could be the equivalent of the kingdom separations in the biological taxonomy, but they are dynamic. He will need to name them and track them through history as they transmigrate through the planes of hegemony, spawning new machines and artifacts as they go, somewhat equivalent to the classes and orders—which then will cross and multiply into ever evolving hybrids, which will be something like the genus and species, but with more fractions.

We all sit in a bar in the sunshine in the little town of Tivoli waiting for the bus back to Rome. I look at them all relaxing in this luscious, faded place: Dan, Sandy, Nina, Michael, and Jaques. The Young Americans. America swallowed up the English hegemony just as England did the Spanish, taking on the custody of the world at the moment that the automation acceleration flowered out of the battlefields of the twentieth century. All that hard work the Germans did on turbines and internal combustion was swallowed up, too. The American is a cars and airplanes hegemony that hovers over its landscape, segueing easily from one continent to the next, its weapon the network-charged airwaves, its fetish individual human rights. We inside it—all the Europeans, all the Japanese, the South Koreans, those isolated Australians, even chunks of Chinese and South Americans—live in a shower of individuation machines and remote controls. Our cameras and laptops and cellphones are the actualization of the American songline.

We order another round of Paninis and Peronis. I comment on the sumptuous leisure of tourism that gives ordinary people like us the wealth of Turkish pashas.

"We're not ordinary people," says Nina, breaking her habitual silence and looking up from her book. She is reading *On the Road*. She tells us how great it is. She tells us how Kerouac's description of the fabulously buoyant early years of modern America, full of glitter and power and deep friendship, is also full of poverty and toil and the wretched task of being alone. As she talks the sun bounces off her spectacles like semaphore from the battlefront, and behind the cedar trees the garden of the Villa d'Este that dominates the life of this little town gradually seems to turn from a treasure chest into a ghostly cavern full of ancient dragons.

———

That night in Rome I doze in my hotel room listening to the sirens and the roar of scooters. Inside my head my brain is turning over the three landscapes of desire and speculating again on what the missing fourth horse of this particular Quadriga might be. I don't want to use tombs—too gloomy. Michel Serres himself suggests an ocean of time, a chaotic milieu to dissolve the excessive redundancy, that is, the static qualities of classification, that are implied by the idea of the three quasi-objects. But I am looking for something a whole deal more pragmatic. This is about machines and architecture, and I want a vision. Nina had a great double-pun phrase for Jaques's landscapes: she called them "fields of vision."

One complication is that hegemonies run their accelerations by the previous acceleration's modes. The Spanish ran colonization like the exploration they rode in on. The English ran industrialization like colonization—McLuhan's rearview mirror at a strategic scale. So here are we Americanos and

Americanas running automation as if it were industrialization. Our fetish is freedom, our weapon is the air itself. Our thing of value is multiple, and available over the counter.

As I drift into sleep, it almost seems clear. We all know about it. We dig the treasure out of the ground and burn it until it turns into something else, and this vanity of bonfires changes the character of the atmosphere. We have discovered that the landscapes of our hegemony are not sustainable: and that what we need to do to perpetuate America is the opposite of what America is.

. . . Galatea, from Parian stone enchanted . . . Pygmalion and Galatea (Jean Leon Gerome, 1824–1904). The Metropolitan Museum of Art, gift of Louis C. Raegner, 1927 [27.200].

M E ! M E ! M E !

"I was the shadow of the waxwing slain," the old man says, holding one finger up in the air. "I was the shadow of the waxwing slain, by the false azure in the windowpane." Chimp copies him, holding up his own little stubby finger all puckered with spit. The two of them are sitting, one in the wheelchair, one on the wheelchair patient's lap, in front of a huge log fire. I was right. A big storm blew in two hours ago and hammered on the roof with hailstones the size of eyeballs. The temperature dropped by twenty degrees and B jumped at the chance to get her fire going. It roasted my back all the way through my humans-have-invaded-the-planet Thanksgiving speech—which went down like a lead balloon. We went around the table each saying thanks for something that had happened to us in the previous year and everyone started with some sort of disclaimer, separating themselves from my remarks. Except for Juliet.

"Okay, honey," said Liberty, "it's your turn. What do you want to say thank you for?"

"For bringing Daddy back!" she squealed into the expectant silence. Her mother's face looked for a second like ground zero. On the other side of the table tears sprang into Ex's black eyes. Duke, meanwhile, munching happily, heard nothing. The sound of himself eating makes him turn off his hearing aid. Isn't that what I was saying? We are the army of occupation. All we have to manage is ourselves.

"Galatea, whom his furious chisel from Parian stone had by greed enchanted, stepped from the pedestal on which she stood and enroyalled his body with her demon blood," says the old man. He is running through his catalog of poetry by old white-haired guys, committed to memory over a long computer-free life. The *waxwing slain* is Nabokov's; this *Galatea, from Parian stone enchanted* is Robert Graves's. It is a grandly generous gesture, reciting poetry aloud. My father's ancient face, illuminated by the flames of the fire, looks as deep as a canyon in sunset. Eroded by a lifetime of experience. The rest of us are perched all round the room listening to the web of peace he is spinning. The greatest gift the old can give to the young is to demonstrate a future filled with hope. And when he launches into the best of them all, the Tennessee Williams poem from the end of the *Night of the Iguana,* the rest of us are in tears. It is a poem written to be spoken by an old man stuck in a wheelchair, his last poem, finished only just in time before the end of his life. "How calmly does the orange branch observe the sky begin to blanch," it starts. "O Courage!" he shouts out in his quavering old voice, his face awash with ambition. "Could you not as well select a second place to dwell, not only in that golden tree but in the frightened heart of me?"

After the meal, John, Chimp, Ex, Duke, my father, and I are all gathered together in the den and full right up to bursting with turkey and pumpkin pie. Way past everyone's bedtime on

Thanksgiving night. One should not give boys of twelve vintage port but it happened anyway and now John's eyes are shining like he has a lamp inside him. The old man demonstrates to the boy his fabulous new state-of-the-art wheelchair. Titanium frame and graphite wheel rims and all.

"Anything else is gaslight!" he exclaims—and he and I know he is quoting Herbert von Karajan, one of the original old white rogues. Alpha males, like Henry Miller and Norman Mailer and Jean-Paul Sartre—and like himself. Lions in the jungle. I call them *Generation Alpha.*

Ex is quiet, moodily sipping his port, brooding about Juliet, but Duke is all over the old man—his father-in-law—joining in with the "oohs" and "ahs" over the wheelchair. He flatters and compliments, and though the old man can see through it like a plate-glass window he doesn't mind because it just feels so good for a disabled man to be treated with a little respect for a change. He starts telling Duke all about the great days in the war when he was designing camouflage for the Air Force.

"We were always one step behind the Germans," he says. "It was astonishing what they did. They could take a two-inch stipple brush to a Messerschmidt just landed in Africa, still painted Abbeville gray, and make it disappear into the desert like a Bedouin." I take this stuff from my dad with a pinch of salt, but the others were enjoying it so I kept quiet.

"We went up to Mildenhall to help the Americans out with their flying fortresses. Two weeks before I'd come across a little painting by Sassetta from the altarpiece at Sansepulcro, a picture of St. Francis relinquishing his crusader's robes, painted in—I don't know, when? Paul?"

"Fourteen thirty?" Take a wild guess.

"Fourteen thirty, absolutely right. And in the corner of the picture, floating in the sky like an angel, is his crusader's castle—his *flying fortress!*" He stopped and searched Duke's face for some acknowledgement of the wit but Duke just held the soft, quizzical frame he'd set his features into and looked like he could hold it forever. "So what does Sassetta do? He has to paint the underneath of this castle, this flying fortress, and how can he do it? No one's ever seen such a thing!" Another pause while he tried to remember the beginning of the story. His eyes swiveled my way.

"Mildenhall," I prompted him.

"That's right! We painted the bombers exactly like the underneath of Sassetta's castle, like brown marbling it was, and they told us afterwards they kept losing each other in formation! That's how good it was!"

By the time Jaques got in from helping to clear the table and stack the dishwasher the rest of us had settled around the room to listen to John's choice of music, which was kind of an endurance test. It sounded like planets crashing together. John was in the middle of the room thrashing about like the kids he's seen on television. It felt like some New Guinea long house in there, some antique preserve of primitive patriarchy.

Now that Jaques had arrived we were all the seven ages together. He was holding a CD in his hand—more planet crashing music?—and another pantaloonic thought flashed through my brain. Perhaps the next generation are planning to flood the world with it. An ocean of sound. A deluge. *Sorry man,* they'll say, *no one over thirty on this ark.* Degendering will be when old men are awarded the same status as old women. But in that case, why was he calling me "sir"? He held out the CD.

"I'd like you to have this, sir. I'd like to thank you for to-day." The label said TDK 700 Mb.

"What is it?"

"My new book, sir." *Book* means CD-ROM already.

"Has it got a title?"

"Yes, sir. It's called *A Field Guide to the Human Beings*."

———————————

At one a.m. on the morning of the day after Thanksgiving, I lay in bed with one arm around B and the other around Chimp, staring at the ceiling. Every so often the lights of a passing car would veer across the room, and I imagined that the house was hurtling through space, spinning as it went, and the moving lights were rushing stars. My turn next to be a pantaloon. It's still fifteen years off but it feels as close as a hug. I remember being Jaques's age, contemplating turning thirty. And being told by thirty-something teachers, listen Paul when you get to my age, you'll realize life just isn't that simple! I remember one guy saying, how many friends have you got? How many people do you know? And I thought a bit and did the math and came up with somewhere between two and three hundred—and he held up one hand with the four fingers and the thumb outstretched and said, *That's how many I have. That's how many people I can count on in this world.* I pitied him. You poor old fart, I thought. And the guy was thirty-two!

Chimp has two people he can count on and that's plenty. Down the hall John is sleeping, half hanging out of the bed with his shut eyes flickering in REM, dreaming of his next phase in life, a dream in which the perfect bodies in MTV videos and the sound of crashing planets figure strongly. He is beginning to smell like a man. Jaques, across the other side of the city in his doublewide, is half awake and luxuriously bending his body to fit Maria's. He is in possession of the best thing on earth: a great idea for a book. *A Field Guide to the Human Beings.* I wish I were doing it. It could be the materialist Bible. Ex, in the room over the garage and all by himself, has just reared out of a nightmare in which he was an inmate of some sort of concentration camp, with everyone crammed into tiny cages, filthy and desperate. But there seemed to be plenty to eat. He suddenly realized they were on a human battery farm, being kept for food; and he woke up in a sweat. And started immediately thinking of his daughter Juliet. He lies awake scheming on how he can steal her back from Liberty and take her to India. Insert her into the teeming mass of the place of the future like a bee in a hive and teach her about the rights and wrongs of life. And what about Duke? All the rest of us are swerving toward our next phase, what about him? He snores. Liberty is getting used to it, but she makes him wear a little plastic nostril dilator that is supposed to open the airways up. So he has to sleep on his back with this thing on his nose, his hearing aid on the table beside him—almost oblivious already. And look, there is the oldest man, last of the bunch, lying downstairs in the den wide awake as always, no time left to waste in sleep, fighting the impulse to urinate, clenching and unclenching his sphincter muscle, locked in battle with his mortality every second of the remains of his life. When Jaques had brought in his CD to give me, the old man had said: "Where's B? I need her. Where's that lovely Maria?" He wanted to flirt a little before he went to bed.

"Is that in the field guide?" I had asked Jaques.

"Oh yes, sir. That's pretty much what it's about. Pretty much exactly that."

"And what happened to *A Field Guide to the Machines*?"

He reached into his back pocket and handed me another CD. Big grin all over his face. "I've got that right here."

Shush now, here's Chimp waking up. He sits up in the darkness and his fat little cheeks fill the room. I lie there and stroke his head and watch him breathe.

"Rocket balloon," he says. He has never said anything before.

"Rocket balloon?" I say. John was playing with one yesterday at the barbecue. You blow it up and let it go and it flies off across the garden with a screeching sound and a wonderful undulation. "Do you like the rocket balloon?"

"Rocket balloon."

CODA

It is the New Year by the time I sit down with Jaques's book. Ex has taught him well. When I open up his CD there is another rainforest homepage littered with icons, except this is more like Shanghai city than a forest; most of the icons throw up banners saying *under construction, no access* when I click on them. *A Field Guide to the Machines* is a far from finished work. I wander about hunting and clicking, searching for a pursuable strain, doing the digital equivalent of turning over stones on the riverbed looking for clams. At last I find one behind a little Mayan god figure, one of those big-nosed, grinning creatures with compact square bodies.

It's an outline of a naming system for the machines. Not a *bi*nomial one like they use for the flora and fauna but a *quadri*-nomial one, based on evolution landscapes. He has attempted to lay out the idea in the context of all the other complications so far uncovered. The cultivations, the accelerations and the landscapes of desire. "Cultivations" are what he's calling the technological plateaus; the geoid-like planes shaped by accelerations and bearing complexes of evolution landscapes of desire, dominated by a few—sometimes, as now, only one—hegemonic tribes. Machines configured by the desires of the hegemons will be hatching out all over them, and rearranging the arrangements surviving from previous cultivations. Eventually the accumulation of new things becomes so complex that all the secure human relationships within the hegemony are distorted. People forget what they set out to do and turn into that bewildered army of occupation I was on about at dinner. And other tribes will be pushing for position, adding to the confusion. Sometimes even wars between colliding landscapes, as the tribal hegemons vie for power. This is not quite a "paradigmatic shift" or an "epistemological break," because what he is trying to describe is a change in the character of desire, rather than of understanding: it is an emotional current. And at this point of confusion, according to Jaques, things are accelerating so fast that sudden clarities appear, and the cultivation transmogrifies into something else. Clarities? He means *action*—technology plus politics. Clarities stand out in tribal histories as huge moments. The revolutions and the regicides and the appearance of heroic figures.

At the bottom of the section is a link saying "Nebula." I click on it and an irregular transparent blob starts appearing on the screen. It comes together in layers, like a reverse striptease, and I can see it is made of bubbles and billows and particles, overlapping and interacting like an astronomical nebula, full of illuminated clumps and traces. It turns out to be Jaques's graphic 3-D model of human history. The clouds are the tribal cultivations, the particles are the machines, and the traces their patterns as they proliferate through the model. It's a bit like that block of fluorite in the geological museum. You can spin it and zoom in on it to see the intricate interactions— some system of coordinates derived from this model will be the first name of four that each machine in the field guide will carry. At least that's the idea: what happens on my screen is a succession of freezes and crashes and exclamation-marked warnings. It's just like a complexity confusion in microcosm, I start thinking—but eventually I manage to navigate through the nebula into the early twentieth century, and onto the rumpled piece of territory of the 1920s and '30s.

A window opens up on the Schneider trophy races. They were air speed competitions that took place during the cease-fire between the two World Wars. It is a tiny, finite evolutionary landscape, more of an evolutionary ledge, that bred the fighter planes of the Second World War. The airplanes were seaplanes, because the variable-pitch propeller had not yet been thought up and the slippery little machines needed long run-ups that could be found only on open stretches of water. Jaques has included clips of these waspish creatures, all cleverly different from each other so as to claim possession of some niche on the ledge, but all as light as possible, with huge engines and with their pilots strapped to their backs like rodeo cowboy heroes. The water all around them adds an amniotic quality to the whole enterprise. National flags glitter in the background and the whiff of man–machine symbiosis futurism is in the air. In 1925 an American company, Curtiss, introduces a water-cooled twelve cylinder in-line engine. It's more trouble than the air-cooled radials the others are using, but it can be inserted into a slim, streamlined shape. While the Germans stand on one side and make detailed notes, the French and Italians and British go at it furiously, pushing toward a culmination in the British Supermarine S6B in the early '30s—meanwhile, back in America at another air race series called the Thompson trophy, almost on the same ledge but on land this time, Howard Hughes is beating all records in a light-weight stressed skin machine with a huge engine. Put the S6 together with the Hughes H1 and you get Reg Mitchell's Spitfire and Willy Messerschmidt's Bf 109, and off to war you go again. This time not in the trenches, but in the air.

I have to stop and think for a moment. This field guide is a peculiar project. It's full of the charge of the French materialists, with their concepts of rupture and change, but inside all that there they are, Howard and Reg and Willy, all the life-travelers falling Maria-style through open skies behind their departing bombers and busying themselves with loving commitment. Sure, everything is relative. But how else do relationships prosper if not with that falling?

My Houston house without the extended family is a huge soft sanctuary full of sweet sounds. Upstairs B is bathing chimp, singing at the top of her voice. In the next room John is sweating and grunting over some PlayStation game. I shut down the field guide and sit back and watch my new screen saver come up. I pulled it off the front page of the *International Herald Tribune* yesterday. It's a picture of four U.S. Special Forces guys on watch at some secret meeting in Afghanistan. They look like a bunch of film stars. They all have scissor-cut beards and Hollywood haircuts and ironic Bruce Willis expressions. They're wearing service handguns and hefting short-barrelled carbines, but there are no uniforms. One has a Helly Hanson snowboard jacket and headwarmer band, another has a hunting gilet and a baseball cap. A third is shooting an *are you looking at me?* glance at the photographer, the cigarette in his mouth distorted by the wide-angle at the edge of the frame so much that it looks like a reefer. It is the most powerful image of the confidence of the American hegemony I've yet seen. More so even than those of B52s unloading sticks of bombs on people in huts twenty thousand feet below them. The bombers remind me of nineteenth-century British gunboats; but these men look like democrat missionaries. Twenty-first-century Jesuits, who want you to do what they say for your own good. And in comes B, radiant with steam and carrying the baby wrapped in a wet towel, his face as pink as a Houston sunset. Look at that bloody photograph, she says. What was wrong with the one we had before, with all the fishes? It's time to make supper, she says. Time for labor.

Before I shut down just now, I clicked on an icon of the Tomb-Raider. It turned out to reveal the missing desire landscape I was looking for in the Villa D'Este. The fourth horse, which pulls the desire trilogy through time. In addition to the three processual landscapes of fetish, weapon, and value there is a wild card, says Jaques—the prevailing hegemony's transcendent desire to last forever. The desire for perpetuity sets off a hunt for how that can be accomplished. Philosophers and artists and scientists all over the tribal territories are involved in this inquiry, accompanied by dissenting philosophers and artists and scientists trying to establish some other clarity. What they discover is not always what they are looking for. The Spanish search for the philosopher's stone, something that would turn the whole world into treasure, resulted in the discovery of chemistry; a material notion that would one day yield far greater riches than treasure. The English desire for title deed to the world—some proof of ownership—came up with the origin not of the English, but of the species. It turned out that no one had title to the wilderness at all.

I look around at B and John and Chimp, Englishly scoffing our meal. We are part of the American tribal hegemony, but we are still aliens in it. So I ponder—what is America's desire for perpetuity? It matters to me because the U.S. domination of the world should last at least another three generations, and so whatever happens here will form the machinic future of my children. Is it a desire to automate the future, so it runs as true as the democratic freedom machine of the American constitution? And could the future be automated like that? Maybe that's what we're looking for in outer space. I recall the jetstream turbulence in the tropopause and think of scientists tracking the weather to determine the future of their satellites and rockets and coming up with chaos theory. Call me what you like, but maybe that is it—maybe "self-organizing" is another way of saying "automatic." And the "sustainable" paradigm is a dream of perfected automation.

―――――――

That whole business of the Nebula and the evolution landscapes is only the first taxon in Jaques's quadrinomial fieldguide-to-be. The first name each machine will have is the string of coordinates that places it in human history. The second name will derive from its generic organization.

Back in seminar two, my Australian friend James and I floated a schematic of architecture based on a four-term sentence: *Rearranging material for human purposes.* "Human" is the catchment for matters of program, we called it "chronotonic," which in Jaques's system is architecture as "objects of desire." Recently I listened to the American architect Don Bates describe the opposition to his firm's beautiful and strange Melbourne Square museum buildings, which were characterized as "camouflaged battleships" by some hostile townspeople. Since I had a few seconds before been thinking how great they were *because* they looked like camouflaged battleships, I reflected that this emotive quality had not been anticipated by the architects. The competition they won had framed the desire-by-use program, but not as object.

The architects themselves were keenest on the building's "architectonic," that is, the arrangement of the parts. They had worked out an apparent randomization of the structure in which six standard components could be permutated by computers to look chaotic—it was this quality that made it seem camouflaged, and their choice of colors, gray, sand, Pacific Ocean blue, that made it look like a battleship. The second taxon in Jaques's field guide corresponds to this architectonic. It is the field of prospective evolutionary lines. If the chronotonic is how a piece of architecture is *desired,* the architectonic is how it's *conceived.*

This field guide could include buildings as well as machines. But buildings, unique and fixed in place on the globe, could be done by a gazetteer instead—an indexed list, with geographical coordinates. A field guide in the old white-hunter mode is like a map for Martians wandering through the Earthen landscape, intersecting with the creatures at large. Jaques's is like that too, but because it's about machines, it has a trainspotting strain running through it. Machines have a strange tension between the general—all three million Toyota Camrys in the world—and the specific—that one over there. That's right, the red one with the dent in the driver's door and 63,336 miles on the clock. What is trainspotting? You go through the world writing down the numbers, but why? Is it in case you see the same one twice? And is that exciting or disappointing?

Machines have number as well as location—prototypes are not complete. They are like mutations—biological sports—until the production versions come along to confirm the species lineage. Machines are like animals. That's why they need a field guide. Which reminds me of the Christmas puppy that appeared last year, that cute mutation with the feet too big and the floppy head—a sad crippled thing, it was, which exaggerated the characteristics of puppy-hood and which some ghoulish corporation was planning to clone as Christmas presents. They would be unstable entities, aberrations, which would not survive for more than a few months—and that was the point. This puppy was just for Christmas. Machine or animal?

So name one is a string of coordinates and name two is a coded concept—D&G would say *percept*—and name three is going to be a specification. A list of actual parts used. We are with the stereotonic, now: the solid presence of the machine in the world.

One way to do it would be to track the presence of the simple machines and their inheritors, wheel and axle passing through the shackle cams of the colonial and the spinning governors of the industrial, picking up electric generators and motors and turbine compressors. Sluice gates moving through railroad points and shut-off valves and accumulating electric switches and silicon chips. All machines are made of these pieces. They are like the cell assemblages that animal bodies are made of—not that these are chronicled in field guides of organic life. It seems possible to do that with machines, however, so here they are. It has occurred to Jaques that the third name a machine could have would be a list of its parts, and species of machines could be homologated purely through shared components. Except that the names are going to get very long, Jaques: your ordinary saloon car has fourteen thousand parts, huge numbers of them being simple nuts and bolts.

Another quadriga is building here. How a piece of architecture is desired, how it's conceived—*perceived*—how it exists and now: how it's used. How it is in action. The fourth name is the tachytronic. We are back to twelve-year-old John holding his screwdriver and saying, "Me plus this screwdriver, plus these subassemblies are a machine! A machine that makes cars."

We make the machines, we are their programs. I find myself speculating again on the peculiar state of anonymity we call celebrity—those strangers we know—and the inflation of our tribal observances into global events. We watch each other all the time on our machines. We make the machines, so we are their programs, and in using them we are watching ourselves. Machines "r" us!

———————

Reluctantly I retrace my steps and climb back out into the streets of Shanghai, and now what's this? An icon in the shape of a Cadillac with my name on it. I click and it opens up an email form, directed to Jaques. It's like a whodunit. He's asking for input, and I am the justice. All this while I've been holding back the floodwaters of structure in my head lest they should swamp Jaques's delicate fledgling. This is about technology, but it's a speculation, not critical theory. It is a one-cloud explanation that attempts to be outside the hegemony, like the globe-skin rug; and in which the solid parts are commitments, made of people and things and ideas.

I recall Gertrude Stein's saying, what is the use of being a boy if you turn into a man? I think, what is the use of being a justice if you forget the lover in you? Or the soldier? First I tell him to dedicate it to all those people who've ever loved a machine. Then I decide to rewrite the whole thing. I'm going to wake Jaques up. To activate him. I start to type: *In the middle of the black Texas night, Jaques—the lover of machines—sits wide awake at the controls of his reconnaissance drone, gathering his wits about the state of the world.*

ANNOTATED INDEX

Accumulation, technological, *continued*
glaciation analogy, 130

A/C dial, 19. *Air conditioning. In the U.K., aircon. In the car trade, air.*

Acid, 18. *The aggressive ingredient in the stings of wasps and bees and bites of ants is formic acid.*

Acropolis (Athens), 172
Elgin Marbles, 77

origins fantasy of, 143. *My Greek observations have four sources. H. D. F. Kitto's* The Greeks *(Penguin, 1957), which has an image of Socrates teaching in the technological milieu of a contemporary African village: Indra McEwan's* Socrates' Ancestor *(MIT Press, 1993), which goes into the matter of Nike and describes the peplos (see* Peplos*) and also the quality of flight imparted by the Parthenon's subtle entasis. Also Joseph Rykwert's* The Dancing Column *(MIT Press, 1998), which describes columns as metaphors of bodies: and Vincent Scully's* The Earth, the Temple and the Gods *(Yale University Press, 1962; revised, 1979) from which was posited the "charged void" (see* Songlines*).*

petrified Athenians, 144

as theme park, 157

Actual, 165. *I am using* actual *to counterpose what has come to mean* virtual, *which used to mean something like "latent" or "potential." I think* real *is more interesting left caught up in the debate about perception that makes sense of having a contemporary "modern art."*

Adam, 118, 119

Adam's House in Paradise, 119. *The book of that name is by Joseph Rykwert (MIT Press, 1981).*

Adelaide (Australia), 72

Aegean, 77

Aero engines, 165

Afghanistan, 105, 192

Africa, 3, 11, 175
eastern, 14
Messerschmidt just landed in, 183
Portuguese exploration of the coast, 133
slave warehouses in, 143

African-Americans, 143

After the City, 20. *By Lars Lerup (MIT Press, 2001).*

Airports, *continued*
  as extended machines, 22
  and hospitals, 23. *Martin Amis commented on the similarity in Experience (Time Warner, 2000).*
  and hospitals and factories, 74
  Jaques's landscape number one, 165
  Leonardo da Vinci (Rome), 165
  no need for, 125
Airside and Landside (airport modern life landscape analogy), 165. *Back in the days when airports were shipping harbors and airliners were flying boats, Gertrude Stein wrote that "a landscape is such a natural setting for a battle or a play that one must write plays." But now that the world has had another fifty years' worth of cover and control, now that even the lions in the jungle are protected by human laws, it is time for more suggestions. Mine is that, in the way that large new buildings tend to be organized as analogues of shopping malls with key client locations used to put hierarchy in the program, contemporary landscapes tend to become analogues of airports. Perhaps because of the prevailing hegemony's use of the air as a weapon?*
Alarm clock/radio, 57
Alberti, Leon Battista (1404–1472), 138. *Alberti was in the front seat of the exploration age clarity. The few buildings he did are as dense as brains. The Rucellai chapel, a building inside a building, is what I mean when I say they have more punch than they should.*
Alchemical, 114
Alcock and Brown, 124. *An airport hotel, so the rooms are themed "aviators." Alcock and Brown were the first to fly the Atlantic non-stop, in 1919.*
Aldrin, Buzz, 145. *Second man on the moon.*
All-glass office, 2. *An office with no paper; everything on computers. Lawyers and insurance companies have ruined that fantasy.*
"All the world's a stage," xii, 94. *This passage is Jaques's "seven ages of man" speech from* As You Like It, *with the verse breaks omitted. Shakespeare's comedies include characters that embody the four humors, a medical-philosophical quadriga that originated with Hippocrates and is related to Anaximander's four elements. The four humors are melancholic, choleric, sanguine, and phlegmatic; in* Twelfth Night, *for example, Toby Belch is the choleric, Touch-*

stone the sanguine, Aguecheek the phlegmatic, and Malvolio the melancholic. In As You Like It, Jaques is the melancholic and the gloomy humor colors the whole idea of the seven ages of man, giving it a fatalist undertone that my use of the idea in this book does not share. The speech is one of the best known of Shakespeare's entire product. I once heard Alan Rickman—one of my generation—doing it with the Royal Shakespeare Company in London. I swear he gulped before embarking on it, so enormous was the expectation of the audience.

Amazons, 160. *Tribe of warrior women in the Greek songlines.*

America
  Ex really feels like he's in, 106
  Kerouac's description of, 177
  mimicry in urban ~ (John McPhee), 20
  swallowed up the English hegemony, 176
  what we need to do to perpetuate ~, 178
  young ~ns, 176

American Academy in Rome, 168, 171

American Airlines, 105, 164

American hegemony, 168, 176

Americanos and Americanas, 177

Anatomy of Architecture, 108. *Northrop Frye's* Anatomy of Criticism *(Atheneum, 1966) is the inspiration for this remark. It is a four-part theory of literature (modes, symbols, myths, and genres). The architectonic, stereotonic, chronotonic, and tachytronic quadriga described in seminar two is the substance of the ambition for an* Anatomy of Architecture.

Androids, 160

Andromeda galaxy, 48

Anesthetist, 42
  stock prices on B's blood chemistry, 46

Anglo, 107, 143

Antigravity machine, 99

Ants. *See also* Nests
  and bees (as hymenoptera), 17
  and bees (have nothing on us), 25
  and the thunderstorm, 16

Antwerp (Belgium), 143

Anura, 90

Aphrodite, 93. *Greek goddess of love.*

Apocalypse Now, 74. *My lover-aged friends insist that the film is based on a true story. Not so: it's based on Joseph Conrad's* Heart of Darkness *(1902). But then* Heart of Darkness *is based on a true story. When I started writing about actuality but using fabricated characters I took the first drafts to Sir John Summerson, doughty historian of the old school, to ask his advice. He was dismayed at the possibility that I might be "poisoning the wells of truth." But if truth is only contained in experience every drama is true, as you experience it.*

Apollo, 128

Apollo and Daphne (Bernini, 1625), 167

Apollo 17, 144

A posteriori, 34

Aquavit, 37

Arachnid, 9

Arachnida, 10

Araneae, 7

Archigram, 165. *See also* Walking city

Archipelago (Australia), 71. *The idea of Australia—which has only eighteen million people in the entire continent—being in effect a densely populated archipelago was described to me by Britt Andreson of the University of Queensland. After the American war of independence, the British thought Australia was their alternative North America, and the disappointment of discovering the interior riverless and waterless and quite unlike the cornucopia that was America still echoes to this day. There is an upside to the lack of development potential, and it appears that the Australians have perceived it just in time.*

Archipelagos of concrete bunkers, 125

Architectonic, 78, 195

Architecture

  with a capital "A" (Roden Crater project), 147

  there's the ~ (work, Arendt), xi

  bent ~s of the Deleuzeians, 36

  big ~, 166

  big ~ (Rome), 163

  but buildings are ~ too, 73

  collecting dust in the ~ libraries, 30

at one end of the scale of ~ are landscapes, 33. *Guy Martin Wetzel has directed my attention to a comparison between Gehry's use of Dassault's Catia software and Lynn's use of evolution landscapes. Catia precisely models 3-D in absolute space and can be directly employed in machining parts, and could be compared to the tradition of stereotomy, he suggests (see below), while evolution landscape algorithms, because virtual, could be compared to the tradition of perspective. The interest for me in the idea is that Gehry is busy transforming his formal studio models into buildings by brute force, using Catia to shoehorn the ideal into the actual and taking up the slack with a noisy architectonic—while Lynn is growing forms pixel by pixel like a chemist growing organic cultures in a petri dish, using actual processes to produce a stereotonic, the equivalent of those studio models.*

petrified ~, 144, 158

Theseus' galley, 91

Athens, 143, 144

Atlantic, 53

ATMs, 15. *Automated teller machines.*

Aurelian Wall (Rome), 166

Austin (Texas), 29

Australia, 77, 105, 108, 165

the continent of ~ is full, 71

"We want to hear about ~!" 74

Australian Central Desert, 76, 77

Australians (part of American hegemony), 176

Auto-barriers, 22

Automata, 61, 63

Automated billing machinery, 114

Automation, ix

Automation acceleration, 176, 178. *Three of my four accelerations (colonization, industrialization, automation) correspond to Manuel De Landa's "motor" technologies of clockwork, combustion, and network as described in* War in the Age of Intelligent Machines *(MIT Press, 1991).*

Automaton

definition of machine, 61

tow-truck driver, 133

Automatons, 63. *I once heard someone in an interview put this position about the more common word "media"—he wanted "mass-mediums." Nit-picking or liberating?*

Autopilots, 22

Axle, 50

Ayers Rock (Uluru), 76

Baby monitor, 156

Back-hoes, 147. *In the U.K., JCBs or diggers.*

Baggage carts, 23

Baggage claim, 22

Baggage handling, 22

Bagpipe music (Judd's place), 149. *See also* Marfa. *The Chinati Foundation at Marfa, Texas has at its center Donald Judd's own house and studio, curated as a museum by people in awe of him. They*

had been part of the front line in the dispute between the Roman and Celtic Christian church. The latter's abbot-centered power structure could not accept Roman usage, particularly the altered date of Easter arising from the Gregorian calendar. They lost; and Bede's history is one of two surviving accounts of the synod that decided the matter at Whitby in 663. His Life of St. Cuthbert *(ca. 720) is full of unlikely miracles, which in the hands of Bede sound like facts. While Cuthbert is busy on his knees praying, waging spiritual warfare on the devil, he is disturbed by the sound of ravens tearing straw from the roof of his hut for their nests. He admonishes them and they fly away guiltily—only to return next day bringing him a gift of sheeps' wool grease with which to waterproof the hide cladding of the hut.*

Beemers, 125. *American abbreviation of* "BMW"; Bavarian Motor Works. *Germans say* BMs.

Bees
  ants and, 17
  birds and, 8, 75
  on a geranium, 153

Bells (on Swiss cows), 159

Berlin (Germany), 77. *"First we take Manhattan, then we take Berlin" is from the Leonard Cohen song, "First we take Manhattan," on* I'm Your Man *(1988).*

Bernini, Gianlorenzo (1598–1680), 140, 167. *See also Santa Maria della Vittoria*
  Apollo and Daphne, 167

B52s, 193

Bidding competition, 123

Biga, 128

Big Bang. *See also* Universe, expanding
  the echo of the ~, 11. *The radiation thought to originate from the Big Bang can still be measured. The whole subject, however, is all hypothesis—hearing astrophysicists talk is like listening to theologians arguing about the size of angels. What if, for example, our universe is but a side aberration of some much bigger picture? And is the universe a perpetually emerging membrane like the Athenian epiphany? Or an inflating balloon?*
  the human ~, 112

Big Bang, *continued*
    force of the human presence in the world, 113
    "right-bam-now," 35
    as taxonomic metaphor, 117
    as they shoot off in their little ~ (machine parts), 132
    we got ~, we got *evolution*, we got *continental drift*, 149

Bigfoot, 43. *Legendary giant ape of the Californian Redwood forest, seen by hunters glazed into hallucination after hours of sitting in their tree perches waiting for deer. Its Himalayan counterpart, the Yeti, similarly appears out of the whiteout to confront hallucinating mountaineers starved of oxygen.*

"Bigger than you and you are not me," 47. *REM, "Losing My Religion," 1990. You still hear this song wherever groups of lovers are gathered in public and someone has a guitar. Perhaps its appeal is the peculiar combination of defiant statement and little-kid whining.*

Bikinis (babes in), 156. *See also* Enewetak. *"Bikini" is an atomic age joke about the garment looking like Bikini atoll.*

Bill of Rights, 154. *Part of the difficulty is that a bill of rights protects individuals against the tyranny of the majority in a democracy, but it is confounded by the intermediary collective of the minority community.*

Biomass, 11

Biplanes, 111

Bird, 114. *Charlie Parker's nickname.*

Birds and the bees, 8, 75

Birmingham (England), 133

Birth canal, 41

Blender, 66, 67

"Bluebird, The," 53. *Song by Charles Villiers Stanford (1852–1924).*

Blue bonnet, 89. *The Texas "national flower," a wild lupin, Lupinus texensis.*

Blue Note, 114. *Definitive bebop jazz record label of the 1960s.*

Bodyguard (Great Khan), 160

Boeing
  big fat bus of a ~, 36
  back in California in ~'s factories, 8
  if you don't do it, ~ will! 157
  that ~ jetliner up there may not be a building, but it is architecture, vii

Boeing boys, 88. *See also* MD-80

Boiling backward (future into the present), 35

Bolt mechanism, 63. *In a machine gun, some of the gases of the exploding cartridge are tapped and fed back inside the gun to act on the front of the bolt, which slides back and allows the compressed spring inside the magazine to push the next round into the breech; another spring immediately drives the bolt back to detonate the cartridge and the process repeats over.*

Bomb(s)

  are going to set themselves off, 8

  atom, 96, 153

  B52s unloading sticks of ~, 193

  hydrogen ~, 153, 154

  jets and ~ and Great Grand Coolie Dams, 157

  "Little Boy," 95. *U.S. military nickname for the first (Hiroshima) atom bomb. The second (Nagasaki) bomb was called "Fat Man."*

  and nothingness of the last century, 125

  super ~, 153

Bomber (evolution), 96

Bombers

  B52s, 193

  flying fortresses, 183

  Linnaean classification of airplanes, 90

Boston (Massachusetts), 143

Bothy Band, 49. *See also* "Good Queen Jane." *An Irish traditional music band who tore into things and comported themselves like a rock band. Their Uilleann piper, Paddy Keenan, used to be known as the "Jimi Hendrix of the pipes" according to the sleeve notes on* The Best of the Bothy Band *(Mulligan CD 041).*

Braque, Georges (1882–1963), 147

Brand, Stewart, 30

Breakdowns (are immanent), 89. *See also* Heideggerian breakdown

Breast management technology, 51

Breasts

  of Second Empire nymphs, 140

  of Swedish woman, 37

  of the Three Graces, 51

Brisbane, 71, 74

Brisbane River, 74

are machine ~ still interesting? 23
machine-~ hybrids, 165
no match for an eighty storey ~ (Houston ground), 21
the ~ was not steel and glass (Cromford), 24
packs more punch than a ~ this size should (Alberti), 138
because it's a roofed program (Parthenon), 80
and landscapes (unlike sculpture and machines), 80
machines and ~, xii
and machines have been playing tag for a hundred years, vii
machine mimicry in ~, 32
Melbourne square museum ~, 195
the period of wishing ~ were machines . . . is over, viii
site (Juliet's milkshake), 66
. . . to stand in for their own bodies (petrified Athenians) 144
and statues that shared their world as if they were the family, 144
a strange ~ project (the Loaf House), 109
story of architecture—read ~, 36
stripped clean aesthetics of modern ~, 32
their ~ all run deep (Victorians, Plantagenets, Napoleon), 73
unique and fixed in place on the globe, 195
unlike ~, be truly useful, 33
why do the ~ look like casualties? 73
you need tall ~ to see the ant's nest from the sky, 69 (*see also* Hancock Building)
Bulldozers, 147
Bullets, 73
Bunkers (Enewetak), 152
Burger King, 129
  baleful gaze of the ~, 130
B.U.R.M.A., 58
Buses, 1
Buttocks, 37, 51
Byrne, David, 17 *See also* City

Cab, 105
Cadillac, 116
  beating up the interstate in the ~, 146
  cost the same as the ~, 53
  desktop icon, 197

Caesarean, 49. *In the U.S., C-section. Availability of pediatric emergency procedures and postnatal care are what reduce the birth rate, not affluence. The Indian province of Karala has for a generation devoted all its limited resources to two things, literacy and pediatric care, ignoring all other infrastructural calls on the treasury. The consequence is that they have child mortality rates the same as Europe and a birth rate that is correspondingly low. People have a lot of children when they are afraid that many of them will die.*
  account of, 46

California, 8, 19, 151, 157

Caliphates, 24, 118. *See also* Persian carpets.

Camera, speed limit enforcement, 133

Cameras
  American songline, 176
  field guides, 12
  four-million-pixel digital, 168, 169, 174
  stamp-sized glowing screens, 170

Camouflage
  fighters, 51
  flying fortresses, 183–184
  Melbourne square, 195

Camper vans, 98. *In the U.S., RVs (recreational vehicles).*

Canada, 15

Can Can, 29. Ribald ballet written by Jaques Offenbach and arranged as part of a suite by Michael Rosenthal as the Gaîté Parisienne.

Can Can philosophy, 35

Cannon (phalanx), 64. *Any gun over 20mm caliber is called a cannon.*

Canova, Antonio (1757–1852), 51. *See also* Three Graces

Cape Kennedy (Cape Canaveral, Florida), 165

Capricorn, 45

Captain Hook (Disney), 171. *See also* Goofy

Capulet, 16

Car(s), 1, 5, 20, 107, 133, 176. *See also* Cadillac; Chevrolet; Lumina; Viper; Volvo
  falling in love with, 6
  gorgeous, 110
  lights of a passing ~, 185
  the living car, 87
  Lumina? 9

meditative distraction of ~ repair, 60

parks, 22. *See also* Parking lots.

Caracalla, Baths of (Rome), 166

Carbines, 192. *A short-barreled rifle, invented for shooting from horseback, now universal for motorized infantry.*

Cargo planes, 23. *No windows, no upholstery, no meals, no videos, no flight attendants.*

Carp, 118, 120

Carpets. *See* Persian carpets

Caryatids, 144, 160. *See also* Elgin marbles

Caspian Sea, 105

Caste, 15. *Michel Serres,* Genesis *(University of Michigan Press, 1997): "India crystallised round the fixed classes in question, whereas we, like the Romans, seek to forget them. India multiplied the barriers and bulkheads between castes, hardening its social system into a series of subsets. . . . India left time, change, evolution, for invariance."*

Cast iron doors, 138

Catamaran, 74

Catastrophist, 126. *See also* Let's kill all the others! *Term for those who consider the world to have originated supernaturally and to have been shaped by catastrophic events, such as the biblical deluge (Noah's Flood). Related to Creationism; catastrophism was to early geologists what Creationism is to evolutionists. The replacement geological frame is called* uniformitarianism, *which states that the processes at work today are the same as they have always been and that the present is uniform with the past. Modern geology started in the late eighteenth century, and was for a time the leading science. The importance of day-by-day increments over catastrophic events was also asserted by Buffon and has an influence on the idea of evolution. However, catastrophism has reemerged— look at the idea that dinosaurs were eliminated by asteroid impact. Indeed, studying the world as a collection of dynamic systems implies catastrophic critical mass events as an element.*

Cathedrals, 110, 157

Cathode-ray screens, 46

CD player, 52

CD-ROM, 185

CDs, 2, 167

Celebrity
   spills out its mixture of ~ and massacre, 5
   strangers we know, 197
   Sweden's Tarantino, 37
Cell-phone (Ex's Web site), 109, 110
Cell-phone aerials, 117
Cell-phones, 20, 176
Celts (flamenco), 52. *The Basques, like the Scots, wear kilts of plaid.*
Centipedes, 10
Central Business Districts, 20
Cerise, 47. *Webster's describes it as a "moderate red" but says that ce-*
   rise comes from the Latin for cherry—so, cherry red—pale maroon.
Chair (automatic/motorized/reclining/vibrating), 1, 3, 5, 8, 92
Challenger (space shuttle), 101
Charged air, 90
Charged void, 77. *See also* Songlines
Chassis, 62
Chevrolet, 8
   by the time the color plates of all the ~s are finished, 95
   family names first, as in Chinese, 87
Chicago, 21, 105, 106
Chimp-pack, 44
China, 62
Chinese
   in American hegemony, 176
   names, 87
Chordata, 10, 90
Christ, 29, 113, 175
Christian keepers of the faith in Portugal and Spain, 133
Christmas puppy, 196
Chronotonic, 80, 108, 195
Cities
   all the ~ in Australia have one-word epithets, 72
   . . . are no more, or less, than human nests, 20
   in these comics (science fiction future), 72
   edge ~ (and Las Vegas), 157. *Term coined by Joel Garreau in 1990 to*
      describe the desire-led formations of material, outside the historic
      downtown areas, that support contemporary American life.
   high-rise dream ~ of the 1920s, 1

the great masonry mounds of the first ~, 113

like Persian carpets, 24

the races take place in generic ~, 117

the interconnectedness of ~ is a spatial necessity (Web analogy), 110

masonry ~ of antiquity, 130

miniature ~ in their own right? (airports), 22

ever thought how much like Web sites ~ are? 110

sluice the old idea of ~ clean out of our architecture, 20

City

a ~ so dark, as David Byrne's song says, 14. *It's a song called "Cities" from the Talking Heads album* Fear of Music *(1979). The same song calls Memphis the "home of Elvis and the ancient Greeks."*

centuries-old ~ of Philadelphia, 139

famous in Australia for being boring (Brisbane), 71

of London sailed on through space, 46

made of these objects (of desire), 131

of peace (Jerusalem and Dar-es-Salaam), 14

shone with its own pale fire (Brisbane), 82

eternal ~ (Rome), 171

every ~ in North America, 20

every day the ~ grows a little more, 1

fourth largest ~ in the U.S. (Houston), 21

floating ~ on the move (*U.S.S. Nimitz,* aircraft carrier), 7

greater whole of the ~ (oriental caliphate), 24

he pointed across the ~ to a green glass tower (Brisbane), 73

ice-bound ~ of a hundred islands (Stockholm), 37

jet noise boomed out across the ~ like a fanfare, 73

jets gliding in across the ~, 19

the ~ looked like scratches on the ground (Delhi), 106

luminous yellow horizon of the ~, 133

Paris heavy ideas of ~ planning, 20

prototypical ~ organization, 131

more like Shanghai ~ than a forest (homepage), 189

strange ~ of machines, 98

traffic that speeds in and out and round about the ~ (Houston), 1

you can sense the ~ from forty miles out, 1

Civil war, English (1642–1651), 72. *Not quite a civil war and not quite a revolution. The old title "The Great Rebellion" may be the right one.*

Cladistics, 100, 117. *See also* Pleached lime

Clams, 189

Clarities, 190

Class (taxonomic), 9, 90

Classification
  binomial, 10, 89, 90
  quadrinomial, 189
  Serres's caution against, 128

Cliffs (best way for an old man to die), 68

Clock (tools and automatons), 60, 61

Clock face, 60

Clockwork
  analogy of human society, 132
  Chinese Jesuit toy, 62

Cockroach, 147. *See also* Roaches

Coconut palms, 151

Cocteau, Jean (1889–1963), 124

Code writers, 107

Coffee machine, 58

Cold War, 62, 152

Coliseum (Rome), 166

Collagen (artificial pout), 37

Colonial
  brick warehouses, 143
  expansion, 129
  names (on wine bottles), 114

Colonization (acceleration), 175, 177. *See also* Automation acceleration
  English gardens, 175

Coltrane (John, 1926–1967), 53

Compact disc, 53, 167

Complex
  any strategy more ~ than [sculpture], 142
  on the contrary, [progress] works to make [the world] more ~, 111. *I mean the world is becoming more complex in its entirety, not necessarily in its individual parts.*
  tool, 62, 63
  the tribe of Athens had billowed into a rich and ~ event, 144
  the "where" and "when" of more ~ architectures, 142

Complexification (of the last two and a half billion years), 35

Complexifying, 130. *The gradual complexifying of the surface of the earth is an image of technological complexity keeping pace with the gradual increase in the human population of the world.*

Complexity

everything that ever there was survives in an altered ~, 111

forget process, 115

satellites, 14

U.S.S. Nimitz in all its massive ~, 7

you had to build a cathedral to house this kind of ~ (of memory theaters), 110

Compressor(s), 48, 50, 65

Computer(s)

as abstract machine, 61

emerging present, viii

development of high-speed ~, 154

Jaques's family of machines, 5, 8

library, 81

wheel and axle, 50

Computer programmers, 107

Comsats, 142. *Abbreviation of* communications satellites.

Concentration camps

Ex's dream, 186

field guides, 11

figure of the twentieth century, 158. *Although concentration camps belong to the industrial acceleration. The British used them to control the Boers; the most enduring are the Indian Reservations, which date from the time when the American West was being consumed (combusted) rather than colonized in the land rushes.*

Concrete bunkers, 125

Condoms (mystery of what they're for), 44

Connochaetes taurinus, 10

Conquistadors (invaders of America), 153

Consensus (lack of in democracy), 116

Constantine, Basilica of (Rome), 166

Continental Airlines, 22

Continental drift (We got *Big Bang,* we got *evolution,* we got ~), 149

Continental style, 20. *As per:* international style.

Contrail, 127. *Abbreviation of* condensation trail—*the white cloud that forms behind the passage of a jetliner as the exhaust condenses. The blue smoke pouring from Dan's Volvo was burning oil.*

Control systems (Airside), 165

Coolant, 61

Coolie Dam (Great Grand), 157. *The Coolidge Dam on the Gila river, Arizona.*

Cormorants, 97

Coronation Drive (Brisbane), 73. *The streets in Brisbane are still named for the British monarchy: King Edward, King George, Queen Anne. Time for a change?*

Cotton mill, 24

Country music, 98

Courtesans (Great Khan), 159

Cousins (machines are our), 8, 109. *Erik Davies in* Techgnosis *(Harmony Books, 1998) uses "brothers and sisters." George Dyson in* Darwin among the Machines *(Perseus Books, 1998) uses "aliens," whom we need to have treaties with. Maria's "cousins" picks up the Shakespearean drift of all this.*

Cowpoke, 52

Cows
  dreadful lowing of the ~ in October, 49
  Swiss, 159

Crabs, 10, 97

Creation (machines as metaphor for), 65

Credit card, 114

Crete, 91

Crickets (insects on studio floor), 141

Cromford, 24. *A town in Derbyshire, England, where Richard Arkwright secured the rights to the river gorge and used it to power his watermills at the end of the eighteenth century. To defend them from Luddite attacks, he built them of stone, like castles, and grouped them around a central court to maintain a continuous curtain wall. There is a single defensible entrance and the external corners are rounded so that corner stones cannot be prized out with crowbars. The windows on the external faces are about thirty feet above street level. The place is now preserved by the English heritage industry.*

Crows, 49

Daisy-cutter, *continued*

"*barrack barrage.*" *It is possible that both were apocryphal. The first was a device that stripped an area down to its subsoil, a sort of instant scorched earth. The second was a shock wave bomb for use against deep dug targets.*

D&G (Deleuze and Guattari), 30, 32, 36, 196

Daphnis and Chloe, 97

Dar-es-Salaam, 14

Daru staircase, 77. *Staircase in the Louvre, Paris, named after Comte Pierre-Antoine Daru (1767–1829).*

Dashboard, 94, 117

Dead-center, 148. *See also* Edge

Debt repayment schedules (dreams of the future), 73

Declaration of independence (Liberty's), 106

Deep House, 126. *House music is contemporary music, not just in time but also in that it is full of shades of genre—it is so relational that everything is defined through reference to others; and the music itself is structurally referential in its use of samples to make sounds. Deep House originated in the West Coast and is—to try and describe it without reference—with spiritual ambitions and powerfully synthetic. Because the computers build in layers, it is polyphonic rather than symphonic. The Deep House pulse is one hundred and thirty beats per minute, which Deep Housers maintain is the neural pulse rate.*

Deleuze, Gilles (1925–1995)

borrowing from Bateson, 170

seminar on, 30. *Deleuze is studied in art and architecture schools for the exciting and scary dynamic of his thinking. In* What Is Philosophy? *(Qu'est-ce que la philosophie? 1991) he and Guattari assert that philosophical concepts do not translate to other fields; indeed what artists call their "concepts" are what they call per-cepts—which I interpret as pieces of perception synthesized into sensual actuality as the work comes into being. (See Gertrude Stein's 1936 lecture* What Are Masterpieces and Why There Are So Few of Them, *which describes how an artist must not know what he is doing until the moment he has just done it.) Scientists have yet another version of the dynamic Deleuze and Guattari call functives.*

Deleuzians, 36. *I am referring to the various attempts to make a liter-*

ally "folded" architecture. However, even "flat-earth" neoclassical architectures are folded into the present—no one can escape it.

Philosophers are aggressive people—question time is for making your opponents cry. The participants of seminar one coined the term "deleuzion" for a quotation from Deleuze and Guattari used as a weapon.

Desire(s), *continued*

    objects of ~ as a sorting system for the idea of machines and architecture, 128 (*see also* Objects of desire)

    product of our immediate and specific ~ (machines), 25

    sixteenth-century ~ for twentieth-century miniaturization, 109. *Desire is the ocean of Deleuze and Guattari's picture of the world. Desire is not in pursuit of something lacking, but is a productive process: itself a machine. An object of desire is "a machine attached to a machine"—see* Anti Oedipus (L'Anti-Oedipe, *1972*).

Desk clerk, 72, 83

Detonator, 63

Deuterium, 153. *An isotope of hydrogen, with an atomic weight of approximately 2. Heavy water is deuterium oxide, prepared by subjecting water to continuous electrolysis, which separates hydrogen gas and leaves deuterium behind in concentrated form. Not until the water is one-hundred-thousandth part of its former volume is the pure oxide obtained. Fusion of deuterium atoms at high temperatures, using the stable solid element lithium deuteride, is what makes the energy in a hydrogen bomb.*

Diaspora, 15. *Means* sow (seeds) apart.

Dickens, Charles (1812–1870), 174

Die Hard, 63. *Series of 1990s blockbusters about one man up against a huge enemy, whose qualities are grit, resourcefulness, and the possession of the element of surprise.*

Differential, 57. *The arrangement of gears in the final drive that allows the driven wheels to rotate at different speeds, as when turning a corner.*

Diotima, 67. *See also* Symposium

Dip slope, 17. *The shallow slope of a finite inclined plane.*

Disc drives (and flat earth), ix

Discoglossidae, 90

Dishwasher, 184

Disney (imagineering), 157. *See also* Simulators; Theme parks. *The problem with Disney's imagineered parks is the problem of the fake: what is authenticity? A thought that it is durational rather than material, of experience rather than use, came to me at a conference in the German city of Münster. Along with many other bombed German cities, reconstruction took place there immedi-*

ately after the war, in many cases not making a new world as in the Netherlands or England, but reclaiming the past. By the standards of present-day reconstruction they are clumsy. Over the last fifty years scientific historicism has produced an ability to replicate precisely: it is the same syndrome that has produced "authentic" music. At Ightam Moat, in Kent, England, the restoration is so acute that holes have been left in wall linings to show the reconstructed timbers inside. Accuracy has become more important than reality—and how can a reconstruction be real? By existing in experience. Disney became a big issue at the Münster conference, but at Disneyland the fake is continuously reaffirmed by trademarking (scripting). It never is allowed to become part of experience.

Disney Hotel Lounge, 171

Divinity (of evolution), 94. *Darwin's account of evolution maintained "divinity in the origins" by implying that humans, in spite of sharing ancestry with primates, were still at the top of the tree. To understand the power of the Victorians you have to imagine the climate in which the theory went forward, and remind yourself at the same time that it did go forward. "Survival of the fittest" suggests a teleology toward the best possible outcome, which could be one planned by god. "Survival of the survivors" is the contemporary version, a tautology that faces the theory's implication that there are no predictable outcomes at all, not even that humans will stay human. Not that the debate has moved on in everyday life. The other day I told a Jehovah's Witness that I was prepared to believe in god, but not that he created the world. (What if god was one of us?) She stood there on the doorstep in her old-fashioned hat with the net across her face, saying "That sounds like an interesting idea"—but I could tell the only interest she had was in how this position could be vanquished.*

Dolce e Gabbana, 30. *Gary Rorbacher told me that the "D&G" joke was part of life at Columbia University in 1994.*

Dolce vita, 166. *See also La Dolce Vita*

Doll, 13, 65

Domination (technology of), 81, 82. *See also* Pejoratives

Donatello (1386–1466), 140. *The sculpture he yelled at was a figure of Habbakuk, a prophet of the Old Testament. The story is related in*

Dunhill (blazer), 146

Dusk, 113. *Houston is just under 30 degrees north of the equator and consequently the days and nights are much more even in length than in northern Europe. Dusk comes on rapidly, like a decision executed, and the long gathering twilights of northern Europe, which feel like time travel, do not obtain.*

Eagle (Boeing F-15), 90

Eames chairs, 30. *Three thousand series frames: Aluminum (aluminium) is alloyed with many different metals for different uses, and each alloy has a thousand series number. Three thousand is a common use alloy—your racing bike may have a seven or eight thousand series frame. The English artist Simon Starling once did a piece where he melted down the frames of an Eames chair and a Marin bicycle and recast them swapping one for the other. It was an exercise in studied pointlessness, Duchampian (or Luddite?) in character. When I pointed out the problem of the materials being different alloys, performance-related and not materially interchangeable (Afterall, issue 1, 1999) my editors assumed I was talking about performance art.*

Earth (Leibniz parody), 33

East African Asian, 15. *The British bought Indians in to help administer the African colony of Tanganyika, but after independence, in 1961, their descendants were forced out of the country, renamed Tanzania, as part of president Nyerere's agrarian and racial reorganizations. Many of them, as holders of British passports, came to the U.K.*

easyEverything, 168

Ecologically balanced, 152. *I am being conventional in opposing an ecologically balanced world to the Bible's grant of dominion over it to man—but another thought is that ecologists do not view the world as an emergence but as a defiled paradise, confusing the ideal with the material all over again. See also Ecologists; and the passage on sustainability on page 178.*

Ecologies (passion the most precarious of a man's ~), 146

Ecologists (Australian), 71. *Ecologists are not necessarily conservationists—it is possible to espouse dynamic ecologies, even nonsustainable ones—but "radical" in ecological circles usually means "fundamentalist."*

Ecosystem, 71

Edelweiss, 159. *Small white alpine flower,* Leontopodium alpinum.

Eden, 173

Edge, 159. *The "edge" is a variation on underground theory: when the world is so territorialized that convention rules everything, relief may be found at the edges of the territories. It has become a cliché,* cutting edge, *which describes innovative work. It has become an adjective,* edgy, *that describes anything that is sharp, or that "pushes the boundaries." Like* underground, *those two ideas assume the presence of a mainstream. The center-field story emerging in this conversation is not about the underground, or pushing boundaries—it is about changing everything. It is finding a position in which art is not "cutting edge," and therefore not critical: but is its own mainstream. A world uncorrupted by hegemonies could be an accumulation of mainstreams.*

Edge City, 20. *By Joel Garreau (1991)—a nuts and bolts description of contemporary land development criteria and practices in the U.S.*

Efflorescence, 102. *In Gulf waters, a vitriolic glow associated with the oil industry.*

Eiffel Tower, 106. *The tall buildings that stick out from their cities and identify them from the air are like everyday colossi. A sort of non-marvelous wonders of the world, they carry the identity of their cities abroad in the minds of tourists. It is dull to imagine Paris without the Eiffel Tower, but it was not erected until the end of the nineteenth century.*

Einsteinian motion and gravity diagrams, 130

Eisenhower age, 63. *I am referring to the period between the end of World War II and the start of Vietnam (or the Kennedy administration): The heroic years of the American hegemony, equivalent to the years after Waterloo for the English. Dwight D. Eisenhower was thirty-fourth president of the U.S., between 1953 and 1961.*

Electric fiddles (modern country music), 98

Electric toothbrushes, 57

Electric tube squeezer, 57

Elephant guns, 12. *See also* Vermin gun. *Heavy-duty .50 caliber guns, single shot, like snipers use for distant targets.*

Elephants, 11

Elevator, 2

Engine bay, 109

England

    airport hotel conference, 124

    Australian abuse of, 74

    in the time of Dickens, 174

    geoid corrections, 1173

    hegemony of, 175

    swallows, 74

    tiny, historic, 139

England to America, 137. *One thing that makes the body of a living organism unlike a machine is that the more you use it, the stronger it gets, whereas machines wear out with use. The body is constantly renewing its own cells; decay arising in old age is a genetic copying problem, where the renewed body cells are defective copies, rather than a result of mechanical wear.*

English

    farmland, 143

    hegemony, 176, 177

    what the ~ did to Native Americans, 153. *Ex is not quite right. The English and the Spanish had different approaches to ethnic cleansing, the former preferring isolation and the latter "intermarriage."*

    natural landscape garden, 175

    typical ~, 127. *The English are fond of saying that Americans are always talking about money—everything comes down to the dollar. But that is because Americans are always busy and need to talk money to facilitate action. Ramon and Juan are saying it is the English who are always talking about money, in their perpetual discussion of the price of petty things.*

Entomologists, 17

Epistemological break, 190. *Part of Gaston Bachelard's description of the process of conceptual changes in science promulgated from the 1920s through the 1950s. For him, scientific history is different from social history, because in the latter the universal of objectivity has to be assumed; but his ideas of rupture and relation have proliferated with the understanding that that distinction no longer holds, and that all histories are partial.*

Epochs, 59. *For a description of the use of these short periods in radar transmissions, see my article "JayTids," published in KSU Architecture's magazine OZ, issue 17 (1995).*

Equal rights (for ethnic language), 153

Erotogenics, 140. *I have used this word instead of "erotica" because it portrays a more systemic prurience—not just an interest in sexual art, but an interest in being interested in it.*

Escalators, 36

Ethnic group (Spanish language), 153

EUR (*Espsizione Universale di Roma,* Rome), 169

Eurocentric (crap), 74, 76

Europe, x

European philosophers (furious), 38. *Actually, it is the one who is not furious, Michel Serres, who points this out (*Genesis, *University of Michigan Press, 1997).*

Everything (as mode of twenty-first century), 148

Evolution

  currently surviving experiments and mutations of, 12

  "Right-bam-now," 35

  the theory of ~ (what goes on behind the scenery), 94. *Here is an accumulated modern problem: to consciously be simultaneously an individual, a member of a tribe, and a part of the machine of evolution.*

  "we got *Big Bang,* we got ~, we got *continental drift*—" (songlines), 149

Evolutionary history, (of machines), 89

Evolutionists (view of contemporary), 94

Exeter (England), 133

Expansion joints, 87

Exploration (acceleration of)

  age of, 129

  Portuguese and Spanish discovery of the New World, 113, 133

  Spanish hegemony, 174, 176

Facemasks (surgical), 46

Factories, 74

Factory-made house, 1. *In the U.S., a factory-made is a prefabricated dwelling. It is not a trailer home on wheels, but a lightweight house that is transported to the site on the back of a truck. When you join*

Factory-made house, *continued*

two units together, it's called a doublewide. *The landscape writer J. B. Jackson applauded them as a component of the unique American landscape. The mobility of the population of the U.S. makes sense of the idea, and new settlements can spring up wherever work is available. They are the closest there is to the periodic dreams of architects to industrialize housing. Unfortunately a social class divide operates that limits their use.*

Factory ship, 111

Falling

in love, 97

Maria's dream of, 95, 96

Family (taxonomic), 9, 10, 90

Family of man, 98, 99. The Family of Man *was the name of an exhibition of photographs curated by Ed Steichen in 1955.*

Fast criticism, x. *Superficial (vs. critical theory)—I recall the story that code writers embarking on new software projects use as building blocks to start with lumps of code whose origins no one can remember, like masons with stones.*

FBI, 63

Fences, 147. *In the western U.S., fences were, with railroads, the prime technology of settlement and figure in tax law as well as folklore.*

Fetish (object of desire), 123, 130, 131, 174, 175, 178

Field (technology as force ~), 83, 130

Field guides, 11, 12, 95

Field Guide to the Fishes of the Great Barrier Reef, A, 95

Field Guide to the Human Beings, A, 185, 186

Field Guide to the Machines, A, 12, 87, 94, 165, 175, 187, 189

Field Guide to the Mammals of East Africa, A, 11. *For good examples of such guides, see the Collins guides:* Nests, Eggs, and Nestlings *(Colin Harrison),* Insects of Britain and North Europe *(Michael Chinery), and* Stars and Planets *(Donald Menzel). For some reason flowers are not possible to trap in this way—their tactile character is too delicate, perhaps. The Collins guide to flowers is beautiful but, like all the other field guides to flowers, hard to reconcile with actual appearances.*

Fields of vision, 177

Fighters (as they stream their vapors fast and level), 51

Figurative

minimalism ~ of nothing, 148

of the partial response to everything, 149

Final assembly shed, 164. *The building where the components of space shuttles are assembled for launching.*

First World War (battlefields), 148. *Or World War I. I have written about battlefields as landscapes in* Memory *in my* The Cultivated Wilderness *(MIT Press, 1997).*

Fishing boat, 111

Fishing rods, 98

Flamenco, 51, 52, 144

Flash cards, 170

Flight traffic control systems, 22

Floodlight (of Shakespeare's stage), 94

Floodlit (her like an actress), 65. *After writing this, I saw the idea used in Adrian Lynne's film of* Lolita. *I re-skip-read the book but could not find it there. I left it in. I had also written about boosting the air-conditioning down to fifty degrees so that the Thanksgiving dinner in chapter 7 could have a roaring open fire; it seemed to fit the idea of the* humans have invaded the planet *speech of thanks. Then I read Tom Wolfe's* A Man in Full *in which the same thing happens. I took it out.*

Fluorescence, 113

Fluorescent (light fixtures), 58

Fluorite, 113, 190. *Also called* fluorspar*: calcium fluoride. A common material used industrially. The museum crystal is unusually big.*

Flying fortresses, 183. *Nickname of the Boeing B-17 bomber, mainstay of the U.S. Eighth Air Force in the U.K. during World War II.*

Fokker triplane, 88

Folding in his grave (Deleuze), 36. *See also* Jeff

Fookwar, Michel, 81, 82. *Michel Foucault.*

Footbrake (the living car), 87

Force

of the human presence in the world, viii, 130. *There are at present four theorized forces; gravity, electromagnetism, and the strong and weak nuclear forces. The search is on for a Grand Unified Theory (GUT) that will join them together. I am calling technology*

Fuel burn (Airside), 165

Fugees, 33. *Late '90s band. "Fugees" means refugees.*

Fujitsu, 78, 155

Function, 80, 109

Fun Palace, 17. *The inventor of the Fun Palace, Cedric Price, was the brain of British architecture in the third quarter of the twentieth century. While Buckminster Fuller used to give five-hour lectures on everything he had ever thought, Cedric Price used to stand up every eighteen months and give a lecture on his latest thoughts; they were full of key phrases—change in level! old age!—and consequently very difficult to understand, but brilliant. His themes of mobility, edge condition and obsolescence were eclipsed by historicism and cultural theory: a revival is soon incoming.*

Galactic model (as taxonomic metaphor), 117

Galatea, 182. *See also Pygmalion and Galatea. The quotation is from Galatea and Pygmalion by Robert Graves.*

Galley (Theseus'), 91

Galley servers (airport machinery), 166

Gallianos, 171. *Refers to the work of John Galliano.*

Gambia, the (Africa), 143

Ganges delta, 105

Garage, 105, 159

Garden-city, x. *Name given to philanthropic late nineteenth- and early twentieth-century settlements designed as healthy living environments in the face of industrial cities; originally Letchworth and Welwyn in Hertfordshire, and the Hampstead Garden suburb in London, England. Their plans have the same sort of densities and community layouts proposed by Peter Calthorpe and others as the antidote to contemporary American suburbs.*

Garden of Eden, 133, 173

Gardens

  English natural landscape, 175

  treasure chest, 175, 177

Garreau, Joel, 20

Garret, 2. *A room in the roofspace: the poorest part of the house. Part of the myth that an artist must be poor to create, which helps artists who are poor to believe in themselves—but does not guarantee it.*

Garret, *continued*

In the Tate Britain gallery, London, there is a portrait by Millais of the poet Chatterton (1752–1770), who killed himself in despair at the age of eighteen. He had been a child prodigy, but entirely self-taught and unrecognized, who was in the van of the creation of the gothic revival in the arts. To slide his poems past the tyranny of Johnson and Reynolds, he wrote them in the fictional person of Thomas Rowley, a fifteenth-century monk, but his efforts were condemned as fraud. England was full of the Palladian revival at the time: Fanny Burney (1752–1840) had this to say about that: "Travel is the ruin of all happiness! There is no looking at buildings here having seen Italy."

Gaskets (rips in the Walking City ~), 115

Gearbox, 61

Gearshift, 87

Geeks (I.T.), 183

Generation Alpha, 183

Generators, 196

Generic (Ridge Racer's world), 117

Genitals

  ancient love stories, 92

  flowers, 89

Genus, 10, 89, 91

Geoid, 172, 173

Geological museum, 113

Geranium (dancing around Maria like a bee around a ~), 153. *Wild geraniums are a bee magnet, like buddliahs for butterflies and echinacea for ants.*

Gere, Richard, 91. *Gere is criticized for his single-mode acting, but distilling everything into one mode is precisely his talent.*

Germans

  camouflage, 183

  at Schneider Trophy races, 191

  work on turbines and internal combustion, 176

Gerome, Jean Leon (1824–1904), 140. *See also Pygmalion and Galatea*

Ghost, 64. *This ghost in the machine is not Arthur Koestler's (1905–1983) of 1967. In that book he advocated the universal use of drugs to counteract human destruction and aggression. He says, "nature has let us down, God seems to have left the receiver off the hook, and time is running out. . . . to use our brain to cure its own shortcomings seems to me a brave and dedicated enterprise." Is that utilitarian materialist? Or pantaloonic?*

God, *continued*

possible to ethicize such a thing, 152. *I say this because you have to believe in the supernatural to have reason enough to power through an atrocity such as this.*

Golden Child, 160. *The successor to (and the reincarnation of) the Dalai Lama, spiritual leader of the Lamaists, Tibetan Buddhists, is chosen while still a child.*

Golden Pond, 21

Golf (VW), 159

Golf courses, 20

"Good Queen Jane," 49. *See also* Bothy Band. *From* After Hours, *by the Bothy Band (1979). The melody is a mournful Celtic refrain, full of strong slow rhythm. The Baby gets stuck; Jane implores the midwives to cut her open and save the life of the child—they and King Henry cannot bring themselves to do it. Henry says, "If I save the flower of England, I shall lose the branch, too." In the end, all through the festival and dancing at the baby's birth, his mother lies "cold as a stone."*

Goofy, 18. *See also* Bambi; Captain Hook. *Who has the difficult job of being the lazybones in Disney's remorseless world, which he exercises with good humor. These characters must be appearing because I have an infant in the house while writing this book.*

Governors, 196. *Steam engines employed a feedback control comprising metal balls that moved up a shaft the faster they went, driven by centrifugal force, and could open relief valves at critical moments. They are one analogy of the complex of "checks and balances" in the American democratic machine.*

Graft, 107. *Petty graft has been described to me like this: when you go to get a driver's license and the man behind the desk in the post office says that the pages must be stapled together. No I haven't got a stapler, he says, go to the back of the queue. On arriving back at the desk he tells you that the papers should be stapled together in a different way, and since forms cannot be restapled, it will require a whole new application. On the street outside, however, is an agent who, for a few rupees, one dollar, will take your application for you and process it with no trouble at all.*

Grand Palais (Paris), 128

Grant, Cary (1904–1986), 23

Grass-skirted inhabitants, 152

Graves, Robert (1895–1985), 182

Gravity (and gravitational field), 83

Great Barrier Reef, 71

Great Khan (Kublai Khan, 1215–1294), 159, 160

Greece

  ancient, and democracy, 156

  the charge of ancient ~, 143

Greek

  ancient ~ landscape, 148

  holy sites, 77

  Island of Samothrace, 77

Greeks, ancient

  question of sculpture, 142

  our story better than theirs—Marfa, 149

  and space rocks, 144

Greenland, 164

Greensward lawns 20. *Millionaires in Texas like to have huge lawns in the English style, but the only grass that will survive is a broad-leafed buffalo grass, which looks okay but does not invite lawn practices like tennis and croquet. Automatic sprinkling systems complete the picture.*

Gremlins, 133. *A gremlin is an unknown cause of a technical malfunction, personified as an elf. The leprechaun is a much older idea, but similar—if you can catch one, it will reveal the location of its treasure.*

Ground zero, 181. *The locus of an explosion.*

Growth and change (question of), 91. *One of the differences between artificial and organic life is the ability of the unit to grow; what you might call internal self-organization. With machines, the in-gene processes are mimicked by developments beyond the prototype—they use us to do it for them—but it is more a matter of continuous reconception than epigenetic growth.*

Grunt, 74. *Vietnam-era "G.I. Joe."*

Guard dogs, 134

Guattari, Felix (1930–1992), 30. *See also* Deleuze, Gilles

Guggenheim, 79

Guided missiles, 76

Gulf of Mexico, 92, 96

Gunboats, 193
Guns, 62, 63
Gutenberg presses, 111

Habitat (and habits), 88
Hailstones, 181
Hair clippers, 57
Hair-splitting factories, 125
Hancock Building, 105. *The John Hancock Building in Chicago was built in 1970 and was the tallest building in the world at 1,127 feet until the World Trade Center was completed in the same year, topping 1,350 feet. In 1973 the Sears Tower was built a few blocks away from the Hancock Building and became the tallest building in the world at 1,454 feet. Some people still think it is; but because these monsters have communication masts on top of them, you can use the aerials to add to the height. In 1996 the Petronas Towers were built in Kuala Lumpur, Malaysia, in such a way that the 242-foot-high masts can be considered an integral part of the design, and give a height of 1,483 feet. Who's next in this game?*
Hard drive, 7, 169
Hawaii-five-O, 16
Hawker Seafury, 138. *The last of the piston-engined monoplane Hawker fighters, the Seafury was based on the Tempest, but tweaked out of all recognition. Its predecessor was the Hurricane, Battle of Britain star, powered by a Rolls Royce Merlin engine, rather than the Bristol Centaurus used in the Seafury. The Merlin has a sound so distinctive that in air shows it makes old men cry, as their dead comrades and their lost youth are mixed together in one painful blur.*
Hawkeye, 64. *The nickname of the hero in James Fenimore Cooper's* The Last of the Mohicans *(1862). In the Hollywood version he carries an extra long musket, which he uses like the finger of God.*
Headbone (the living car), 87
Headman (Enewetak), 152
Health (technologies of the self), 81
Hearing aid, 62, 181, 186
Heartbeat monitor, 41
Hegemonic
  plane of the, 168

~ tribes, 189

Hegemonies, xi, 174, 177
  are tribal events, 174

Hegemony. *A word from Greek meaning* leadership*: applied to dominant states of ancient Greece similar to the "king of kings" of clan alliances. Used here in the twentieth-century sense of power "blocs."*
  American ~, 168, 174, 193, 194
  cars and airplanes ~, 176
  English ~, 175, 176, 177
  geoid as metaphor for the plane of ~, 173
  is a fact of human life, 155
  Judd's pink-painted ~, 145
  landscapes of our ~ are not sustainable, 178
  a one-cloud explanation that attempts to be outside the ~, 198
  over the power switches, 54
  planes of ~, 176
  Spanish ~, 168, 174, 176, 177
  strike against (American) ~, 163
  prevailing ~'s transcendent desire to last forever, 193
  when ~ passed to England, 175

Hegemons, 189, 190

Heiddegerian breakdown, 127. *When the unity of the articulated moments of being in the world is ruptured (Martin Heidegger, 1889–1976).*

Helen (of Troy), 77

Hellenistic, 160. *The name given to the period of Greek world hegemony that followed Alexander the Great's conquests. Sculpture and painting became exaggeratedly realistic, and statuary was characterized by big composite marble groups such as the* Laocoon. *The* Nike Samothrace *and the* Venus de Milo *are Hellenistic.*

Helly Hanson, 192

Heterogeneous materials, 142. Uniformity and Variability: An Essay in the Philosophy of Matter, *Manuel De Landa, doors of perception 3 conference, 1998. The homogeneous metals—like bronze, but principally steel—promote unification and central control by the nature of their production. Heterogeneous materials, because unpredictable and unique, are better typifications of nonlinear processes.*

Houston, *continued*

  it's ten hours out of ~ (Marfa), 146

  slipped through ~'s roadways, 19

  triple garage of my ~ home, 105

  this turbulent, machinic ~, 20

Houstonites, 21. *Or* Houstonians?

How Buildings Learn (Stewart Brand, 1994), 30

Howling Wolf, 88. *Urban blues man, Chess piece, contemporary of Muddy Waters, Bo Diddley, and Buddy Guy.*

Hubble telescope, vii

Hughes, Howard (1905–1976), 192

Hughes H1, 192

Hulk, the, 138

Human artifice (Arendt), vii, xi, 20. *All life is artificial—see page 10. Are birds' nests architecture? The* avian artifice?

Human columns (Acropolis origins), 144

Human condition

  Arendt, xi

  Can-Can, 35

  four histories, 38

  ~ statement, 34

  technology is the ~, 82. Condition *has the sense of* contract—*with God in the sixteenth century when the term appears? In the* All the world's a stage *speech the contract is with action. And now? It has not escaped me that this idea itself, indeed all of this book could be a fragment of the North American hegemonic attitude.*

Humanist, 111

Humanity (as opposed to humans), 83, 158

Humanoid, 111

Human predicament, 81

Hummers (hand-held), 95. *Machines that imitate the traditional Indian practice of pulling hairs out using threads rubbed to a twist across the flesh.*

Hydraulic flaps, 22

Hydroponically, 75. *Industrialized agricultural method of growing things in nutrient-enriched water, which enables plants to be grown in multistorey buildings instead of fields.*

Hyena, 4, 10, 11. *Most Hyenas are carrion feeders.* Hyaena brunnea

Indians, *continued*

> *themselves? "They call themselves Omaha," he said. The Indians of the Houston area were probably the* Natchez, *or perhaps a cat clan called* Caddo.

Indonesians (boat people), 71

Industrialization (acceleration), 177. *See also* Automation (acceleration)

Industrial revolution (Arkwright), 24

Inertial guidance gyros (crystal block), 22. *See Donald MacKenzie's chapter on the development of these gyroscopes in his* Knowing Machines *(MIT Press, 1996). He suggests that the glamour of the new technology was so great that huge investments were made to get it to work in real airplanes, when old-style spinning metal gyros could have done the job just as well for a fraction of the cost.*

Information

~ concentration camps, 11

~ explosion (terrorists making bombs), 154

great pile of ~, 92

what use is an ~ explosion if it doesn't blow away the poverty? 154

~ wilderness (of the Web), 11

Information technology, 90

Inorganic, 6. *See also* Nonorganic

Insight, 83

Interceptoridae, 90

Interceptors, 90. *Latin:* catch. *Name given to fighters.*

Intercontinental ballistic missiles, 95

Interdictors, 90. *Latin:* prohibit. *Name given to strike fighters (fighter bombers).*

Intergalactic air force, 72

Internal combustion, 176

International Herald Tribune, 192

Internet

deeply phlegmatic ~ watchers, 38. *Who sometimes look on the internet as a new sort of wilderness—in which the search engines are the equivalent of aboriginal guides, who say they can read the tracks.*

place of in the nonplace global civilization, 125

Internet art, 93

Interstate (to Marfa), 146

Interstate 10, 1. *The interstate system of the U.S. is named like this: the nine roads that cross the continent from west to east are numbered 10 through 90, from the south. The first, Interstate 10, runs from El Paso to Florida. The forth, I-40, is the one that crosses the center from Los Angeles via Arizona to Philadelphia. I-90 is the route from Seattle to Chicago. The north-south roads are numbered 15 through 65, this time from the west. 15 runs up behind the coastal mountains from California to Oregon: 35 is the road that goes all the way from Corpus Christi in the Gulf to Buffalo, up on the Canadian Border. The interstate junction numbers are the mileage measured from the western or southern origin of the road: so you exit from Interstate 10 for Houston at Junction 762, which is 762 miles from El Paso.*

Ireland, 175

Iron (asteroids), 141

Irony (the world of art has become sodden with), 31

Ishmael, 119

Islam

  and exploration acceleration, 133

  in flamenco, 52

Islay (Isle of, Scotland), 147

Italian museums (erotic sculpture), 140

Italy, 163

Ivy League, 139. *The Ivy League is a group of colleges in the northeast U.S. that consider themselves the best. The League itself was originally the football league to which they all belong.*

Jackson, Janet, 117. *Her album* Runway *came out in 1995.*

Japan, 111

Jeff, 36. *See also* Deleuze, Gilles. *Jeff Krolicki. It's a pretty obvious joke, but when you're all sitting around a table drinking and smartassing, the important thing is to get there first. He was referring to the Deleuzeian writings of "The Fold."*

Jellyfish, viii

Jeremiah, 126. *Hebrew prophet who proclaimed times of strife for his people at the break-up of the Assyrian hegemony in the sixth century B.C.*

Jericho, vii, 53

Jerusalem, 14, 133

Jesuits

    Chinese automaton, 62

    Counter Reformation's army, 175

    twenty-first century ~s, 193. *The Jesuits were innovators. They spearheaded the Counter Reformation. Their spiritual exercises were a sort of focused meditation, they invented tutorials as an educational tool to replace didactic pedagogy, and the first Baroque thing was their church in Rome. They became one of the primary vehicles of the exploration acceleration, going as missionaries all over the world. The South American proselytization fell to them, and in North America, in England (where hanging, drawing, and quartering was invented especially for them) and in China and Japan, they frequently found martyrdom.*

Jesus

    man leaning forward into time, 35

    washing feet, 39. *Or, people in Jesus' time washed their feet and anointed them to ward against infections picked up by scratches on the road.*

    "Ye shall know the truth and the truth shall make you free," 29

Jet (prop plane almost as fast as a), 139

Jet-lagged, 115. Arnica *is the remedy for jet lag's background headaches.*

Jetliners, viii, 50

Jets

    and bombs and Great Grand Coolie dams, 157

    gliding in across the city, 19

    gulp down kerosene, 8

    three hundred thousand people in the air at any one time, 19

John (three students called John)

    bam! 34

    consumer monadology, Leibniz parody, 33

    five simple machines, 33

Joker, the (Batman), 163

Judd, Ashley, 164

Judd, Donald (1928–1944), 95. *See also* Marfa. *The description of his pugnacious nature on page 146 is adapted from Michael Rotundi's.*

Juliet (Juliet's doll), 13, 65

Jupiter, 160

Landscape, *continued*
    buildings and ~ (unlike sculpture and machines), 80
    a ~, a building, and a machine (inclined plane), 34
    colliding ~, 190
    construction of *A Field Guide to the Machines,* 175
    of desire, 189
    the English natural ~ garden, 175. *Usually referred to as driven by art and literature theories rather than technological change.*
    a ~ so empty (minimalism in Texas), 145
    evolution ~, 170, 189
    ~s of fetish, weapon, and value, 193
    fields of vision, 177
    I guess the ~s would be the fields? (Field guide), 165
    fitness ~s (Greg Lynn), 170
    ~ free of competition, 47
    geoid and hegemony, 173
    glacial moraine ~ (golf courses), 20
    giants who made the ancient Greek ~, 148
    gods stalk the ~ (ancient Greece), 92
    ~s of our hegemony are not sustainable, 178
    the herd is so big that it has become the ~ (wildebeest), 3
    a link between the ~ and machines, 76
    machines-~s hybrid, 165
    machines and ~s, xii
    ~s of objects of desire, 174
    organizing . . . machines . . . by their origins in certain ~s, 170
    as plateaus, 170
    resultant, machine made ~s, 158. *Resultant as opposed to* intentional.
    at one end of the scale of architecture are ~s (*What Is Architecture?*), 33
    as though some giant had scoured the ~ with sandpaper (Delhi), 106
    technological events as, 130
    tribal affiliations are intertwined with the ~ (Australian songlines), 76
    white hunters wandering through the Earthen ~, 195
    the world ~ in this Ridge Racer game, 117
Landside (airport automation landscape analogy), 165, 167
Language
    technologies of sign systems, 82. *Paradox of: see Deleuze and Guattari in* A Thousand Plateaus: *"if there is language, it is fundamen-*

tally between those who do not speak the same tongue. Language
is made for that, for translation, not for communication."

Laptop, 111, 117, 169, 176

Last of the Mohicans, The, 64. *See also* Hawkeye. *One of James Fenimore Cooper's* Leatherstocking Tales *(1826) featuring the wilderness scout Natty Bumppo.*

Las Vegas (Nevada), 157

Laurel, 167. *Laurels are genus Daphne.*

Laz-y-boy, 8

Le Corbusier (1887–1965), viii

Ledbetter, Huddie ("Leadbelly,"1885–1949), 111

Leibniz, Gottfreid Wilhelm (1646–1716), 32

Lennox, 8

Lerup, Lars, 20

Let's kill all the others, 47. *Information on this hypothesis of human
origins came from an outline of ideas contained in* The Last Nean-
derthal *and other works by Ian Tattershall summarized in* Scientific American *(January 2000).*

Levelers, 72. *The English civil wars proceeded on a revolutionary
promise, that the King and the lords were to be abolished and that
Parliament would represent an enfranchised people. Two groups,
the levelers and the Diggers, arose as factions demanding these
radical reforms toward the end of the war; the levelers were the less
extreme of the two but commanded part of the army. Both groups
were put down in 1649, and the leveler's leader, John Lilburne, was
arrested and imprisoned.*

Lever (the five simple machines), 33

License plates, 127

Lick Your Wounds, 49

Life of Theseus, 91. *Plutarch's* Life of Theseus *is from his* Parallel
Lives, *comparing Greek and Roman statesmen. His biographies are
intense and anecdotal; reading them is like loving. The passage
quoted here is from Ian Scott-Kilbert's translation for Penguin
books. The classical short biography was revived by Montaigne
and Bacon and later by John Aubrey (1626–1697), whose* Brief
Lives *of the celebrities of his own time in England is even shorter
and more lovelike.*

Linguatherapy, 49

Linnaeus, 89. *Real name, Carl von Linné (1707–1778): studied the reproductive structures of plants and the locomotion and function of animals to establish a systematic naming of all species. The Linnaean hierarchy was* kingdom, class, order, genus, species, *and* variety. *"Variety" is subspecies and refers, for example, to the range of colors of human skin. Linnaeus' program sprang from ancient logic texts, which had established* genus, species *(definition),* differentia, property, *and* accident *to classify substance. Compare this with the historical and material program initiated by Georges-Louis Buffon (1725–1753) in pre-Revolutionary France. The two methodical foundations were subsequently systematized as a Linnaean natural history of space and a Buffonian natural history of time. Efforts to drive the two together (space-time, geography-history, nature-culture) are the more fertile for that difference.*

Lions, 11

Liquor store, 114

Lissamphibia, 90

Literature (an abbreviating art), 60

Live oaks, 115. Quercus virginiana. *The grand tree of the south and southwest, as beautiful as the sequoias of the northwest Pacific and the beeches of northwest Europe. They are evergreen oaks, with leaves like elongated ivy—indeed the Latin name of the similar species that grows in Europe, the Holm oak, is* Quercus ilex, *which means ivy oak. "Live oak" and "ivy oak" prompt etymological speculations.*

Living car, the, 87

Loaf House, 109. *See also* Memory theater. *This is an interpretation of Ben Nicholson's* Loaf House *project. Program in architecture might be the efficient cause, but it might be another way of describing human life—or, in the Loaf House, lives. The project seems to evade spatial necessity by making a conflation of several life durations; almost more like music than architecture. See Nicholson's CD-ROM* Thinking the Unthinkable House *(Renaissance Society at the University of Chicago, 1996), which also contains his studies of the geometric encyclopedia installed in the pavement of the San Laurentian library, Florence. See also the idea about two different sorts of solid, page 142.*

Localities, 20. *The cliché of Italy—when in Rome do as the Romans do—is apt in global times. The Italians seem to be able to maintain local identity in coexistence with adjacent different local identities. They are* global *rather than* globalized. *During the last half of the twentieth century they suffered repeated coalitions and fragmentary democracies, seen by others at the time as weakness but, as it turns out, pioneering of political multiplicity.*

Log fire, 181. *See also* Floodlit

London, 14, 41, 105, 133

   canal art, 123

   the city of ~ sailed on through space, 46

   empty the museums of enchanted rubble, 77

   Wellington monument (quadriga), 128

Londoners, young, 134. *See also* House (music). *Most of whom would not live anywhere else. "It's a London thing" is their concept of club life.*

Long house, 184. *The New Guinea long house is a large building where the men live communally, which is surrounded by small buildings where the women and children live in family groups.*

Looms, 24

Los Angeles, 21, 30

Los Malaguenos, 53. *Their name means* the people from Malaga.

Loudspeakers, 52

Louvre, the (Paris), 76

Love

   falling in, 97

   how do you ~ yourself? 102

   is the human condition, 101

Love stories (ancient), 92, 97. *As well as* Cupid and Psyche *and* Daphnis and Chloe, *Jaques might have done* Acis and Galatea *(Galatea was one of the Nereids, daughter of the sea god Nereus. She loved Acis, her suitor; the cyclops Polyphemus crushed him under a rock, and she rescued him by turning him into a river);* Philemon and Baucis *(an old couple who entertained Zeus in disguise. They were granted their wish to die together and became trees intertwined); and* Cephalus and Procris *(she gave him a spear that would never miss that Artemis had given her to patch up a quarrel between them. Still jealous, she spied on him out hunting and was hit by his marvelous spear, he thinking her his quarry).*

Low earth orbit, 142. *About 300 miles up; the orbit will eventually decay and the artificial asteroids come crashing back to earth.*

Loxosceles reclusa, 9
Loxoscelidae, 9
Loyola, Ignatius (1491–1556), 175
Lubbock, (Texas), 34
Luddites, 24. *See also* Levelers. *Ned Ludd was an early industrial organizer (1779) who favored the direct action of smashing up the first stocking frames (machine looms). The Luddites were a group formed in his honor (he may have been a fiction of theirs created to mislead the authorities) to continue his work; they operated between 1811 and 1816.*
Luggage loaders, 166
Lumber, 23. *In the U.K.:* timber. *In the U.S. lumber also means "stuff," or "baggage," all those dead-weight memories that clutter your attic. See Nicholson Baker's* The Size of Thoughts *(Random House, 1996).*
Lumina, 8, 87, 116. *In Europe, the equivalent GM vehicle at the turn of the century was the Omega. The grass is always greener, however— in the U.S. the Omega was sold as a Cadillac, badged "Catena."*
Lurex, 16
Lynn, Gregg, viii, 170. *Both quotations in this book are taken from an article published on the Eindhoven Technical University Web site.*

Machine. *See also* Machines
  the idea of a ~ aesthetic, viii
  ~-age poetic scansion, 59
  Airside is full of . . . ~s—that's our actual life, 165
  ~ analogies to describe human society, 132
  or animal? (Christmas puppy), 196
  ~ animals would be more interesting, 91
  antigravity ~, 99
  it was an armoured ~ (Cromford), 24
  ~ because of its instrumentality in the Pan-Athenian annual procession (Parthenon), 80
  biblical impact, ~ revealed to Liberty with, 53
  is it only a ~ when (the pieces) are bolted together? 60
  blowing up was as valid to the ~ as pursuing on course, 101
  as if the ~ had broken! 132
  ~ buildings (Australia), 74
  ~-building hybrid, 165

are ~ buildings still interesting? 23
a computer abstracts the automaton from the ~, 61
a ~ that makes cars (John and the screwdriver), 64, 197
spectacular color of the ~ against those grays, 139
his computer, the abstract ~, 5
if a ~ compromises with time (highly styled building), 108
is community some sort of ~? 131
when arranged to work in concert, is the ~, 64
can you call something so loosely connected a ~? 22
clicking his little ~ to bring up a new image, 112
~ dependent and therefore out of our direct control, 154
the whole complex dynamic of our ~ dependency, 12
dismantling of ~ assemblies under repair, 131
drinks ~, 48
is this the foundation of a ~ ethics? 64
has looked up ~ in the encyclopedia, 33
evacuating his lungs on one ~, 47
the ~ I'm writing this on would have to forgo its fans and disc
   drives, ix
the freedom ~ of the American constitution, 194
what is a ~ gun? 63
human workers had been reduced to machine parts, 24
the invisibility of ~ functions, 32
killing ~, 124
landscape, building, sculpture and ~, 80
a landscape, a building, and a machine (inclined plane), 34
litter ~, 131
all those people who've ever loved a ~,198
to anyone who's loved a ~, xii
a ~ is only machinic when it's running, 64
the whiff of man-~ symbiosis, 191
~ mimicry in buildings, 32
the ~ world slicing through human history (D&G), 32
the first name of four that each ~ in the field guide will carry, 190
the third name of a ~ could be a list of its parts, 197
~ nurturing. It sounds . . . expensive, 75
passengers were turned into ~ components, 23
resultant, ~-made landscapes (of the twentieth century), 158. Resultant *as opposed to* intentional.

now that ~ are sharing our world as though they were our cousins, 8

(the Loaf House) has to join us in the world, as Maria says of ~, as a
   cousin, 109

we were busy defining ~, 61

configured by the desires of the hegemons, 189

that distort space and time, 15

drum ~, 98

families of ~, 170

his own little family of ~, 5

don't have fear and laughing, 101

A Field Guide to the ~, 12

this field guide could include buildings as well as ~, 195

have you figured out the difference between ~ and buildings yet?
   108

forget about the ~ (all airplanes are bastards), 97

and globalism, 73

when we make ~, we aren't playing god, 8

what kind of ~ are (guns)? 62

habitats for ~, 170

implicate humans in their operations, 111

a shower of individuation ~, 176

aren't *in*organic, they're *non*organic, 6

and landscapes, xii

landscapes, buildings, and ~ (anatomy of architecture), 108

another landscape that ~ emerge from (hegemonic plane), 168

~-landscapes hybrid, 165

a link between the landscape and the ~ (Smart Rocks), 76

it's local thanks to the ~, 25

how can ~ be lovable? 6

the lover of ~, 1, 12, 16, 165, 198

loves these ~ as if they were his people, 5

the meal I wanted to offer here was ~, vii

are a metaphor for creation, 65

we are not Frankensteins but midwives, 7

names of Jaques's ~, 8

have number as well as location (stereotonic), 196

go obsolete, alright (species extinction), 111

are not organic life (cladistics), 100

with their talent for describing a partial life in a general world, 145

Machine, *continued*

the particles are the machines and the traces their patterns (nebula), 190

the passive life of ~, 101

the phenomenon of ~ . . . is complicated by our inside knowledge of them, 89

are all these pieces ~? 60

all ~ are made of these pieces, 197

the ~ carry pieces of our lives for us, 25

a potential origin landscape for ~, 167

we are the programs of our ~, 197

purchase their special character of peculiarity, 88

at the other end of the scale (to landscapes) are the ~ (*What Is Architecture?*), 33

and sculpture, xii

it includes ~ and sculpture in architecture (Australian Quadriga schematic), 79

become obsolete and sculpture becomes timeless, 80

don't have sex . . . but they do reproduce, 8

the five simple ~, 33

track the presence of the simple ~, 196

they think ~ are slaves, 8

a sorting system for the idea of ~ and architecture, 128

sometimes it's about ~, sometimes about technology, 72

spawning new ~ and artifacts as they go (planes of hegemony), 176

spawning grounds for new city of ~, 170

the tombs and temples . . . as well as the ~,viii

because it's ~, it has a trainspotting strain, 195

the way we turn ~ against our fellow human beings? 25

this twenty-first century boy, born into a world of ~, 50

the unpredictable syntheses our ~ put together, 25

jets and bombs and Great Grand Coolie dam's–eye view of the world of ~, 157

to the ~, we are the wilderness, 95

what would be the point of making ~ whose function was to worship us? 65

Machinic

Loaf House, 109

Houston, 20

Machinic qualities (of ants), 19. *The qualities of nerveless endurance of* Terminator *were tempered in the sequel by going beyond the "clinical and emotionless" cliché to accept that first, machines can learn, and second, that "machinic" is not a synonym for "passion-free." Coleridge's reference to "the machine of instinct" and "the spirit of reason" suggests that, contrary to current use of the word, it is rationalists who need a religious foundation, as they require a prime cause to found reason on; and the fabulous complexity of life in an ants' nest supports the idea that material instinct is not an automated joylessness. William James's* Pragmatism *(1907) was partly about resolving the contradictions and paradoxes contained in this conundrum. See his illuminating diagram entitled "Tender minded and Tough minded."*

Machu Piccu, 147

Magazine, 63. *The automaton that holds the bullets of a gun, spring-loaded in a stack so they can click into place one by one.*

Magic (unseen workings of technology), 114. *An ordinary idea, that technology is somehow magical: see* Techgnosis *by Erik Davies (2000) for an updated version of the orientalist transcendence of hippie days. But I am linking it here with the idea of "enchanted rocks." It is not the transcendence of a higher authority so much as awe at the invisible electricity of material life.*

Magistrate, 81

Magus, 109. Magic *is a Greek word; a magus is a magician or sorcerer. (Majesty in the monarchic sense is tied to the Latin* major.*)*

Mailer, Norman, 183

Mammal (Taxonomic group), 10, 11

Mammals (mother and child, simple mammals again), 48

Manhattan (first we take), 77. *See also* Berlin

Manhattan Island, 21

Manhattan project, 153. *The project to build the atom bomb, at Los Alamos, New Mexico, was led by Robert Oppenheimer. His opposition to hydrogen bomb development after the war was negated by information from the spy Fuchs that the Soviets had their secrets: and Teller was the man chosen over Oppenheimer's head to create the first thermonuclear weapon. He exploded his first bomb at Enewetak in 1952. A second nuclear weapons establishment, the Lawrence Livermore Laboratory, was set up in California with Teller in charge, in the same year.*

Microsoftian, 2

Midwives, 7, 42, 45

  robot, 75

Mildenhall (England), 183. *Still an operational U.S. Air Force base. Used by the USAAF in World War Two.*

Miller, Henry (1891–1980), 183

Millipedes, 10

Miniaturization, 109

Mini-bar, 78

Minimalism, 147

Minimalist, 145. *A school of art originating in the 1960s that posited the aesthetics of modernism as modernism's real quality. That's one explanation: see Hal Foster's* The Return of the Real *(MIT Press, 1996). But see also the raunch definition on page 97—to say minimalism is "figurative of nothing" (and figurative might not mean realistic as opposed to abstract, as in common usage, but iconic— which is representative in a different way) may be a caricature, but, like the "speculation" and "fast criticism" described in the preface, caricature is a way of countering the dense substantiation that has to go on with any theorizing after postmodernism by surfing clean over it. The problem of that substantiation is that it works against action by using relations as equalizers rather than differentiators.*

Minotaur, 60

Missile, 64, 95

Mississippi (absence of Australian equivalent), 71

Mississippi deckhand, 18. *These guys are legendary in the south for their profane machismo—people say they capture and rape wild horses in the darkness of the Mississippi shore on Saturday nights.*

Mitchell, Reginald, airplane designer (1895–1937), 192

Mites, 9

Modems, 15, 126

Modern

  there is your ~ architecture (777), 73

  a baroque ~ thinker (Giordano Bruno), 109

  the blown-apart character of ~ life, xi

  in every crevice of the ~ world, 73

  fabulously buoyant early years of ~ America (Kerouac), 177

  global ~ world, 24

  ~ medical robots, 41

this ~ mobile place (Houston), 1

~ mode country (music), 98. *Also called new country. Not the same as alternative country.*

partial, human, ~ world (Thanksgiving), 25. *I am using modern to mean* contemporary—*but the term is loaded. Although the end of World War I changed everything in terms of automation (1918), "modern" often refers to everything since the French Revolution (1798). British historians sometimes use the accession of the Hanoverians (1714), who were the first monarchs free of the ancient taint of the house of Stuart. The invention of the blast furnace (1708) could be a starting point for the technologized modern world. Or to go even further back: the Baroque is the exploration acceleration complexity, and can be seen not as the end of the Renaissance, but as the start of the modern. The first baroque thing was the Jesuit church of Il Gesù, Rome (1568).*

rolling cultivation of ~ times, 127

not symbolically ~, like free verse, 59

too much turbulence in the ~ to solve it, 31. *Because of antirevisionist anxieties?*

triumphs of the ~ world, 15

"wise saws and ~ instances," xii, 51

Modernism (Hi-Tek description), 24. *See also* Hi-Tek

Modernist

  Cocteau, Jean, 124

  inflammatory excitement of the ~s, 124

  steel house architect, 157. *Modeled on Pierre Koenig, who has escaped the pantaloon phase using humor as a tunnel.*

  carriers of the ~ torch, 30

Moderns, 25

Mojo, 88. *Voodoo sex fetish.*

Monadology, 32

Mongol war machine, 32

Monroe, Marilyn (her belly), 46

Montague and Capulet, 16. *The warring houses in Shakespeare's* Romeo and Juliet.

Moon, men on the, 83

Moonrock, 144

Moonroof, 21. *The same thing as a sunroof, but in the air-conditioned states of the south and southwest, you do not open it during the day.*

Motorola, 33

"Mr. High and Mighty," 146

MTV videos, 185

Multicultural (transformation of tribes into nations), 159

Multiculturalist (idea), 148. *Ethnic groups living side by side (toler-ance) or ethnic groups living together (symbiosis)?*

Musicians (digiphile Catalans), 126. *The substantial analogy for mu-sic is "Oceanic." Musicians swim in an ocean of sound that en-velops all of us all of the time; they make it audible. (See David Toop's* Ocean of Sound, Serpents Tail, *1996.) But people writing music on computers behave like builders building brick walls. First they make the clay—sampling sounds—then they make the bricks—blocks of sound—then they arrange them in patterns. A tabulated computer score is not architectonically unlike sheet mu-sic, except that the dynamic execution of the music is contained within it. The idea of musical time as duration is very clear to these people; hence the analogy of music with being alive. If the analogy extends through to brick walls, as I suggest, then the idea of lived existence as a solid block of time comes swimming into view, and if that picture is clear, then the picture of technology as a complex accumulating field itself analogous to a solid may also be more clear.*

Muslim (flak for being Muslim in India), 108

Mussolini, Benito (1883–1945), 115, 169

Mussolini blackshirt, 114

Mutations, 12, 152

Muzak, 36, 165

My Digital Dad, 107. *The idea came out of a conversation with David Heymann.*

Naafi, 58. *World War II five-letter acronym:* Navy Army Air Force Institute.

Nabokov, Vladimir (1899–1977), 182

Napoleon (1769–1821), 57, 73

Narratives, 142. *The problem with narratives in the dumb arts (sculp-ture, architecture, and landscape) is that they obviate conclusions. That is what my* What Is Architecture? *(MIT Press, 1994) is about. Machines can handle it, like they handle everything else, by being precise in the short term (like us).*

NASA, 99, 138, 141, 142, 164. *National Aeronautics and Space Administration, founded in 1958 after the Russians launched their* Sputnik *satellite.*

Native American (blankets for nudes), 139

Native Americans (ethnic minority), 153. *See also* Indians

Naughty Nineties, 29, 31. *Last ten years of the nineteenth century.*

Navy (U.S.), 20, 59, 64

Navy, Royal (U.K.), 138

Nebula, 190. *Cloud of interstellar gas; distinct from a galaxy, which is the group of stars themselves.* Galaxy *derives from the Greek word for milk and was once used only for our own system: other visible accumulations in outer space were once all called* nebulae.

Nest(s)

  as artificial wilderness, 167

  as community, 17

  description of, 16

  Jaques's landscape number two, 166

  human, 20, 22. *Extended city analogies—there is no rural and no city; everything is one human landscape with varying densities of voices—are closest to these nest analogies. The human response is, perhaps, generically—"but how do we build this corner of it?" The ant response is, "no—this is our nest and none other will do."*

  little old-fashioned ~, 8

  urban, 21, 25, 105, 106

Newcastle (England), 23. *Where coal first came from in England, hence bringing coals there is a redundant action. Newcastle is pronounced with a short "a" and with no emphasis: New-kass-il.*

New Guinea (eastern Malay archipelago), 184

New Jersey, 154

New World, 2, 107, 133

New York City

  art world, 145

  imitations of, 20, 21

  largest city, 21

  movie with Ashley Judd, 164

New Zealand, 114

Niagara, 106

Night of the Iguana (1961), 182

Nihilism, 26. *The old nihilism would be against truth: relationism*

Nihilism, *continued*

   and God-is-deadism. The new nihilism could also be "no-logoism" and loss of faith in political change: is that apathy or anarchy?

Nike, 77, 128. *Nike was the warlike manifestation of Athena; she has the wings of victory. The temple of* Nike Apteros *(apteros means without wings) on the acropolis, Athens, is dedicated to a paradoxical mutation in which the winged Athena is deprived of flight. See* Indra McEwen's Socrates' Ancestor *(MIT Press, 1993) for an explanation.*

Nile (Egypt), 165

Nit-picking, 108

Noah's flood, 119

Nokia, 36, 73

Nomadic, 130. *See also* Agricultural revolution. *The alternative proposition includes the idea that nomadism was a challenge to city organization, invented after the event. See also page 47.*

Nomadology, 33. *See also* Deleuze, Gilles. *Part of Deleuze and Guattari's* A Thousand Plateaus *(1987).*

Nonorganic 6, 8. *See also* Artificial life. *The distinction on page 6 between nonorganic and inorganic rests on the inadequacy of organic and inorganic as an opposition. Organic chemistry is carbon based, inorganic is everything else; and life is carbon based. Maria is making a point about the vitality of machines; "vitalism" as a chemical theory of life force was upset in 1828 when urea, which had been considered a purely animal product, was synthesized from ammonium cyanate, an inorganic compound. The mode of being that characterizes organic life in this passage is emotion: a process rather than a substance.*

Normalization, 82. *See also* Pejoratives

North America, 20, 74

North American continent, 53

North American culture (balloon of), 38

North Sea, 68, 141

Northwest (camping trip), 6

Nostril dilator, 186

Nothing

   how do we go from ~ to something? 125

   minimalism, 148

   staring ~ right in the face (Judd), 148

as mode of twentieth century, 148

Nothingness
of the last century, 125
metaphysics of, 29. *It was not nothing, but it was invisible.*

Nuclear deterrent, 124

Nudes, 140. *The idea for this came from the artist Becky Young. In her version it was women with no clothes on.*

Nymphs (erotic statues), 140. *See also* Voluptuous bronze

Objects of desire, 123, 128, 131, 175, 195. *See also* Quasi-objects. *Michel Serres, in* Genesis (Genèse, *1982), extending from Georges Dumezil, calls these things quasi-objects, perhaps to distinguish them from the it-matters-not objectivity of modern science. They are the quality of hominid culture, what separates us from "an unstable band of baboons, [for whom] social changes are flaring up every minute." Serres speaks of them as* universal solutions—"*do you know a human group without religion, warrior, exchange?"— and says of the objects arising—the fetish, the weapon, and the thing-of-value—that they are more contracts than things, and they are quasi-objects in so much as they remain a "quasi us." Quasis* "ʀ" us! *This speculation can be found in the "Quasi-Objects" section of the chapter "Birth of Time" in* Genesis, *which has been translated into English for the University of Michigan by Geneviève James and James Nielson (1995).*

Off-switch (for Duke's androids), 106

O'Hare (Chicago), 105

Olive tree (Athena's), 143

Olympus (mountain of the gods), 93

Omega Speedmasters, 126

On the Road (Kerouac, 1957), 177

Onyx table, 156

Operating theater, 46

Order (taxonomic), 10, 90

Organic. *See also* Nonorganic
we cleave the world into ~ and inorganic, 6
~ life as humans know it (ants' life), 18
~ life forms copy themselves onto their offspring, 94

Orgasms (digital), 99

Original sin, 47

Ossified, 156. *Turned to bone.*

Owl, 51. *He is a long-eared owl,* Asio otis. *The great gray owl of Scandinavia is called* Strix nebulosa: *good name for a sci-fi hero.*

Oxytocin, 42. *The hormone that provokes lactation in nursing mothers. When synthetic oxytocin is introduced in the last stages of pregnancy, it causes the smooth muscles of the uterine wall to contract.*

Pacific
  Australian archipelago, 71
  Enewetak Island, 151
  ~ rim, 71

Packs, 15, 44. *The first humans must have lived in packs of twenty or so, as the other big primates do—the word* tribe *refers to something later and larger, as the tribe of Athens. See also page 112.*

Padre Island (Texas), 96. *There are North and South Padre Islands—they are part of a series of low-lying sand spits formed by the currents flowing east (counterclockwise) all along the Gulf coast. Behind the spits is a protected channel of water called the "Intra Coastal Waterway," which, partly canalized, can be followed all the way around Florida and up the eastern seaboard behind similar spits formed by coastal currents flowing north as far as the Carolinas.*

Pager, 45

Palace (object of desire), 131

Pan-Athenian procession, 80. *Annual reconfirmation of the origin myth of Athens. See also page 143.*

Pantheon (Rome), viii, 166

Paradigmatic shift, 190. *Thomas Kuhn's (1962) characterization of the process of conceptual change. I interpret it as the American hegemonic (democracy machine) version of epistemological break. Equates to* accelerations *but without the sense of accumulation I am trying to stress. See Whitney Balliet's description of the coming of bebop jazz outlined under* Parker, Charlie, *below.*

Parallel universes (John's Leibniz parody), 33, 145

Paris (France)
  from the air, 106
  Apollo quadriga, 128
  artist's garret, 2 (*see also* Garret). *Gertrude Stein relates how impressed she was with the slim figures and athletic bounce of the*

artists she mixed with in Paris in the years before the First World War—they explained it was all a question of going up and down stairs all day to their attic studios.

heavy ideas of city planning, 20

Nike Samothrace in the Louvre, 76

statues in, 140

Ex's Web-city explanation, 115

Parker, Charlie (1920–1955), 114. *Like Mozart, died at 35. Nicknamed "Bird." Whitney Balliet, in a 1959 essay on bebop drumming, observed how Parker had transformed jazz from swing to bop by being so innovative that every other musician wanted to play like him. Not just saxophonists; first trumpeters, then piano players, then bass players and finally drummers were all trying to turn their instruments into alto saxophones. The drums never sprang back after this distortion, and that's what really changed the music. This is analogous with what I'm saying about technological accelerations in seminar three. The acceleration—in this case the arrival of Parker—has consequences that are themselves the fundamental change.*

Parking lots, 22. *The British expression* car parks *sounds like a landscape event by comparison. However, in Houston and other car-heavy cities of the U.S., every threshold experience is made similar by the walk from the parking lot to the building through ranks of cars; it is a powerful but not unpleasant phenomenon and a real landscape event.*

Parkway, 115. *Memorial Drive and Allen Parkway, Houston.*

Parrots, 74

Parterres (English gardens), 175

Parthenon (Athens), viii, 77, 79, 80

Partial pictures, 24. *Another word for partial could be* quantized*: through analogy with quantum physics, which will not attempt to predict universal pictures, because only the local can be interpreted. Postmodernism could be to international modernism by a similar analogy.*

Passion

the etymology of ~ is *suffering*, 100. *I guess that passion in the common sense of* emotion *depends on a conception of humans as the clay of God, which is reactive to his will—so confused with emotion, which denotes an excitement to action.*

Passion, *continued*

the most precarious of a man's ecologies, 146. *And people think they suffer love, when it is that they do love.*

Passive (mode of machines), 101. *The "passive synthesis" used by D&G in* Anti Oedipus *refers to a much more complex idea of "machine" than that of this book with its view of machines as/are/and architecture, but suggests ways of understanding that such machines can produce the conditions of their own continuation.*

Patriarchy

obsolete, 51

primitive, 184

Pecking orders, 34

Pejoratives, 82. *I know the matter is more complex than this, but in caricature these words carry the ring of 1968 and the Paris barricades. Is a U.S. parallel the "raunch epistemology" of the Woodstock days? See Dave Hickey's* Air Guitar *(Foundation for Advanced Critical Studies, 1997) and Robert Persig's* Zen and the Art of Motorcycle Maintenance *(William Morrow, 1974), where academicism is pilloried and "quotidian" individuality-in-democracy championed. The synthetic world that Microsoft and the image media have fabricated WERE still over the horizon for these people.*

Penknife (with a rabbit's-foot key ring), 130

Peplos, 77. *See also* Plaid; Persian carpets. *The cloth worn by Nike and Athena and renewed annually as part of the Pan-Athenian ceremonies (as is the* kiswa, *the cover of the Ka'aba in Mecca). Implicated in the idea that the tribal people are woven together like a piece of cloth, and that its coming into being is the tribe's epiphany. See also page 144.*

Percept, 196. *See also* Deleuze, Gilles. *An artist's concept.*

Pericles (495–429 B.C.), 144

Peristyle, 91. *The outer perimeter of columns.*

Peroni(s), 176. *Peroni is an Italian beer.*

Perpetuity, 193–194. *Michael Serres (Genesis): "The vestals in Rome . . . kept watch over the fire, but above all the most venerable and sacred objects, only the supreme pontiff had the power they had, to know and see them. The secret was so well protected that it has not come down to us. Perhaps it was the secret of Rome's perpetuation."*

Persian carpets, 24. *The idea is that the pattern of a Persian carpet is a representation of paradise, like a Muslim garden. You are, like Adam, a particle in among the absolute authority of God. Your life is configured by that reality, but you are not aware of the details of the configuration. In my picture of a partial world, God is replaced by the force of the human presence in the world.*

Personal message, 59. *Forty words, the exact length a personal message should take up? Compare the standard Dear John letter:* Dear John, dear John, I've found another. I can't love two, so I must lose you, dear John, dear John. *Twenty words.*

Perth, 72

Petrified Athenians, 144

Phalanx, 64, 165. *These automated guns are the only thing securing the future of navies, hence hegemonic power projection, in their current technological acceleration as floating airbases; appropriately, the Pentagon has named them after a key feature of the classical war machine, a solid block of heavy infantry standing shoulder to shoulder. The theater defense radar systems are likewise called* Aegis *after the breastplate of Zeus. Other Pentagonian naming modes include the biocentric (Eagle, Raptor), the systematic (C-17, F22), the coded (Foxbat, Bear—Cold War Warsaw pact fighters names began with F, bombers with B), the Acronymic (UCAV), and the clever (see* Smart rocks).

Pheromones, 29. *A chemical substance that excites a response in one of the same species.*

Pheromonic (ant's nest bondage), 17. *"Smell" could be a shorthand for a sense so far undescribed.*

Philadelphia (Pennsylvania), 139

Philosopher's stone, 114, 129, 193. *Base metal into gold? Alchemy is also analogous to the desire to turn savages into Christian saved souls.*

Philosophies of emergence, viii

Philosophy (in schools of architecture), 31

Phoenix (Arizona), 23

Phonograph, 111

Phosphor bronze, 138. *Bronze is a ductile metal alloy made of copper and tin. Other metals are added to produce different properties— for instance statuary bronze has less than ten percent tin, but has*

Phosphor bronze, *continued*
    lead and zinc added (so is technically a brass). Phosphor, added in minute quantities, improves the hardness of the alloy and imparts a sparkling sheen to the metal on wearing surfaces.

Phylum (taxonomic), 10.90

Piazza Navona (Rome), 170

Piazza Popolo (Rome), 166

Picasso, 31. *The story about Picasso and Alice Toklas comes from Gertrude Stein's* Autobiography of Alice B. Toklas *(1933).*

Pick-up, 1, 19, 21, 25, 159. *A small truck with a two- or four-seat cab and an open bed at the back. In the western U.S. they are an icon of the country but also thrive in the cities, which helps to illustrate the idea that western cities are accumulations rather than institutions. Contemporary pick-ups have A/C and cruise control, power everything—steering, windows, door mirrors, seats, the whole nine yards.*

Picture.it, 156. *See also* www.picture.it

Pigeons, 47. *Family* Columbidae *(after* Columba, *the dove that led the Argonauts to safety through the clashing rocks) and genus* Columba *or* Streptopilia. *The European species are: wood pigeon, rock dove, stock dove, collared dove, palm dove, and turtle dove. "Dove" is onomatopoeic of the call.*

Pilot EasyTouch ballpoint pen, 33

Pilot lights, 5

Pinions, 57. *The small gears in the differential that mesh between and mediate between the two-axle drive ring gears.*

Pittsburgh (Pennsylvania), 151. *Why Pittsburgh? My mental image of Pittsburgh is the opposite of my mental image of Enewetak.*

Placental beds (artificial wombs), 75

Plaid, 16. *See also* Peplos; Persian carpets. *A multicolored checked cloth; I am using it here in the sense of a metaphor for a people woven together as in a tribe. The kilts of Celtic clans have unique checks and the colors are derived from plants and earths particular to the clan homelands, hence offer camouflage as well as identity—or is that the same thing?*

Plane-spotting, 90

Planet Earth, 155

Plantagenets, 73

Plateaus ("evolution" and "fitness" landscapes), 170, 189

Plato (ca. 428–348 B.C.), 67

Playboy-magazine-style console, 78

PlayStation, 192

Pleached lime, 100. *"Pleaching" is a way of making plants grow to-gether and in strange shapes by interlacing partially cut stems. I am using this rather than the obvious* rhizome *as a metaphorical alternative to cladistics to capture the quality of human desire in machines as architecture.*

Plexiglas, 47. *In the U.K.,* Perspex.

Plutarch (45–120 A.D.), 91, 92. *See also Life of Theseus*

Pollock, Jackson (1912–1956), 147

Pollution (consequence of social program), 157

Pool, 18, 156

Population explosion, 147. *See also* Caesarean

Port, vintage, 183

Portugal, 133. *The agreement between Portugal and Spain to divide the world either side of line drawn 370 leagues (about a thousand miles) west of the Canaries was made in Tordesillas in 1494. Spain was to have everything west of the line, and Portugal everything east of it. The line had first been set up by papal bull in 1493 at 100 leagues: but Portugal claimed there was not enough room to carry out the African adventure. The new line was between 48 and 49 degrees West of Greenwich, and turned out to take in the bulge of South America that is Brazil—which is why the Brazilians speak Portuguese. None of the other maritime nations took any notice of the Tordesillas agreement.*

   The Portuguese explorers carried with them stone pillars called padrões *to mark the furthest point of their searches, to help those following on subsequent missions. One of Bartolomeu Dias's* padrões—*his was the first ship to round the cape, in 1488—has been recovered from the sea at Padrão de São Gregório and erected on False Island, near the Cape of Good Hope, South Africa.*

Poseidon, 143

Postcard (exchanges with Ex), 107

Postmodern, 47, 123. *See also* Partial pictures. *How do you define postmodern in a way that describes both the banality and the pro-fundity of it? The prefix "post-" is interesting in respect of the accum-ulations described in seminar three, because it would be clearer if it operated like* B.C. *and* A.D., *pre-Christ and post-Christ—so that*

Postmodern, *continued*
  if something is postmodern it includes the modern movement but
  does not eliminate it.
Poverty (ending), 156
Power switches (hegemony over), 54
Prada, 73
Prayer (technology of the self), 81
Price, Cedric, 23. *See also* Fun Palace
Primates, 11, 15
Printing (techniques of the exploration), 133. *See also* Techniques
Process (architectural term), 30. *Especially potent in the hands of the*
  ecologist landscapers, Lawrence Halpin and Iain McHarg: first-
  generation sustainability. The sustainability machine—that is, the
  perpetuity machine—that is explicit in new urbanism's depend-
  ence on building codes was implicit in Halprin's use of scores
  (RSVP Cycles) and MacHarg's sieve map procedure.
Processors, 100. *I mean the "process" philosophers who explain emer-*
  gence: that means, for me, Bergson, Deleuze (and because of him,
  Liebniz) and Serres.
Processual, 193. *Anthropologists' term referring to temporal changes*
  in pattern of long-lasting structures.
Product engineers (planning babies), 44
Projection screen, 114. *Story relayed by Paul Baker.*
Program
  we are the ~s of our machines, 197
  and use, 108
Progress, 110
Progresses, 35, 38. *There are four in this description: the expanding*
  universe, the evolution of life, the wandering of the tribes, and the
  growth of your self. In seminar one these are progresses *and histo-*
  ries; in seminar two they are frontiers. *Maria's idea of love as the*
  human condition on page 101 corresponds to them: see also the
  summary of quadrigas on page 128. These progresses are not lin-
  ear, but expansive and historical: a teleology seems to be implied
  because of the historical quality but a progress has no known or
  predictable end.
Promised Land, 133
Prophylactics, 44
Prototypes, 90, 196

Psyche (and Cupid), 93
Pulley (the five simple machines), 33
Punctuation (in encrypted messages), 59
Puppy (cloned Christmas product), 196
Puritans (*Mayflower*), 107
Purple Heart, 73. *Every U.S. soldier wounded in action is awarded the Purple Heart medal.*
Pygmalion and Galatea, 140. *Painting by Gerome in the Metropolitan Museum, New York. I imagine him finding a rivulet of blood under his chisel. The alternative story to that given on page 140, probably a Naughty Nineties version, is that Pygmalion, despairing of finding a good woman, decides to make one for himself. See also quotation from Robert Graves on page 182.*
Pylons (electricity), 159. *The derivation of the word* pylon *is Greek for* gate: *a structure that denotes the way through the edge.*
Pyramid(s), viii, 131
  big building, 165
  construction of the Great ~, 34

Quadriga, 82, 128, 177. *See also* Nike. *A four-horsed chariot: metaphor for four-part theories explained on page 128. One of the qualities of such four-part structures as these (another example is Northrop Frye's* Anatomy of Criticism, Atheneum, 1966) *is that each part of the theory works in concert with the others, rather than as a hierarchy.*
Quadrinomial (taxonomy), 189, 194
Quasi-objects, 128, 177. *See also* Objects of desire
Queensland (Australia), 71

Rabbit's foot (key ring), 130. *A rabbit's foot used to be a lucky charm, along with a lucky penny and a horseshoe—Grimms brothers–era superstitions.*
Race-car, 65, 67
Radar
  landing ~s, 22
  Phalanx weapon system, 64
  ~ platform airplanes, 90
  shoal detector, 111
Radio control, 62

Radio-controlled car, 57

Railroad points, 196

Rainforest

  Ex's cell-phone screen, 110

  Gambian, 143

  Queensland, Australia, 74

Real ("the real world"), 30. *As Northrop Frye demonstrates in his* Educated Imagination *(Indiana University Press, 1964), "the real world" in this context should be called "the conventional world." His image is of the heavily coiffured men and women who occupy that "real world."*

Reality (as truth and as material), 152

Rear axle, 61

Rearranging material for human purposes, 79, 194

Reconnaissance drone, 198. *"Drone" is used to denote a pilotless airplane, remotely controlled.*

Recovery ward, 23, 48

Red Baron, 88. *Manfred von Richthofen (1882–1918), the first air ace, remembered now as a cartoon figure and comic cliché. He was Prussian, and fought in World War I, which makes him an acceleration breakpoint icon between industrialization and automation. (Along with Henry the Navigator—age of prayer/exploration—Charles the Beheaded of England—exploration/colonization—and Napoleon—colonization/industrialization.)*

Refrigerator, 5, 8, 65

Remote control, 52, 176

Renaissance Society (IIT), 109. *On the Loaf House CD, IIT is credited with "assistance." The Renaissance Society is based in the University of Chicago.*

Rescue module, 102

Rest stop, 127. *In the U.K.:* service area.

Retirement homes, 5

Rickman, Alan, 63. *See also* "All the world's a stage"

Ridge Racer, 117

Ritual (tribal custom, tribal taboo and tribal ~, as technologies of domination), 82

Rivercat, 74, 82

Roaches, 141. *Cockroaches. In the northeast they have* Blatella germanica, *but in Texas it's* Periplanata americana, *bigger and darker*

*and with a slither that makes your blood run cold: provoking
thoughts of some ancient evolved-in conflict between humans and
animals like that.*

Robots (medical), 41

Rocket balloon, 187

Rocket motors (artificial asteroids), 142, 149

Rockets, 194

Rock/paper/scissors, 165. *In the U.K. it used to be* hic hac hoc.

Rocky Mountain rainsheds (absence of in Australia), 71

Romans (persecution of St. Lucia), 36

Rome (Italy), 128, 140, 163

  Bernini in, 167

  digital camera in streets of, 169

  computer-generated reconstruction of, 164

  EUR, 169

  full of big things, 164

  Holy ~, 174

  sites of ~, 166

  Spanish hegemony and, 168

  that night in ~ I doze in my hotel room, 177

  Tivoli and, 176

  Villa D'Este, 173

Romulus, 164. *The founder of ancient Rome. According to Roman historian Varro Marcus Terentius and the Michelin guide, in 735 B.C.*

Rose garden, 89

Rostra, 164. *Plural of* rostrum, *which was the name given to the beak-
head prows of ships. The rostra was the platform in the Forum of
ancient Rome from which speakers addressed the crowd, and was
hung with the hacked off prows of captured battleships.*

Rug-rats (hospital robots), 41

Russians, 153

Safety belt, 10, 133

Sagittarius, 45

Saint Andrews (Scotland), 20

Saint Cuthbert, 141. *See also* Bede

Saint Francis, 183

Saint Lucia, 36. *St. Lucia's day is December 13.*

Samothrace (Greece), 77

Sampler (32 Bit), 53

Samson, 163

Samsung, 73

San Fransisco (California), 36

San Jacinto (Houston), 108. *Houston street named after Houston's river and also the name of the battle fought on its shore in 1836, which was the decisive event in the Texas war of independence from Mexico. The commander of the Texas troops was Sam Houston.*

Sansepulcro (Italy), 183

Santa Claus, 5

Santa Maria della Vittoria (Rome), 140. *See also* Bernini. *Bernini's Saint Theresa in the church of Santa Maria della Vittoria has a coin-operated floodlight for the better examination of her face. Theresa's love story is that she was overcome one day with rapture from the presence of god, a rapture spiritual, she said, but also most definitely physical. Her fevered, orgasmic raptures were famous—theological scholars came from all over to watch her going through it. There they are carved into the niche that holds the statue, chatting and making notes while she writhes in ecstasy on a couch of clouds. Bernini has rendered her hot flesh in white marble, her eyes closed, her half-open mouth issuing cries of bliss.*

Sant Andrea al Quirinale (Rome), 170

Sartre, Jean-Paul (1905–1980), 183

Sassetta (d. ca. 1450), 183. *Sienese painter of the early Renaissance. The St. Francis altarpiece took seven years, between 1437 and 1444. Some of it can be seen in the National Gallery, London.*

Satanic Verses, The (Salman Rushdie, 1988), 164

Satellite(s), 107, 141, 142, 172, 194

Saturn Five, 145. *Launch vehicle for the Apollo moon missions.*

Satyrs (erotic sculptures), 140. *See also* Voluptuous bronze

Saudi Arabia, 20

Saxony, 143

Scarecrow (in a wind tunnel), 44

Scarp, 17. *The steep face of a finite inclined plane.*

Schneider Trophy, 191

Schumacher, Dan, 127. *Referring to Michael: German driver ace of Formula One (Grand Prix) racing.*

Science-fiction comics, 72

Scooters, 177

Scorpions, 9

Scotland

  English colonization of, 175

  golf courses little pieces of, 20

Screen saver, 192

Screw

  the five simple machines, 33

  fixing screws, 58

  a ~ is a tool, 60

Screwdriver, 5, 9

  while he was working on it, the ~ had the same status as the pieces of the car, 60

Scuba suit, 95

Sculptor, 138, 147

Sculpture

  because of its . . . entasis (Parthenon), 80

  included in architecture, xii, 79. *If poetry is a form of music, and painting a form of literature, so sculpture is to architecture. Northrop Frye has an expression in* Anatomy of Criticism *to describe lyric poetry: as not heard but "overheard."*

  Donatello yelled at his ~s, 140

  and machines (obsolescence and timelessness), 80

  is carrying the survival of the entire real world on its back, 142

  right here! and right now! 142

Scuttle, 127. *The weatherproofing plate between the car's front bulkhead and the windscreen/windshield, under the bonnet/hood.*

Second Empire, 140. *The time of Napoleon the third as emperor of France (1852–1870) and a name given to the neoclassical sculpture of that period.*

Second World War, 191

Seimen's, 155

Seine (River), 115

Selective breeding (as art), 147

Seminar with Michel Foucault, A (Fookwar), 81. *The etymology of the word* seminar *is* seed bed. *See* Technologies of the Self.

Sensor devices (at Enewetak), 152

Serres, Michel, 123, 128, 177. *See also* Objects of desire

Service vehicles (airports), 165

Servo-motors, 62. *The motors that provide motion for secondary assemblies; in the case of the race-car for the steering rack and the speed regulator.*

Seth, 119

Seven ages of man, ix, 16, 51, 67, 138. *See also* "All the world's a stage"

Sevenoaks (England), 133

Seventy percent water contents, ix. *We land dwellers carry our own little salt sea oceans with us; this idea comes from* Hypersea *(Mark McMenamin and Diana McMenamin, 1994), quoted in Sadie Plant's* Zeros and Ones *(Doubleday, 1998).*

Sexual harassment, 29. *See also* Teledildonics. *Paul Virilio's assertion in* Open Sky *(Norton, 1997) is that sexual harassment is not a social issue but a technical one that arises out of remote human relationships conducted through modern media. Since touching is eliminated in cybersex, or "teledildonics," any form of touching is suspect. (Joel Garreau reports in* Edge City *a calculation that electronically transmitted sex will require a modem running at three billion bits per second.) Virilio is anxious that people will be driven to be single by mutual repulsion and that, as a consequence, the human species is in danger of dying out altogether. Is this ironic? Or did it just start out ironic? See also page 99.*

Shabak, 33, 145. *German toy manufacturer: makes airliners at 1:500 scale, somehow without the wheels looking too big.*

Shackle cams, 196

Shakespeare, William (1564–1616), ix, xii, 16, 67, 94, 166

Shaman, 48. *In the English hegemony it used to be* witch doctor, *or* medicine man.

Shelley, Percy Bysshe (1792–1822), 137

Shocks (shock absorbers), 61

Sibelius, Jean (1865–1967), 53

Sigg-Steyrh, 63. *Austrian gun manufacturer.*

Silicon chips, 196

Silk shirts (like Swiss Bankers), 143. *Alison and Peter Smithson have observed how their legendary mentor, Mies van der Rohe, always wore cream silk shirts and black knitted ties, "like a Swiss Banker." The modernists reacted against the smocks and berets of the impressionists by wearing conventional clothes.*

Simulators, 152. *I am using the word as a collective noun, but it means all of us: copying is a difficult subject for idealists and materialists* alike. *In all its guises, from Disney to cloning, from simulacrums to downloads, from artificial life to iteration, it is the miracle of the modern world. Our ability to stamp out one identical piece after another, to have machines in factories working tirelessly to turn out Hyundai after Hyundai after Hyundai is like the Bible come true— and has a similar effect on disbelief.*

Singapore Airlines 777, 73

Sirens, 177

Six-shooter, 52

Skin and skeleton, 74. *See also* Hi-Tek. *The anthropomorphic analogy of building fabric with skin and bones (cladding and structure) is a fantasy of the Hi-Tek crew. I was introduced in Australia to an extended idea that a building had a head (roof), a body (carcass), and feet (foundation). An alternative would be that a building is a building and not a body at all.*

Skunk works, 168. *Nickname given to a special projects division of Lockheed (Aerospace) that manufactured high-flying and superfast spy planes during the Cold War.*

Slave transit depots, 143

Sleeping beauty (Maria), 92

Sloth and superstition (army of occupation), 26

Sluice gates, 196

Small Arms of the World, twelfth edition, 63. *Edited by Edward Clinton Ezell et al. (Stackpole Books, 1983).*

Smart rock(s), 76. *See also* Phalanx. *The developed version has smaller, smarter devices called* brilliant pebbles. *A Pentagon joke.*

Smith and Wesson, 63. *American gun manufacturer.*

Smithereens, 24

Smithsonian, 144. *Museum and Institution of American Art and Science, Washington, D.C.*

Snafu, 58. *U.S. Army World War II five letter acronym:* Situation Normal, All Fouled Up.

Snails, viii

Soap dispenser (battery powered), 57

Soap opera, ix. *The meaning of a drama written to sell soap in the advertisement breaks holds good here. The seven men and four women are intended to be mouthpieces to make the argument by emotion. I've heard it said that a good soap can't be written by a first-rate writer at idle speed, but only by a second-rate writer going flat out.*

Social insects, 17. *See also* Hymenopteran Fascist

Social program, 154. *See "standard program" on page 156.*

Society for the Repatriation of Enchanted Rubble, 77

Socrates (ca. 470–399 B.C.), 67

Sofa, 123. *"Velveteen" is a synthetic velvet.*

SoHo (New York), 145

Soldier ants, 18

Solenoid, 61. *Uses an electrical signal to trigger a small mechanical movement.*

Songlines, 76, 77, 174, 178. *See also* Acropolis. *An Australian aboriginal perception that the past exists in an eternal present. The landscape itself was made by giants, their tribal ancestors, who are now asleep. The story of the fabrication of each place is embodied in the associated idea of the* dreamtime. *Their human condition is framed by passing along the lines that connect each tribe's places in the landscape, bought to the present plane by the reiteration of specific songs. As a world picture, this is similar to that of the ancient Aegean as described by Vincent Scully in* The Earth, the Temple, and the Gods *(Yale University Press, 1962; revised, 1979). He and his archaeologist colleagues nicknamed that the "charged void": they said the Greek temple precinct buildings are not related to each other but set down into the charged void of the myth rich landscape. See also page 94.*

South Americans, 176

South Central Texas, 15. *Texas has three main geological parts: the flat orange oil laden plateau that reaches out to the northern and western borders; the hill country, a shallow crinkle of limestone forming an archaic fault dividing the state; and the coastal plain, on which the city of Houston stands and which runs down to the Gulf. To these three parts geography adds three more. The "panhandle" is the piece of the west that sticks out into what might otherwise be Oklahoma. "Centex" (central Texas) is a regional name for the dynamic economic region triangulated by Dallas, Houston, and San Antonio. The "third coast" refers to the Gulf, and is Texas's bid to be taken seriously as another cultural engine of the U.S. along with the east and west coast. Californians and New Yorkers snort with derision when they hear that.*

South Koreans, 176

Southwestern U.S., 153

Sowbugs, 10. *In the U.K.:* woodlice.

Spaceships

  comic book, 72

  free fall, 96

Space shuttle

  Challenger catastrophe, 101

  free fall, 96

Space-time, 130

Spain, 54, 133, 173, 174. *See also* Portugal

Spanish (language of the conquistadors), 153

Spanish hegemony, 168, 174, 176, 171

Spanish Steps (Rome), 166. *A baroque piazza built on the side of a hill in the form of steps, in which lateral movements as well as vertical movements are accommodated.*

Spears, 124

Species

  biological sports, 196. *A "sport" is a chance mutation that is grown on, but is sterile and has to be propagated by grafting. The Lombardy poplar that lines the roads of France is a sport.*

  origin not of the English, but of the ~, 194. *Refers to Charles Darwin's book,* The Origin of Species *(1859).*

  phylum, class, order, family, genus, ~ (Brown recluse), 10

Species (taxonomic), 89

Speculations, x. *See also* Apocalypse Now. *It has occurred to me that historians don't speculate enough: the problem being that they equalize everything through authentication and render themselves indiscriminate. Speculation is risk, like a wound: and an opening to some new process, like an infection.*

Spiders, 10, 11

  brown recluse, 9

  curled up in death like a tiny flower, 141

Spinal cord (epidural procedure), 42

Spinner (propeller), 139

Spitfire, 192

Spotter books, 90

Sprawl (suburban), x

Spray-cans, 132

Springs, 61, 63, 131

Standard program, 156. *The Western social democratic program of the postwar period.*

Stanford, Sir Charles Villiers (1852–1924), 53

Star Wars, 76

Statues (voluptuous bronze), 140

Steel houses (chic in California), 157. *The Case Study houses.*

Stein, Gertrude (1874–1946), 31, 198. *See also* Picasso

Stereo, 5, 8, 53

Stereotomic, 79. *Means* cutting of solids *and is used in architecture to describe the technology of stone cutting, notably in the Gothic mode and then in the Baroque, but also in respect of a building's shape:* stereometric *could also be used for that.*

Stereotonic, 79, 196. *The confusion with* stereotomic *is aural and depends on* architectonic. Stereo *means* solid. Tonic *means* characteristic sound.

Stipple brush (camouflage), 183

Stockholm (Sweden), 36

Stoplight, 109, 116

Strait of Hormuz, 7

Stroller, ix. *In the U.K.:* pushchair.

Structure, 124, 198. *Or* structuralism—*murky because attacked by poststructuralists for its universal tendencies, but not dispensed with, perhaps for its value to the tribe?*

Styrofoam, 23

Subassembly (definition of machine), 41

Subjectification, 82. *See also* pejoratives

Submarines, 58

Subphylum, 61

Suburban (wagon train circles), 98. *The factory-made housing settlements in the U.S. are one step less mobile than this, but are still part of what J. B. Jackson called* Landscape Three. *(See* Discovering the Vernacular Landscape, Yale University Press, 1986.*) Suburbs got their start as the garden cities of Europe, where they were not about mobility but part of the socializing impulse to eradicate the dense slum housing of the late industrial era and replace it with something more healthy. Now that the idea has come full circle, fueled by concerns about energy consumption, and urbanists talk* *about redensifying cities again, "sprawl" has replaced "slum" as the negative word. See page x. We can continue with both forms because the accumulative nature of technology militates against* carte blanche *reforms.*

Taboo (tribal custom, tribal ~ and tribal ritual, as technologies of domination), 82

Tabula rasa, 141. *Means* clear table.

Tachytronic, 80, 108, 197

Taco, 90

Tall poppy syndrome, 72

Tanzania, 14. *Formally—in Ex's childhood—Tanganyika.*

Tarantino (Sweden's Quentin), 37

Task group (Enewetak), 152. *A U.S. Navy task group is a tactic for defending an aircraft carrier on offensive duty with an anti-aircraft and antisubmarine screen comprised of its own aircraft, battleships, cruisers, and destroyers. The screen is deployed in a circle around the carrier so that sudden synchronized turns can be achieved. The diameter of the circle is varied according to the threat.*

Taxon (quadrinomial), 194, 195

Taxonomy, 12, 175. *A systematic classification. From* tax *plus* nomie; *literally, the "naming of the parts."*

    cladistic ~, 117

Teatro Marcellus (Rome), 166

Tech-junkie, 109

Techniques

  of the exploration, 133. *Hair splitting: Because I am mostly using "technologies" for the principal accelerations, I am here trying to distinguish those technologies that are characteristic of an acceleration. In the Masonic, I suggest astronomy and accounting, for their layered bits. The exploration technologies are expeditions setting out from the main body. They are too temporary to be colonizing movements; the main body is paramount. The case for banking is the way loans are excursions to be returned to the center. The case for printing depends on an idea that the pieces of type are sent out from the font to be arranged into book order as an expeditionary force and then returned to the font when the job is done. Charles I is the exploration/colonization wave breakpoint icon. (See Red Baron.) His severed head was never returned to the main body. (See also field, and Jacques's naming system described on page 189.)*

  new ~ that clatter around the world like gremlins at a wake, 133

Technological accumulation, 129

Technologies. *See also* Technology
  continuous ocean of automation ~, 159
  cuckoo's eggs of new ~, 8
  of domination, 81
  one of four ~ (Foucault: signs, production, power, self), 81
  individual freedom and aerospace ~ (American hegemony), 168
  new ~ don't replace old ones, 111, 120
  paradox of, 82 (*see also* Language)
  of power, 81, 82
  of printing and banking, 133
  of production, 81
  of sign systems, 81
  of the self, 81
  transformational ~, 20
  continual transformations forced by individual ~, 112
Technologies of the Self, 81. Technologies of the Self: A Seminar with
    Michel Foucault, *Martin et al. (1988)*.
Technology. *See also* Technologies
  action—~ plus politics, 190
  astonishing as a piece of high technology (Bernini), 168
  each billow of the ~ cloud, 132
  changes of ~ are made in the emotional flow of these evolved reali-
    ties, ix
  communication ~ related, 59
  that's our dependence on ~ (Airside), 165
  that fabulous, denigrated subject, vii
  is a force of nature (human presence in the world), viii, 112
  is not a flow, it's a force field, 130
  this great new ~ of theirs (wired up guys and the social program), 156
  he makes ~ sound like a force of nature, 83
  he was wrong about ~ (obsolescence), 126
  what he means by ~ is the accumulation of human action, 83
  that picture of ~ as the "human artifice" is hers (Arendt), xi
  is the human condition, 82, 83, 123
  he shows me ~ raised to be a description of everything humans do, 82
  what humans do is ~, 82
  when love was the prime ~, 92
  new ~ of banking, 16, 133
  searching ~ and health in the library computer, 81

Technology, *continued*
  seminar on ~ and Michel Serres's quasi-objects, 128
  (this book is) sometimes about ~, but it's not about the future, 72.
    George Dyson also says this at some point in Darwin among the
    Machines *(Perseus Books, 1998)—the assumption that technology
    is tied to the future runs deep. Is that America speaking?*
  speculation about the origins of ~ (Serres), 123
  this is ~ here, and therefore conclusive, 60
  the Victorians were ~-minded, 73
  ~ which has bought this family to this particular climax, 54
  a world that could be solved by democracy plus ~ (social program),
    158
Teenage hatchet, 60
Teledildonics, 99. *See also* Sexual harassment
Telephone
  monadic, 33
  on the onyx table, 156
Telescopes, 12
Television, 1, 4, 5, 8, 98
  Fujitsu black, 78
  Richard Gere as Plutarch, 60, 91
  kids thrashing about on ~, 184
  switch a ~ on and you are shown your place in the world, 4
  like watching ~, 153, 156
  wildebeest, 3
Teller, Edward, 153. *See also* Manhattan project
Temple (object of desire), 131
Terminals (airport departure), 22
Terminator, 19. *See also* Machinic qualities
Terrorists (attack on America), 163
Tesseract, 169, 172
Testicles, 47
Test tubes, 83
Texan(s), 145, 148
Texas
  academic life here in ~, 138
  black ~ night, 1
  brown recluse spider in, 9
  club sandwich in, vii

Thompson Trophy (air speed competition), 191

Three Graces, 51, 52. *By the early industrial wave sculptor Antonio Canova (1757–1822). The* Three Graces *are in the National Museum of Scotland, Edinburgh—there is a* Cupid and Psyche *of his in the Louvre. The* Oxford Companion to Art *says he "combined classicism with sentimentality": a very judgmental judgment. (The* Oxford Companion to Music *condemns Bruckner for repetition, which is like condemning Beethoven for melody.)*

Three hundred thousand people in the air, 19. *Passenger trips in the U.S. are running at one billion trips a year. 300,000 people is a city the size of Wichita, Kansas.*

Three thousand series (aluminium), 30. *See also* Eames chairs. *Aluminum (in the U.K.: aluminium) is alloyed with many different metals for different uses, and each alloy has a thousand series number.*

Thunderbolts (and insight), 83

Thunderheads, 23

Ticks, 9

Tires, 61, 87

Tivoli (Italy), 176

Toads (fire bellied, midwife, proper, and natterjack), 90

Toga, 91

Toklas, Alice B., 31. *Gertrude Stein's* Autobiography of Alice B. Toklas *(1935), together with her* Lectures in America *(1935) is the clearest account of modern—not modernism—that I know.*

Tokyo Bay, 165

Tool (definition of machine), 60

Tornado (Panavia Interceptor/interdictor), 90

Toronto (Canada), 106

Torture chambers (immigration service), 22

Toshiba, 8, 33

Tower-crane, 66

Tow truck, 130, 133

Toyota Camrys, 73, 195

Tractors (airport push-out), 166

Trafalgar Square (London), 134

Traffic jams, 83

Trailer (articulated), 87

Train-spotting, 195

Transglobal (saber rattling), 152

Trastavere (Rome), 171

Trawler, 111

Trevi Fountain (Rome), 166

Treasure chest
  gardens, 175
  Villa d'Este, 177

Tribe
  distinction between the ~ and the species, 76
  the monstrous state complexes that demand our loyalties, 82
  on top of the rock a ~ of people gather (Acropolis), 144
  what these separated ~s do to the people within them, 82

Tribespersons, 114

Trickle charger, 57

Triga, 128

Troy, 77

Trucks, 1

Truth
  love of the pursuit of truth, 101. *Maria's idea is that even with relativity you have truth—but the word describes the action—the pursuit—and not the goal.*
  reality and material, 152
  ye shall know the ~ and the ~ shall make you free, 29. *Not "set" you free, note, but "make": John, 8.32. The truth in question is that Christ is God's son.*

Tuohy needle, 42. *Technical information on the procedure of spinal tap (lumbar puncture) was given to me by Andrew Parsons, anesthetist of Sydney, Australia.*

Turbines, 176, 196

Turkey, yams, and pumpkin pie, 137. *The customary Thanksgiving meal. The nineteenth-century institution of Thanksgiving depends on a story that the first settlers had this meal to commemorate their first year of survival in the new world, and that what they ate was what they found there: wild turkeys, sweet potatoes, and pumpkins.*

Turn-arounds, 22. *The hub-to-spoke journeys these airplanes make are shuttle journeys. A turn-around is the time it takes to empty the plane, clean it and fill it up again for the return flight.*

Tuscan shutters, 138. *All timber, the casement-glazed lights have wooden baffles on the inside for darkness and adjustable shutters with top-hung louvered panels for afternoon shade on the outside.*
Tweezers (hickory handled barbecue), 153
Typewriter, 111

UCAVs, 90
Uluru (Australia), 76
Uni, 74, 81. *Australian abbreviation for* University.
Uniformitarianism, 149. *See also* Catastrophist. *The opposite of catastrophism.*
United States, 173. *See also* U.S.
  attack on, 163
Universe (expanding), 35. *See also* Big Bang
University of Texas (at Austin), xii, 29, 168
University of Virginia, 163
Urbanism, 24, 167. *If the urban nest is not this, is it then a vision? Or a practicality?*
U.S. *See also* United States
  Air Force, 76
  government, 154
  special forces, 192
Useful, 33. *The difference between function and use that clouds discussion about buildings is illuminated by the study of machines. Function is what the designer needs to set the material in relation to its arrangement and form, and corresponds to human program (chronotonic). Use (useful) describes the machine when it's running or operating (tachytronic), and corresponds to what people do with a building, which is rarely the same as the designer's intention, because of the looser fit and because of the long life of buildings. The difference accounts for the possibility of using* form follows function *buildings such as power stations as art galleries. In a sense, the makers of architecture abandon their works when finished and leave them to their users.*
U.S.S. Nimitz, 7. *The* Nimitz (CVN 68), *which went into service 1975, is one of the biggest class of U.S. aircraft carriers, which also includes* Dwight D. Eisenhower (CVN 69) *and the* Carl Vinson (CVN 70). *They displace 93,405 tons and have crews of 6,280 people.*

They carry 95 airplanes and have three Phalanx systems each (see Phalanx). They are powered by two Westinghouse A4W pressure water reactors, which have a running capacity of thirteen years and can propel the ships for one million nautical miles. "U.S.S." is a TLA for United States Ship.

Vacuum-powered toilets, 22

Valentine's day, 58

Valves, 196

Van Gogh, Vincent (1853–1890), 57

Variable pitch propeller, 191. *The pitch of the propeller is the relationship of the blade to the air; in variable pitch, it can be altered to provide more pull at low speeds, and less drag at high speeds.*

Veldt, 3. Veldt *is Afrikaans for "open country": distinct from* wilde, *meaning "wild." It is a metaphor for "rustic" and so belongs to the great family of things that were laughable preindustrial, but desirable postindustrial.*

Venetians, 73

Venus de Milo, 77 140

Vermin gun, 16. *At the opposite end of the scale to the elephant gun, a .22 rifle for shooting rats and pigeons.*

Versace, 73

Vertebrae, 42

Vertebrata, 90

Via Barberini (Rome), 169

Via Veneto (Rome), 166

Vibrator (Howling Wolf), 88

Victor Emmanuel monument (Rome), 128

Victoria (Empress of an empire now lost), 46

Victorians, 73

Video-conferencing, 137

Villa Borghese (Rome), 167

Villa d'Este (Rome), 173, 177, 193

Viper (Dodge muscle-car), 110, 116

Virilio, Paul, 99. *See also note under* Sexual harassment

Virtuality, 115. *See also* Actual

Vita activa, xi. *See also* Arendt, Hannah. *The "active life." Arendt revives the correlative* vita contemplativa, *the "contemplative life"*

Vita activa, *continued*

> *as a valid duality. The second is the return for the activities of the first. But isn't it possible that contemplation is purely sensual, which would be action of a fourth sort?*

Volcano, 147. *This parody of James Turrell is based on an encounter in Austin, Texas, in 1997.*

Volkswagen, 10

Voluptuous bronze, 140. *The statues in L'Opera, Paris, France are the apogee—both the* torchères *inside by Carrier Beleuse and those outside at the back of the building. Also, voluptuous stone in Italy: see* Eulalia *by Franchesci (at Rome) and* Slave *by Ginotti (at Turin).*

Volvo, 126, 127, 133

Vulture, 3

Waders, 97

Wagon train (of Winnebagos), 98

Wales, 175

Walking City, 115. *Archigram was a group of architectural thinkers in the late nineteen sixties. The Walking City is the Archigram project that has lived longest in the memory, because Ron Herron was the one who could draw best. It was a vision of a giant megalopolis on stilts so extreme that it became a caricature of the group's emphasis on flexibility and nomadicity by going cleanly in pursuit of their underlying motive: the desire for spectacle. The real architecture that came out of their paperwork is the set designs for the U2 and Rolling Stones tours by Mark Fisher. Those cities don't walk, however: they are multiples; one traveling, one erecting, one performing, leapfrogging each other across the globe.*

Walkmans, 95

War (materially effective), 38

Warehouses (slaves), 143

Warheads, 76

Warlords, 155

Wars, faith, 113. *The rise of Islam, the crusades, the schisms of the Christian church.*

Washington, D.C., 152

Waterproof (notepad, and camera), 95

Waxwing, 181. *A songbird of the Northern forests,* Bombycilla garrulus. *Named for the shiny beads on its wing feathers.* I was the shadow of the waxwing slain *is the first line of the poem from Nabokov's* Pale Fire *(1961).*

Waypoint markers, 22. *In flight traffic control, airplanes are given precise instructions by ground controllers, but over the deep oceans they are handled automatically by radio waypoint markers, which give a safe check to their inertial guidance systems. The conspiracy theory about that Korean airliner that strayed into Russian airspace and w̶a̶s̶ shot down was: how could he have missed his waypoint marker unless it was intentional?*

Weapon (object of desire), 124, 130, 131, 174, 178

Web and city analogy, 110, 115. *See also* Loaf House. *A lot of this conversation with Ex is derived from conversations with Ben Nicholson.*

Webber, Melvin, 30. *His essay "The Urban Place and the Non-Place Urban Realm" in* Explorations into Urban Structure, *ed. M. Webber et al. (University of Pennsylvania Press, 1963), was an attempt to explain Los Angeles as the way the future was going to be. Urban planners often exclude the blood and guts from their analyses, and Webber was no exception. No wonder he was shelved. But a revival of the content has dawned—see Lars Lerup's* After the City *(MIT Press, 2001).*

Web-links hand, 110

Web site

  Department of State, 163

  Ex's, 109

  My Digital Dad, 107

Web surfers, 115

Wedge (the five simple machines), 33

Wellington monument (London), 128

Westinghouse, 8. *See also U.S.S. Nimitz*

What Is Architecture? An Essay on Landscape, Buildings, and Machines (1994), 33

What Is Philosophy (Qu'est-ce que la philosophie? Deleuze and Guattari, Columbia University Press, 1994), 36

Wheel (the five simple machines), 33

Wheel and axle (and disc drives), ix, 196

Wheelchair, ix, 9, 50, 68, 137, 159, 160, 181, 182

Wheels, 61

Whopper, 129, 130, 131

Wildebeest, 3, 4, 10, 111. *Wildebeest is Afrikaans for* gnu: wilde *(wild)*

Wildebeest, *continued*
    *and bees (ox). Gnu is the Khoisan/Hottentot word for the animal.
    See also Connochates taurinus on page 10.*
Wilderness (and cultivation), xii
Williams, Tennessee (1911–1983), 182
Willis, Bruce, 192
Windshield, 19
Winnebagos, 98. *An RV (recreational vehicle) made in the town of the
    same name.*
Wired-up guys, 156
World Trade Center, 164
World War Three, 50
www.picture.it, 109. *Ex is reviving the idea of the "picturesque" with
    this name, emphasizing it as visionary, a complete picture of the
    world, rather than simply scenographic.*

Xanadu, 37, 159. *The summer capital of the Great Khan, as phoneti-
    cized by Coleridge, still visible in atlases as the inner Mongolian
    city of Shang-du in contemporary China.*
Xerox, 111

Zebras, 11. *See Manuel De Landa's* A Thousand Years of Nonlinear
    History *(MIT Press, 1997) on evolution—it is not that there is an
    ideal zebra of which all living zebras are imperfect copies; rather it
    is that the zebra population of the world at any time constitutes the
    basket of possibilities that the species is.*
Zeus, 93
Ziggurats, 131
Zits, 15
Zook (Zurich), 14
Zurich, 15